SAMUEL BUTLER

THE INCARNATE BACHELOR

SAMUEL BUTLER

The Incarnate Bachelor

by

PHILIP HENDERSON

NEW YORK

BARNES & NOBLE, INC.

*Published in the United States
of America, 1967 by
Barnes & Noble, Inc.*

Printed in Great Britain

FOR BELINDA

'The lady students at Heatherley's used to call Butler the incarnate bachelor.'—FESTING JONES, *Memoir*.

PREFACE

FEW MEN HAVE TOLD US SO MUCH ABOUT themselves as Samuel Butler. Six large *Notebooks*, scrupulously indexed, with long accounts of his personal relationships; sixteen volumes of general correspondence; the autobiographical chapters of *The Way of all Flesh*—Butler took care that we should know all about him. Festing Jones carried on the tradition with one of the most detailed biographies in the language. Jones was, nevertheless, hampered by his inability, or unwillingness, to make use of the family correspondence, and what he gives us in the *Memoir* (1919) is substantially Butler's own view of himself and his father. Canon Butler may have been very like Theobald Pontifex; but, except for Mrs R. S. Garnett's *Samuel Butler and his Family Relations* (1926), his case has never been really presented. Since he was the most important person in Butler's life, the source from which his whole revolt against Victorian ideology derives, any book about Butler must be to some extent a book about his father. Mrs Garnett wrote with charm and good sense; she had the advantage of a family connection with Butler's younger sister; but her portraits are nevertheless based mainly upon hearsay.

Festing Jones's *Memoir* has an enduring fascination and is still the main source of our knowledge of Butler. But one cannot help feeling that Jones, in his piety, almost buried his friend beneath the accumulated detail of his two bulky volumes, and with much of this detail the harassed reader of today is likely to feel a little impatient —unless he is already a Butler devotee. There are also serious gaps in Jones's account and more than a suspicion of an attempt to conventionalize his subject. Of the more important side of Butler's private life we are told practically nothing.

There would seem, therefore, to be room for a more compact biography dealing principally with the man rather than his works—in spite of the fact that he has warned us that there is more of him in his books than anywhere else. But every writer, it is to be hoped, has a life apart from his books. With Butler the dominant emotional pattern was established early and changed little in later life, as Hugh Kingsmill has pointed out in his admirably perceptive essay in *After Puritanism* (1929). Kingsmill having indicated the main lines which any future biography of Butler must take, Malcolm Muggeridge leapt into the breach with *The Earnest Atheist* (1936), which appears to have been written out of a detestation of Butler and all his works. Butler was, after all, his own severest critic and there was surely no point in taking advantage of such transparent integrity.

But it is still usual to dismiss him as a brilliant amateur of science and letters, an odd and amusing character who attacked the family because he hated his father, turned Victorian morality upside down in a witty Utopia, set up the earlier evolutionists against Charles Darwin, and thought the *Odyssey* was written by a woman in Sicily. It is true that Bernard Shaw hailed him as 'in his own department the greatest English writer of the latter half of the nineteenth century'. But Shaw was really only interested in him as a Creative Evolutionist and the forerunner of *Man and Superman* and *Back to Methuselah*. It may be that Butler was most original in his scientific books, which, as Professor G. D. H. Cole has emphasized, are in reality pioneer works in social psychology, and not merely attacks upon Darwin's 'mindless' universe. But his total achievement falls into many departments—far too many to be more than briefly touched upon in the following pages, which have been very largely influenced by his own repeated assertion that 'the personality of the author is what interests me more than the work'. It was his delight in the personality of Nausicaa that gave rise to his fascinating Odyssean theories and his love of Shakespeare the man that made him 'reconsider' the Sonnets. It is my delight in the personality of Butler that is responsible for the present book. Those who wish to explore the intricacies of his thought cannot do better than turn to Clara Stillman's *Samuel Butler: A Mid-Victorian Modern* (1932).

I am greatly indebted to Butler's Literary Trustees, Mr Geoffrey Keynes and Mr Brian Hill, for permission to draw so extensively upon the General Correspondence and the *Notebooks* and for permission to quote from Henry Festing Jones's *Memoir*; and to them and to the Master and Fellows of St John's College, Cambridge, for allowing me to reproduce the photographs from the Samuel Butler Collection which illustrate this volume. I am indebted to Messrs Emery Walker Ltd for permission to reproduce the portrait sketch of Butler by James Ferguson. For the quotations from the published works my best thanks are due to Mr Jonathan Cape, Butler's publisher, who has generously allowed me to make use of much copyright material. I am also grateful to Messrs J. M. Dent for permission to make use of material from Mrs Garnett's *Samuel Butler and his Family Relations*, to the Public Trustee and to the Society of Authors for permission to quote from a letter of Bernard Shaw, and to the Editor of *John O'London's Weekly* for allowing me to quote from A. G. Macdonell's interview with Alfred Emery Cathie, 'Samuel Butler as I Knew Him', which appeared on 23 November 1935. Mr P. N. Furbank, of Emmanuel College, Cambridge, and the author of a brilliant short critical study of Butler, has very kindly read my book in manuscript and given me the benefit of his advice on several important points. No less helpful has been the patient criticism of my wife, with whom I have discussed my book at all its successive stages, and who has helped me to clarify many things that would otherwise have remained obscure.

CONTENTS

xi

ILLUSTRATIONS

Between pages 130–131

No man should try even to allude to the greater part of what he sees in his subject, and there is hardly a limit to what he may omit. What is required is that he shall say what he elects to say discreetly; that he be quick to see the gist of a matter, and give it pithily without either prolixity or stint of words.

The Note-Books of Samuel Butler

CHAPTER I

LANGAR

SAMUEL BUTLER WAS CHRISTENED WITH A bottle of Jordan water by his grandfather, Bishop Butler, in the autumn of 1836. He was born in the previous year, on 4 December, at Langar Rectory, near Bingham, Nottinghamshire, the second child of the Rev. Thomas Butler and Fanny Worsley. He was preceded by an elder sister, Harriet, and followed by a brother, Thomas, another brother, William, who died in infancy, and a younger sister, Mary. He used to say in later life that the delay between his birth and his christening 'was a very risky business, because during all those months the devil had the run of him'. But Dr Butler had much else to attend to. In April 1835 he resigned his headmastership of Shrewsbury, one of the great Victorian public schools, which, like Dr Arnold of Rugby, he had 'made', and in July he was consecrated Bishop of Lichfield and Coventry. Only then could he find time to go up to Langar, where his son was rector, and christen his grandson.

After the ceremony the bishop made sure of a good dinner, having ordered it himself beforehand. But when 'the turbot from Groves' came to the table and the cover was removed, he turned to his daughter-in-law and exclaimed in disgust: 'Good God, Fanny, it's skinned!'—an episode from clerical life which Butler improved upon in *The Way of All Flesh*, when George Pontifex complains furiously at Ernest's christening dinner that the sauce has been made from a hen instead of a cock lobster. It is doubtful whether Dr Butler, like George Pontifex, had, the night before, dropped the bottle of Jordan water on to the steps of his wine cellar and baptized his grandson with what he and his man managed to mop up off the floor. In point of fact, his disagreeable portrait in *The Way of All Flesh* is founded upon what Canon Butler told Butler about his own father.

The epitaphs of the various members of the Pontifex family, as they appear in the novel, are taken from the family tombs in that corner of Kenilworth Church known as the 'Butlers' Pantry'. Of William Butler, who died in 1760, we learn: 'He now awaiteth a joyful resurrection at the Last Day. What manner of man he was that day will discover.' This Butler incorporated into the epitaph of George Pontifex, Theobald's father, a context in which the original pious eighteenth-century sentiments sound particularly ironical.

The Butlers were a Warwickshire yeoman family. William Butler I was buried at Kenilworth in 1709; William Butler II bought the Stone House there in 1711; William Butler III (old Mr Pontifex, the carpenter, who played Handel)[1] carried on the trade of linen-draper in the town, and it was his son who became Bishop Butler. If on his father's side Sam came of two generations of clerical stock, his mother, Fanny Worsley, was the daughter of a Bristol sugar refiner. Needless to say, Butler always felt that he had more in common with his distinguished grandfather than with his more humdrum father. He remembered his grandfather's death in 1839 because it was his birthday, and he had been given a pot of honey and a string of birds' eggs. When his father came into the nursery to announce the solemn event, he took away the honey, 'saying it would not be good for me' —an early event which set the pattern for all Butler's subsequent relations with his father.

[1] *The Way of All Flesh*, Ch. I.

The childhood of Ernest Pontifex, according to Festing Jones, is faithfully drawn from Butler's own childhood, 'Theobald and Christina being portraits of his father and mother as accurate as he could make them, with no softening and no exaggeration'. But against this statement must be set the fact that Jones does not seem to have found out anything for himself about Butler's parents. At any rate, Butler tells us that as a child he could not remember having had any feeling for his father but shrinking and fear, though Thomas Butler does not seem to have been a particularly formidable person. He merely disapproved of everything his son wanted to do, the example of disapproval having been already set for him by his own father. Dr Butler, doubling the roles of head-master *and* father, must have been very formidable indeed. In *The Way of All Flesh* Ernest's parents act on principles derived from a contemporary manual on how to bring up a family—Theobald and Christina are unoriginal even in this—and the first principle inculcated by the manual was 'Break your child's will early, or he will break yours later on'. This appears barbarous today, when it is usually the child who succeeds in breaking the parents' will. But in those days the breaking process was reinforced by daily beatings. Doubtless the Rev. Thomas Butler would have been scandalized had anybody told him that he was addicted to what was known on the Continent as 'the English vice'. But then he was only doing as most parents did. 'Mr Pontifex may have been a little sterner with his children than some of his neighbours, but not much', Butler tells us of Theobald's father. 'He thrashed his boys two or three times a week and some weeks a good deal oftener, but in those days fathers were always thrashing their boys.' And he reminds us that it is easy to have juster views when everyone else has them, and that what one has to consider when passing judgment on people of

2

another age is 'whether a sufficient number of reasonable people placed as the actor was placed would have done as the actor had done'. Those were the days before Freud had revealed to us how discreditable the majority of our habits and preoccupations are, though Butler was himself a pioneer in the realization that 'it is our less conscious thoughts and our less conscious actions which mainly mould our lives and the lives of those who spring from us'.

Cruelty to children is a constant theme in Victorian novels, particularly in Dickens, who was obsessed by it. But Theobald had never liked children—'he had always got away from them as soon as he could, and so had they from him'. Perhaps it was his father's want of affection that hurt Sam even more than the beatings, though, if we can believe *The Way of All Flesh*, his father began to teach him to read in his second year and 'began to whip him two days after he had begun to teach him'. At the age of three he beat him for pronouncing 'come' as 'tum', when reciting a hymn—which sounds slightly incredible. Before he could crawl, we are told of Ernest, he was taught to kneel; before he could well speak he was taught the Lord's Prayer and told that he was a miserable sinner, and 'before he was three years old he could read and, after a fashion, write'. Before he was four he was learning Latin at the point of the stick. As he grew older to his father's bullying was added his mother's emotional blackmail. During their 'sofa talks' Ernest was induced to confide in his mother. His mother passed on the information extracted by kisses and caresses to his father, who then summoned him to the dining room for punishment. The mere smell of the furniture polish associated with this room gave Sam the same sensations as he experienced later in life when sitting in a dentist's waiting room.

Like Ernest, Sam was of a naturally affectionate and trustful nature. In these sofa talks he knew well how careful he ought to be, and yet his fondness for his mother invariably overcame his reserve. It was, of course, part of the blackmail to make him feel guilty for not being sufficiently grateful for all his parents had done for him. And though in time he grew wise to this particular 'domestic confidence trick', the guilt-feelings remained, and as he grew older he was never free from 'a pervading sense of wrong . . . felt as a dull, dead-weight ever present day by day, and if he woke at night-time still continually present'. It was still there when he grew up. As a man Butler continued to resent his childhood; he never forgave his father for his treatment of him, and any suggestion of paternal authority, whether in the world of science, art, or letters, set up the automatic reaction of resentment and defiance. His dislike and distrust of women, and his fear of surrendering himself to emotion, derived in the same way from his mother's betrayal of his confidence in their sofa talks.

If in *The Way of All Flesh* Butler paints his father in the darkest colours, we are intended to see him as the victim of a particular kind of environment—the graceless, life-hating, Puritanical environment of nineteenth-century England. 'I should say', he wrote in the 1880's, 'that I had drawn the better rather than the worse side of the life of an English country parson of some fifty years ago.' Theobald, like Thomas Butler, his original, had had no vocation for the Church, nor had he been particularly anxious to marry; he had allowed himself to be bullied into both, first by his father, then by his future father-in-law. It had become a habit to do what was expected of him rather than what he wanted to do himself. Thomas Butler's tragedy was that he was deficient in any strong feeling: his impulses and emotions had been too carefully ironed out by his father, the dread headmaster of Shrewsbury, who made a fortune out of his boarders while he birched them and exercised them remorselessly in Latin and Greek. All Thomas Butler really wanted to do was to get into a comfortable groove and stay there, and this he was able to do as Rector of Langar. He was comfortably off, he had a pleasant Georgian house to live in, his parochial duties were not heavy, and he was respected on all hands as a model clergyman, unworldly in his tastes and scrupulous in his devotions. He visited the sick and administered 'what he was pleased to call spiritual consolation', as his son acidly remarks. He also gave his sons the best education available in his day. What other feelings he may have had were too deeply repressed ever to come to the surface of his mind; and in course of time, all emotion, except devotion to his own comfort and doing what was expected of him, withered and died. But so well were appearances kept up that when visitors called or stayed at the rectory they saw what they took to be a happy, united family.

In spite of everything, Butler was in reality deeply attached to both his parents. If he sees his father as a gloomy and pitiable tyrant, his mother appears in *The Way of All Flesh* as a figure of high comedy, one of his happiest creations. She used to tell him 'to have his loins girt about with the breastplate of purity'. Butler hesitated to attribute this particular *mot* to Christina, as being almost too strange for fiction, but, as he says, all the most far-fetched things in his books are taken straight from life. When he was five, Fanny Butler, not expecting to recover from her last confinement, wrote a letter addressed 'To my two dear boys', which did not come into Butler's hands until after her death in 1873—just in time for him to put it, word for word, into *The Way of All Flesh*, only changing the names Sam and Tom to Ernest and Joey.

The only place at Langar where Sam ever felt at ease was the kitchen, talking to the cook, the footman and the

housemaid—Ellen of *The Way of All Flesh*. The fact that
Ernest finally marries Ellen, after she has been driven on
to the streets by Theobald—she was pregnant by the
footman—is perhaps an indication of how attractive Sam
found her original.

How was it possible for a child reared in such an
atmosphere as Langar to grow up healthy and vigorous?
Since 'our parents are our yesterdays', our todays are
what they have made us. Even if we react against them,
as Butler and his brother Tom did, the emotional pattern
we thus establish is often compulsive and neurotic. But it
is often of such neurotic conflict that creative work is
born. Butler's work, in nearly all its aspects, derives from
his struggle with his father and his early clerical environment, and the enormous effort it cost him to establish his
independence. At the same time, the effort needed to free
himself was so great and so prolonged—for Butler was
not free of his father even in middle age—that it not only
took the greater part of his emotional vitality, it incapacitated him for any normal relationship with anyone else.
Fortunately, he was able to canalize the emotions
generated in this struggle into creative and critical work,
whereas the reaction of his brother Tom to the same
environment, though equally violent, was purely self-
destructive. As for his sisters, Harrie and May, they were
everything that a Victorian country parson's daughters
should be.

Mrs R. S. Garnett, in her *Samuel Butler and His
Family Relations*, says that *The Way of All Flesh* should
never have been written and pities Canon Butler and his
wife for having had such a son as Sam. 'We all feel', she
writes, 'that there are some things we want to see respected.
There is a certain decency in family life. Our mothers, at
least, should be safe from attack. No: we cannot forgive
Butler for his exposure of Christina.' But this is

7

surely to miss the point. Butler felt that the kind of family life lived at Langar was particularly indecent in its cruelty and stultifying hypocrisy, and thought that it should be exposed. As for his mother, she did him just as much harm, in her more insidious way, as his father.

The object of Mrs Garnett's book is to correct the picture of Canon Butler and his wife and daughters given in *The Way of All Flesh* by showing us how they appeared to other members of the family. Her grandfather was Philip Worsley, Butler's uncle—a man he particularly disliked—and Butler's sister May was Mrs Garnett's mother's 'very dearest friend'. Her book is illuminating, not because it contradicts *The Way of All Flesh*, but because it largely confirms it. It is true that Canon Butler appears as 'dear kindly humorous Uncle Butler, full of pleasant jest and quip', and so to other people he may have been. Not, however, to his sons. One of his grandchildren wrote to Mrs Garnett: 'To understand something of the atmosphere of Langar which so strongly reacted on Uncle Sam, it is necessary to go back to the early life of his father. My grandfather had been brought up at Shrewsbury School, as a boy greatly in subjection to his father, the headmaster, later, as a junior master under him, always under his eye and his control. He wished to go into the Navy, but was compelled by his father to take orders, and was appointed curate at Meole Brace, then a small village about a mile from Shrewsbury. Here he was still under family control, for Archdeacon Bather, Vicar of Meole, had married his eldest sister. From Meole Brace he went to his first and only living of Langar-cum-Barnston: and in that small village all his children were born and brought up, seeing little of the world for over forty years. He settled down to a monotonous life; and did much for the improvement of the church and village.

. . . He was a very quiet and retiring man, as open and simple-hearted as a child; and I think Uncle Sam's writings not only irritated but amazed him. He saw no way of dealing with the problem but by treating Uncle Sam as severely as he would have treated a recalcitrant boy at the schools; and though he would fly into a great passion and write letters in a white heat, he never failed to repent of having been harsh, afterwards'[1]—when, that is to say, the harm was already done.

As an example of 'the sparkle and fun in the dear old grandfather' Mrs Garnett relates the following story. Soon after his marriage he was going to Bristol to fetch his wife home, and she had evidently written to ask him to bring her two crinolines, to which he replied: 'My dear, I do not know how I can bring both your hoops unless I wear one.' During his wife's illness in the spring of 1836 he sent her daily a bunch of flowers accompanied by amusing little impromptu verses, such as:

> Hocus pocus
> Here's a crocus.

> There's no rhyme to Polyanthus
> So I must manage as I can, thus:
> Will my wife accept a posy
> For her pretty little nosey?

> I, in the innermost
> Part of my cranium,
> Thought you might like
> A scarlet geranium.

This does not sound very like Theobald. But perhaps Sam never saw his father's playful and affectionate side. He makes Theobald so dull and stupid that it comes as a surprise to learn that he was a Fellow of his college at Cambridge and was for that reason able to get Ernest

[1] *Samuel Butler and His Family Relations*, pp. 13–14.

some of the best rooms overlooking the Fellows' garden. There were inevitable similarities between father and son. Before he died Canon Butler had collected one of the finest herbariums in the country, and presented to the museum at Shrewsbury sixty-five volumes of dried plants, each containing forty to fifty specimens. The six volumes of Butler's *Notebooks*, written on sermon paper, lovingly revised, indexed and preserved in duplicate pressed copies, are themselves a species of herbarium; while his leather-bound, gilt-edged account books, preserved at St John's, might easily be mistaken for prayer books—which, in a sense, they were. Butler does, indeed, mention Theobald's *hortus siccus*, though he tells us that his main occupation was pasting parallel Biblical texts into a book in order to make what he called a harmony of the Old and New Testaments. As for Theobald's sermons, we read that at his death they were sold for ninepence a barrow load. An entry in the *Notebooks* makes it clear that this does not refer to Canon Butler.

Much of the bitterness of *The Way of All Flesh* was due to frustrated affection. Butler wanted to love his parents, and the fact that his early affection for them was gradually extinguished by their treatment of him does not argue very forcibly for the lovableness of either of them. Moreover, they look so exactly like Theobald and Christina in their photographs that one cannot help feeling that Butler's portraits of them were very near the originals. 'A diffident, affectionate, generous nature' is Mrs Garnett's final verdict, 'warped for life by the repressions and severities of childhood.' On the other hand, she thinks that 'physical punishment has not in the main been bad for English boyhood'. Butler, however, had 'too much sensibility'. One expects a writer to have more sensibility than the average boy, though Butler himself would have been the last person to desire such a painful sensitivity for a son of his own. It is for that reason, among others, that Ernest in *The Way of All Flesh* has his children brought up as bargees.

By the time Sam went to his public school at the age of thirteen he was, like Ernest, 'a mere bag of bones, with upper arms about as thick as the wrists of other boys of his age; his little chest was pigeon-breasted; he appeared to have no strength or stamina whatever. . . . After he had had the breath knocked out of him and been well shinned half a dozen times in scrimmages at football—scrimmages in which he had become involved sorely against his will—he ceased to see any further fun in football, and shirked that noble game in a way that got him into trouble with the elder boys. . . . He was as useless and ill at ease with cricket as with football.' In fact, he found the atmosphere of Shrewsbury 'so gusty that he was glad to shrink out of sight and out of mind whenever he could'. His heroes, however, were strong and vigorous and 'the less they inclined to him the more he worshipped them'. It is impercipient of Mrs Garnett to blame Sam for not possessing 'that cheerful frankness, that upright self-confidence, which would have gained him both esteem from others and his own self-respect'. Such qualities could hardly have come out of such an upbringing as that at Langar; nor were they to be suddenly acquired by a brisk game of 'rugger', a cold shower and a rub down with a rough towel. Dr Skinner, the headmaster of the Rough-borough of *The Way of All Flesh*, is founded upon Dr Kennedy of Shrewsbury who, in other accounts, appears as a great personality. To Butler he appeared 'a passionate, half turkey-cock, half gander of a man whose sallow bilious face and hobble-gobble voice could scare the timid, but who would take to his heels rapidly enough if he were firmly met'.

As in Dr Butler's day, the curriculum of Shrewsbury

was still confined almost entirely to Greek and Latin literature. Dr Kennedy's teaching of these subjects is reputed to have been superb, but it only implanted in Sam a still greater dislike for the classics. Like Ernest in *The Way of All Flesh* he survived, thanks to the promptings of his unconscious self, a self 'more real than the Ernest of which he was conscious. The dumb Ernest persuaded with inarticulate feelings too swift and sure to be translated into such debatable things as words, but practically insisted as follows: ". . . You are surrounded on every side with lies which would deceive even the elect, if the elect were not generally so uncommonly wideawake; the self of which you are conscious, your reasoning and reflecting self, will believe these lies and bid you act in accordance with them. This conscious self of yours, Ernest, is a prig begotten of prigs and trained in priggishness; I will not allow it to shape your actions, though it will doubtless shape your words for many a year to come. . . . Obey *me*, your true self, and things will go tolerably well with you, but only listen to that outward and visible old husk of yours which is called your father, and I will rend you in pieces even unto the third and fourth generation as one who has hated God; for I, Ernest, am the God who made you." ' Sam's unconscious self told him to frequent the pubs and to begin smoking at the age of thirteen or fourteen, both practices of which 'that outward and visible old husk' would have disapproved. Otherwise, Sam was a rather priggish little boy, writing to his mother in September 1851: 'In the first place Tom and I think that a hamper at the end of November just before coming home is rather a paradox, and therefore if it could be managed to be sent whilst Aunt Bather is at home she would see after it and it would come about a week after long holiday which begins next Tuesday: it would be very pleasant provided it was convenient, the inside could be left to Aunt Bather provided only that among other things it contains a veal pie. . . . I get on very smoothly with Mr Browne [his drawing master]. I really think him a very clever little man in other respects besides drawing, his conversation is always very sensible. Tom has not been quite well, he being very sick the other night. I do not think he eats much trash on the whole but that day he had been eating some, and I do not think he will eat much more for some time in consequence. . . . ' It is noticeable that at the age of sixteen Sam does not trust his mother even with the contents of a school hamper.

The Way of All Flesh is so close to Butler's childhood that one can only conclude that the incident of his father putting him through a third-degree examination about the moral character of each boy in the school, with the school list in front of them, and then tabulating the results so obtained and giving them to Dr Skinner, is based on fact. The result of this in the novel is that on his return after the holidays Ernest is severely punished by Dr Skinner for telling tales out of school, and the pubs and food shops of Roughborough are put out of bounds. Horrified at what he has done, Ernest makes a clean breast of the whole affair to the senior boys, who realize that he has been bullied into giving them away, and revenge themselves upon Theobald by burning him in effigy on the fifth of November.

Though music was not encouraged at Shrewsbury, it was while he was there that Sam discovered Handel. Festing Jones conjectures that this discovery may have dated from hearing his Aunt Bather play the overtures to *Rodelinda* and *Atalanta* on her piano at Meole Brace. This aunt was the first relation to be kind to him; and ever afterwards Handel's music was associated in Butler's mind with a mood of kindness and serenity.

The family visited Italy twice during Sam's childhood and youth, once in 1843, when he was eight, and again in 1853. On the first occasion they travelled, like their contemporaries the Ruskins, in their own carriage through Switzerland to Rome. All that his father and mother seem to have noticed was that the bread was sour, the butter rank, and that they were pestered by beggars, who ran after their carriage and, when they received nothing, shouted 'Eretici!' On their second visit, when Sam was eighteen, they stayed half the winter in Naples and Rome, and he had lessons in Italian from a Signora Capocci, who told him of a poor young friend of hers who had been 'so unfortunate' as to murder his uncle and his aunt—an attitude to crime which at once suggests *Erewhon*. 'Thenceforward', writes Festing Jones, 'Italy and Handel were always present with him as a double pedal to every thought, word, and deed.' For Butler, Handel was not only the greatest of musicians and poets (he ranked him above Shakespeare in his knowledge of the human heart), but Handel's music became the central fact of his life. 'All day long', he tells us, 'whether I am writing or painting or walking—but always—I have his music in my head.' He tried to like Bach and Beethoven, but Bach seemed to him to lose himself in cold labyrinths of contrapuntal abstraction, and Beethoven to be continually working himself up into frenzies of emotion and showing off. 'If Bach wriggles', he notes, 'Wagner writhes.' In Handel alone he found the strength and poise of perfect health: a mellow golden beauty such as existed nowhere else, except in Italian painting. Handel represented to him that golden mean which he tried to follow all his life, and it is this Handelian quality he aimed at, and often achieved, in his first book, *Erewhon*.

Butler's views on a public school education are, like so many of his views, more in tune with our own age than his, when the professional middle classes had it all their own way. 'A public school education', he writes, 'cuts off a boy's retreat; he can no longer become a labourer, or a mechanic, and these are the only people whose tenure of independence is not precarious.' A constant nostalgia for the greater freedoms of working-class life runs through *The Way of All Flesh*, and Butler contrasts the high-spirited children he saw playing in London alleys with his own depressed, sickly childhood at Langar, surrounded as it was with every material comfort and yet so comfortless. But even if children are very unhappy, it is astonishing, as he observes, how easily they can be prevented from realizing it. 'A man first quarrels with his father about three-quarters of a year before he is born. It is then he insists on setting up a separate establishment.'

It is not surprising if Butler looked with suspicion upon the sort of people who are in the habit of saying that their schooldays were the happiest time of their lives. The first place where he was 'consciously and continuously happy' was Cambridge, where he had a room of his own, at last.

CHAPTER II

CAMBRIDGE

BUTLER'S ROOMS AT ST JOHN'S WERE AT D, New Court—that Gothic Revival folly at the north end of the Backs. In a congenial atmosphere he began to realize for the first time what life might be, and on 6 November 1854 he wrote to his father, with calculated casualness: 'The scholarships have come out this morning, and I have got one; only five other freshmen have; how much mine is worth I do not know; but shall some day I suppose. Parkinson and Headlam and France are awfully jolly dons, far the nicest in the college; Rayner and Mayor are brutes. Bateson stopped me in the courts a day or two ago and let me dandle his two fat fingers, which was very kind.'

Butler tells us very little about life at Cambridge in *The Way of All Flesh* because, as he says, undergraduate life has been described in a score of novels. But of Ernest we read that 'a straightforwardness of character was stamped upon his face, a love of humour, and a temper which was more easily appeased than ruffled made up for some awkwardness and want of *savoir faire*. He soon became a not unpopular member of the best set of his year.' Next March Butler is proposing to do a tour of the churches of Northern France. Possibly he had read William Morris's splendid essay on Amiens in the first number of the *Oxford and Cambridge Magazine*. 'The funds are ample for my purpose', he writes to his father, 'for, in the first place, first class from London to Caen, including everything, is one pound (I am not joking), and

I would stop as long as my money lasted, but I have a pressing and hearty invitation from a friend who lives at Caen to stay with him. . . . There are excursion tickets from London to Lucerne in the summer (railroad all the way—every inch of it) at a very low price indeed, and from London to Paris is but 28s. first class (via Dieppe) and'—he could not resist adding—'we might find our-selves cutting the churches if we got loose on the spree. . . . ' It is not recorded whether Butler ever made this trip. In July his father sent him a case of wine.

Whatever friends Butler made at Cambridge were regarded by his mother, he always felt, as potential husbands for his sisters, especially if they happened to be 'well connected'. Fanny Butler never forgot a name and would take occasion, one way or another, to extract in-formation that might be of use to her in her husband hunt. A husband caught in this way, perhaps, was George L. Bridges, the brother of Robert Bridges the poet, who married Harriet ('Harrie') Butler. May was less successful and followed her mother in 'otherworldliness'.

Butler worked so hard at Cambridge that he strained his eyes. 'I don't care about beginning small print candle reading too soon as it seems to try them', he wrote to his father in October 1857. 'Daylight reading does not in the least affect them, so I have been out of bed by a quarter past 5 every morning lately and into bed by 10 at night, get a cup of tea by 6 in the morning, and read till break-fast and amusement till 10, read from 10 to one, go to Shilleto [his classics tutor] ½ past 6 to ½ past 7 (I don't care about that at all). Well, then, there is music from 1 to 2 and exercise from 2 to 4, and music from 4 to 5 and dinner at 5, so when I come back from Shilleto I am pretty glad to have done the day's work. Of course drawing goes to the dogs. I am exceedingly well in every respect but my eyes, and they are mending. This is all about myself but I can think of no more agreeable topic (!). It is pouring wet, the river flooded, and Snow says I am to steer at 2 o'clock which hour is just on the point of approaching. I shall not steer for Snow or anybody else.' In the same letter he refers to the proposed sale to his cousin of the Whitehall Manor at Shrewsbury, of which he was under his grandfather's will joint owner with his father and his aunt Lloyd. He says that he really does not know what to say on the matter; all he cares about is having his fair share: 'I don't care about being better off by the bargain but I don't want to be worse, that is all'. In 1901 he added a note to the foot of this letter: 'How they bamboozled me!' Later the Whitehall property became one of the many bones of contention between Butler and his father.

Butler joined the boat club, and even steered and coached his college boat. He occasionally also watched a cricket match, but otherwise he was not interested in sport, and was considered a reading man. It was an accepted thing in the family that he should follow his grandfather and his father into the Church, but as long as ordination remained a fairly remote possibility he did not let it bother him, and attended chapel only as often as he was compelled to do. His dislike of religion and all that went with it was summed up for him in the persons of the Simeonites. The 'Sims', as they were called, were all that remained of the Evangelical awakening of more than a generation before. The Simeonites were further discredited in Butler's eyes by being almost entirely confined to the poorest undergraduates who lived in dingy, tumbledown rooms behind the chapel of Caius. These quarters were known as the labyrinth. To many even at St John's the existence or whereabouts of the labyrinth in which the sizars lived was unknown, he tells us in *The Way of All Flesh*. 'Some men in Ernest's time who had rooms in the first court, had never found their way through the sinuous passage which led to it.' Here lived men of all ages, from mere lads to grey-haired old men who had entered late in life. 'They were rarely seen except in hall or chapel or at a lecture where their manners of feeding, praying and studying were considered alike objectionable; no one knew whence they came, whither they went, nor what they did, for they never showed at cricket or the boats; they were a gloomy, seedy-looking *confrérie* who had as little glory in clothes and manners as in the flesh itself.'

A few of them would sometimes 'emerge' after winning valuable scholarships, and would even become tutors and dons; some even rose to high positions in politics and science, but they never completely shook off the uncouthness they had brought with them to the university. Their ways were not the ways of Butler and his friends, for they would meet in one another's rooms for tea and prayer.

Ordination, therefore, became synonymous with associating with men who would never be accepted by 'nice people'—that is, the healthy, the good-looking and the elegant, people who gave the impression that they were on good terms both with themselves and with the world. So, when the seedy-looking Simeonites had the temerity to drop their tracts into the letter-boxes of the nice people, Butler wrote parodies of them which he dropped into the letter-boxes of the labyrinth. The subject he chose for his tract was personal cleanliness, which, he reminded the Simeonites, was next to godliness. Butler's friends, he tells us, thought that his dislike of the Simeonites was due to his being the son of a clergyman.

On coming of age, Butler inherited £5,000 which brought him in an income of £250 a year. But he did not realize that this made him independent of his father, for it took more than an independent income to free him from the parental stranglehold. Until well past middle-age he had, like Ernest, 'fierce and reproachful encounters with Dr Skinner and Theobald in his sleep'. Tom was also at St John's with him, but the two brothers do not seem to have had much in common. Most of the references to Tom in Butler's letters are slightly contemptuous.

His mother had evidently written to him about one of his college acquaintances, L——, who may have struck her as a possible son-in-law. From Butler's reply it sounds as though L—— was a 'Sim'. 'L—— is good enough himself', he writes in May 1857, 'he is only gawky and uncouth: but he is not a man that I could ever become in any way intimate with: and so, I suppose, considering me a "bloated aristocrat", in company with all the rest of the Lady Margaret Boat Club he has determined to have none of us.' In June he went on his projected continental tour with his friend Joseph Green, whose name he Italianized into Giuseppe Verdi. They went to Grenoble and from there through Dauphiné by diligence and on foot, one day walking forty-two miles. From Turin they went to Arona and rowed over to the other side of the lake, then Austrian territory. They went up Lago Maggiore, crossed the Simplon, and returned by Grindelwald, Meiringen, the Furca, Hospenthal, Amsteg, Lucerne, Basel, Strasbourg, Paris and Dieppe. They were away three weeks and spent only £25. Butler wrote an account of the tour, which appeared in the fifth number of *The Eagle*, the St John's College magazine. *The Eagle* began publication in the Lent term of 1859, and for the first number Butler had written an article signed 'Cellarius' *On English Composition and Other Matters*. It is remarkable as showing that his ideas on style were already fully developed. He wrote:

A man should be clear first of his meaning before he endeavours to give it any kind of public utterance and,

having made up his mind what to say, the less thought
he takes how to say it, more than briefly, pointedly, and
plainly, the better.

During his last year at the university he overworked
himself in deference to his father's wish that he should
take an honours degree. This made him so unwell that it
became doubtful whether he would be able to go in for
his degree at all; but he managed to do so, and was
bracketed twelfth in the first class of the Classical Tripos
for 1858. Nevertheless he disliked classical studies and
in *The Way of All Flesh* makes Ernest contribute an article
to his college magazine arguing that Aristophanes, 'this
keen, witty outspoken writer', expressed the general dislike of the Athenians for their tragic dramatists. In fact,
he concludes, going to the theatre was for the Greeks very
much what going to church was for Ernest's contemporaries. They went because everyone else went, but in
reality they were bored to death. But of course Butler only
disliked the Greek and Latin poets because he had had
them thrashed into him by his father and had to grind
away at them for his degree. This early grounding in the
poets, and the veneration in which Canon Butler held
Tennyson, were responsible for his lifelong antipathy to
poetry, an antipathy that extended to nearly everything
except Homer and Shakespeare. 'I am a prose man', he
would say defiantly. He particularly disliked Tennyson
and took pleasure in recording in the *Notebooks* that the
laureate was in private singularly foul-mouthed and fond
of dirty stories.

At Battersby, after he had taken his degree, Ernest's
mother, we read, tactfully broached the subject of his
becoming a clergyman. This time it was during a turn
taken in the garden and not on the sofa—which was
reserved for supreme occasions. His mother said how

anxious Papa was that he should not go into the Church blindly, without fully realizing the difficulties of a clergyman's position. Theobald shrank from pointing out these difficulties himself to his son, and Christina was no more precise. She contented herself by saying: 'Oh, no! Such questions are far better avoided by women, and, I should have thought, by men, but Papa wished me to speak to you upon the subject, so that there might be no mistake hereafter, and I have done so. Now, therefore, you know all' —an incident which must surely have occurred at Langar.

So Butler returned to Cambridge for the May term of 1858 ostensibly to read for ordination, and also to find husbands for his sisters, first for Harrie, who was supposed to be so clever. 'All young ladies are either very pretty or very clever or very sweet', he observes acidly in *The Way of All Flesh*. 'They may take their choice as to which category they will go in for, but go in for one of the three they must. It was hopeless to try and pass Charlotte off as either pretty or sweet.[1] So she became clever as the only remaining alternative . . . Not one, however, of all the friends whom Ernest had been inveigled into trying to inveigle had shown the least sign of being so far struck with Charlotte's commanding powers.' And now his mother asked him to bring Towneley to Battersby— Towneley who 'belonged to one of the most exclusive sets in Cambridge, and was perhaps the most popular man among the whole number of undergraduates. He was big and handsome—as it seemed to Ernest the handsomest man whom he ever had seen or ever could see. . . .' The most he had ever done was to admire him from a distance. Towneley at Battersby was unthinkable!

As for ordination, the more Butler thought about it the

[1] In *The Way of All Flesh*, Butler rolled his two sisters into one, under the name of Charlotte.

more unpleasant did it appear. Nevertheless, he set to work to make a comparative study of the four Evangelists in the Greek Testament, to find out what it was exactly he would be required to believe, and the closer he studied the Testaments the clearer it became to him that there were discrepancies between the four accounts of the life and death of Jesus Christ which raised serious doubts in his mind as to whether reliance could be placed upon any of them. And Butler was not prepared to take the story on trust. But he had not yet given up all idea of the Church, for no other reasonable alternative had so far presented itself to him.

As a preparation for the holy life he left Cambridge and went to live and work among the poor in London as an amateur lay assistant under the Rev. Philip Perring (the original to some extent, perhaps, of Pryer in *The Way of All Flesh*), curate in the parish of St James's, Piccadilly. He lived in Heddon Street, a dingy and notorious district behind the elegant façade of Nash's Regent Street, in a house like Ernest's in Ashpit Place. He was, Festing Jones reminds us, fortunately not quite so inexperienced as Ernest. There was nothing in Butler's life to correspond to the Miss Maitland episode; 'on the contrary', writes Jones, 'there had already been incidents which would have disqualified him from deserving the reproaches addressed by the magistrate to Ernest, that, in spite of education, he had not even the common sense to be able to distinguish between a respectable girl and one of a different sort'. He did not hoodwink himself into thinking that there was anything in common between his tastes and those of the people among whom he lived. There could hardly have been a more incongruous figure in such an environment than Samuel Butler—the dandified young man of the early photographs with his flowered silk waistcoat. Perhaps it was the conscience-stricken, miserable and Langar-ridden youth in the photograph with the riding crop that went to live in Heddon Street.

'He lived among the poor, but he did not find that he got to know them', we read of Ernest in *The Way of All Flesh*. 'The idea that they would come to him proved to be a mistaken one. He did indeed visit a few tame pets whom his rector desired him to look after. There was an old man and his wife who lived next door but one to Ernest himself; then there was a plumber of the name of Chesterfield; an aged lady of the name of Gover, blind and bed-ridden, who munched and munched her feeble old toothless jaws as Ernest spoke or read to her, but who could do little more; a Mr Brookes, a rag-and-bottle merchant in Birdsey's Rents, in the last stage of dropsy, and perhaps half a dozen or so others. What did it all come to, when he did go to see them? The plumber wanted to be flattered, and liked fooling a gentleman into wasting his time by scratching his ears for him. Mrs Gover, poor old woman, wanted money; she was very good and meek, and when Ernest got her a shilling from Lady Anne Jones's bequest, she said it was "small but seasonable", and munched and munched in gratitude. Ernest sometimes gave her a little money himself, but not, as he says now, half what he ought to have given. What could he do else that would have been of the smallest use to her? Nothing indeed; but giving occasional half-crowns to Mrs Gover was not regenerating the universe, and Ernest wanted nothing short of this. The world was all out of joint, and instead of feeling it to be a cursed spite that he was born to set it right, he thought he was just the kind of person that was wanted for the job. . . .'

Many young people have felt the same. The Victorians in particular had a bad conscience about the poor, building hideous blocks of flats like prisons for 'the industrious classes', which were nevertheless an improvement on the old slums of the eighteenth century, and accompanying their gifts with the soothing syrup of religion. Butler felt very uncomfortable about it all. He realized that he only made the condition of the dying rag-and-bottle merchant worse by his talk of the Last Judgment and the Saved and the Damned. There were some fifteen or twenty thousand poor in the parish of St James's, Piccadilly, and of those by far the greater number were, he discovered, if not actively hostile, at any rate indifferent to religion, while many were avowed atheists and admirers of Tom Paine. What on earth, as a prospective clergyman, 'a human Sunday', was he to do? Was he to go into the highways and byways and compel people to come in? 'Was he doing this? Or were not they rather compelling him to keep out—outside their doors at any rate?' It was a pretty hopeless situation.

His faith was still more rudely shaken when he discovered at his evening Bible classes that there was nothing to choose in conduct or character between the boys who had been baptized and those who had not. This was a serious matter. It was only eight years before that Church and State had been convulsed on the subject of infant baptism, as to whether baptism was merely a symbol or a means to regeneration. In any case, it was asked, were infants worthy to receive it? The bitter controversy that ensued caused the greatest doctrinal crisis in the English Church since the Reformation. Butler did his best to take his position seriously. But he still failed to see the poor as blessed. Living in Heddon Street made it very difficult. It may have been easier from a country rectory or a cathedral close.

After about six months Butler went back to Cambridge —a far more congenial place—in the hope of getting pupils and a fellowship at another college, having missed a very good chance of one at his own. Apart from that, his plans were rather vague. His father, naturally, wanted to know what he intended to do, and a long series of letters, increasingly acrimonious on both sides, passed between Cambridge and Langar. Matters were coming to a head in the spring and summer of 1859. Festing Jones gives the impression, an impression reinforced by *The Way of All Flesh*, that Canon Butler tried to force ordination upon his son by threatening to cut off supplies if he did not obey, but there is nothing in the letters that passed between them at this time to support such a view. Canon Butler was puzzled and disappointed that Sam did not want to follow him into the Church, but he only insisted that Sam should decide upon *some* profession—a profession, admittedly, of which he could approve—and he wrote to Cambridge on 9 March: 'Dear Sam, To-day your letter is come. It does not strike me as satisfactory. I don't want you to be a schoolmaster any more than I want you to be ordained. But I mean you to do *something* for your living, for your own sake. And if you can show me anything else that you like the sooner it is done the better I shall be pleased. If you say "I'm very well contented as I am and would rather live on my allowance and improve my mind", I shall not sanction your throwing away your best years, so I shall cut yr. allowance down. I don't want to force upon you any life that is objectionable to you, but I want to drive you to halt no longer between two opinions and to choose some course. The college life you are now leading seems the worse sort of life for opening the mind.—Yr. affe^te father T. B.' Not a very pleasant letter perhaps, but no worse than many fathers in those days wrote to their sons, and certainly not as bad as the letters received by Theobald from *his* father in *The Way of All Flesh*, which Festing Jones says are taken with small change from Canon Butler's letters to Sam.

Sam replied angrily on 10 March: 'Dear Papa, I hope that you will reconsider your wish that I should immediately leave the University. . . . If, however, you still desire me to leave this place I really know nothing in this country to which I could turn my hand: a person when once he adopts ideas out of the common way, whether he be right or whether he be wrong, he is done for here. I see that very plainly. The thing I would most gladly do is emigrate. I have long wished to do so, but said nothing about it because Tom has already gone, but upon my word, if you bid me suggest anything, it is the only thing I can think of which would be at once congenial to my feelings and likely to fill my pocket. I believe the promotion of cotton growing to be one of the finest openings in the world; when we consider that the failure of the cotton crop in America would ruin half England—that is, when we consider that this plant lies at the root of the prosperity of England to such an enormous extent, it becomes doubly important that its production should be diffused over as large a space as possible: and people assisting such diffusion become public benefactors as well as good speculators. What say you to my going to Liberia, for instance? . . .'

The same day he wrote to his mother, saying that he hoped that his answer to Papa's note 'was not calculated to annoy him . . . though I fear it was not very sane, for I had to answer the same day of course, and had little time to concoct any scheme whatever. . . . I wish I had never said a word about not wishing to be ordained and then all would have been well. You, I know, will understand how galling it must be to a person to have the threat of docking one's allowance (as if I had done something scandalous) offered on so short notice. You cannot imagine how cut up I have been about it and how thoroughly undeserved I feel such language to be.' He adds that he feels like throwing up the allowance and trying to live without it—'only I know Papa didn't mean that, and know that it would be cutting off my nose to spite my face'.

On 12 March Canon Butler wrote again: 'Dear Sam, I don't want to drive you into any line of life you dislike, neither will I object to your staying up till October. But you write indefinitely, say you are working but not a word to lead me to grasp how or at what. But that your mother forwarded a letter this morning, I should have no knowledge whatever but that you had become some way or other discontented with the notion of taking Orders and have no other distinct view. I see no distinct view now—Liberia is the wildest conceivable vision with a tropical climate on the African coast. And wherever cotton is grown the European constitution will with difficulty stand it. In America it is confined to the slave states, and they are slave states *because* cotton is grown. This is so wild that it shakes my opinion of your judgment. I should greatly regret to see you leave England. There is plenty of work to be done, and that good work. And I don't feel sure that a man out of Orders may not be more useful than if he were ordained. . . . But I want a path. I see nothing but tangled brambles. I take it you know less of farming than I do . . . By writing you might pick up a poor and scanty subsistence. School books are the only ones that pay, and it may be you won't be read. I care as little about money as I believe most men, neither am I anxious about your being rich or about saving your allowance, but I think you're working now on a false plan—reading with a number of young men who easily take up a view or an interpretation and then see *that* in everything. When perhaps three words of explanation from an older head might have set all straight, though now the bias is formed there may be a good deal of difficulty in meeting it. Do you mean to go in for your Voluntary Theological? I most earnestly hope so, ordained or not. Do you go in for the Carus? You see I know nothing about your doings but a vague feeling that you like nothing. This last I stoutly oppose, seeing clearly enough that it is wrong, and till you can show me what you're wishing or aiming at as your course of life I am not satisfied. We must talk it all over when you come. . . . Take a fellowship, if official, with coach.'

These letters, which do not appear in Festing Jones's *Memoir*, put a rather different complexion upon Butler's quarrel with his father at this time. Not only is Canon Butler *not* trying to force his son to be ordained, but it appears he only heard in a roundabout way that Sam had any objection to being ordained. Evidently Butler did not have the courage to tell his father of his objections straight out, so that his father's bewilderment is understandable. Everything Canon Butler says in the foregoing letter would be endorsed by any other father—particularly his sensible remarks about authorship. Sam replied on 15 March:

'Either I have a bad way of expressing myself or else you mistook my meaning when you thought that I ever thought of doing *nothing*. All I wanted, and all I asked for, was permission to stay here *till October* and look about me instead of hurrying into the first thing that turned up; but you are by yourself, and not having Mama with you fancy my state of mind very different from what it is. I assure you when I come down at Easter you will find me very rational and very submissive. . . .' Nevertheless he goes on: 'Having read so much at subjects which I never cared a straw about I am naturally anxious to make use of the opportunity you gave me to apply what little I may have learnt to practical use in subjects wherein I take a lively interest, and only pleaded for till October, and that too with a chance (which still remains) of getting work in the meantime. I would take anything now this minute that offers itself, barring a school, and will take that at October if nothing better can be hit on between us. I write so plainly and baldly to show you that it is no mere vague and ill-defined notion that I "like nothing", but rather that I don't wish to engage in anything until I have had fair survey of the prospect to see what may be the most advantageous; whatever I take to I shall stick to once I take it, you may be quite sure, if I once get my hand in. I am reading for my Voluntary now and also the Greek Testament, but not with a view to the Carus; though if the Carus is the searching examination that the Classical Tripos is I ought to be in a fair way to do well in it.' In his next letter the Canon says that he is glad to see that Sam has had the sense to abandon Liberia, but that he still does not see exactly what he *does* like. 'My object rather is to urge you to go in for the Voluntary and the Carus too, and let me know when the examinations for each of them come off. Why should you not make your reading tell?' Sam was to make his reading tell, but scarcely in a way that his father would approve of, for the upshot of his study of the Greek Testament was *The Fair Haven*, ridiculing the supernatural element in Christianity. The school plan, his father reminds him in the same letter, was his own proposal 'and what you thought you would like till I passed it'.

By April, Butler had two pupils and on the fifth he writes cheerfully to his father: 'I am getting on very nicely with my drawing: I go twice a week from eleven till one to the art school. I commenced with curved symmetrical lines—very difficult indeed to copy accurately. I then went through a course of hands and am now going through a course of feet; I have just blocked out the Venus de' Medici's toes.' This seems to have been too much for the Canon: 'I greatly regret your not going in for the Theological without still further procrastination', he wrote. 'I wish you had spoken out about your professions. Yr. mother conjectures that you look to bookselling. To this I should have no objection if I thought you fit for it, but you have not the mercantile element in your character necessary to insure success and I can't advance capital to be sunk in some overwhelming breakdown. The steps necessary to it would be, 1st two years in a counting house; then a junior partnership, if you could get it, in some firm of whose concerns neither of us know anything but what they tell us. . . . I have said 50 times I don't want to force you into the Church, but what has the law done to your conscience that you should not be a barrister? Do, pray, put life into some practical shape. You refuse the plan I had looked to and refuse it at the 9th hour when time and education had been laid out for it. Still I don't quarrel with that, but it rests with you to find a substitute.' On 15 April Butler wrote to his mother to say that he wanted to be a painter. 'This is a very matured and deliberate proposition, very unlike the Liberian one. I have formed my opinion on the subject and nothing can change it; but, as I said before, if Papa should not like it I will say no more.' In another letter he suggested going into the army, only to take it back again when his father looked like favouring it.

But by now the Canon was coming to the end of his patience. 'If you choose to act in utter contradiction to our judgment and wishes', he wrote on 9 May, 'and that before having acquired the slightest knowledge of your powers, which I see you overrate in other points, you can of course act as you like. But I think it right to tell you that not one sixpence will you receive from me after the Michaelmas payment till you come to your senses. You speak justly about the army. The necessity for obeying was the chief inducement in my mind to make the sacrifice which would be necessary to buy your commission. But the risk not only of your not liking it but of your getting into difficulties with your superior officers is too great. Remember the proposal originated with you, not with us.' He adds that he will not contribute to Sam's going abroad, but will continue his allowance as far as £100 a year in law, which, taking into account the heavy fees and other expenses, is all he can do. 'Neither am I disposed to sacrifice the other children to you. If you will not take that profession and can get a tutorship, good. If you can get a mastership in a school, good but not so good. If you can devise another plan of your own I'll hear it, but under no fetter to accede. You take no notice of my last letter which required an answer. God give you a seeing eye some day!—Still your affectionate father, T. B.'

Sam did not reply to this angry letter, but wrote next day to his mother and asked her to pass it on to his father. It was a long restatement of the position as he saw it. He is willing, he says, to emigrate, to farm in England, to turn homœopathic doctor, to be a painter—to all of which suggestions his father says 'No'. His father suggests the law or schoolmastering—to which suggestions he says 'No' not less decidedly. 'And knowing that I have duties to myself to perform even more binding on me than those to my parents, with all respect adopt the alternative of rejecting the pounds shillings and pence and going in search of my own bread in my own way. No man has any right to undertake any profession for which he does not honestly believe himself well qualified, to please another person. . . . I am old enough by this time to know my own mind and deliberately accede to my father's proposal that I should receive no more money from him if I refuse to do what he wishes; it is fair play;

I don't question his right to do what he likes with his own—I question his wisdom greatly, but neither his motives nor his determination to stick to them. One thing I trust—that is, that I shall be allowed to correspond with Langar. . . . I should be very sorry to think that any connection other than a money connection should cease. That I regard as ceased already. . . .' His plans are, he says, to ask Hallyar if he thinks there is a good chance of his earning his living as a painter in four or five years' time, and if the answer is favourable he will move to London and, with pupils, make the £270 he has in hand last three years, raise what he can from friends and borrow on his reversion of the Whitehall estate. If at the end of a year in London he feels that he is going to fail as a painter, he will then emigrate to New Zealand, with whatever money he can raise, or go in for the Civil Service examinations.

After all, he was not so badly off; he had £250 a year besides money in hand, and this was worth considerably more then than it is now. Many a young painter would consider himself lucky indeed to have £250 a year to fall back upon. On the same day as he wrote to his mother, Butler sent a shorter letter to his father 'to resign the money I never asked for (so far from wishing you "to sacrifice the others to me")', and to say that he 'will endeavour with the small capital I have at my command to make my own bread for myself'. The letter repeats substantially all he had said to his mother and begs his father to send him 'a *quiet* letter' in reply. 'You offer me alternatives which I cannot accept without rendering my life unhappy and unprofitable under penalty of losing all future monies from you. I with all submission accept the penalty and refuse the alternatives. The alternative of grinding my seven or eight hours a day—for I cannot tell how long—in London—at work I hate—on £100 a year —that is the law. The alternative of continuing a master on £150 or £200 per annum during the best years of my life—this is the school. Hard work and little to eat with hope at the end of it and a heart and soul in the work—this is the artist. Can you wonder which I choose?'

The Canon replied at once: 'Most fathers would, I believe, on the receipt of this morning's letter have been intensely angry. I am much distressed—distressed at your obliquity of vision, distressed at your opinion of myself, distressed at your seeming [altered lightly in pencil from "obvious"] callousness of heart.' He has not, he says, favoured an artistic career, 'and this is my sole motive for refusing to assist you in it—because you have shown no decided genius for drawing', and 'to all except men of a decided professional talent it is a very uphill and hopeless task, and I think still I should do wrong to afford you the slightest possible encouragement to a course for which, for all I know, you may be just as unfitted as for a soldier, lawyer, schoolmaster, tutor ["or farmer" crossed out]. You speak as if I had thrust these things upon you. Do let me beg and beseech you to consider with whom they originated. I believe I may perhaps have suggested the law (I'm not sure about it), but the army was yours, the mastership in a school was your own earnest wish when you went to college. The tutorship was yours—I mention these things because I thought they were such things as you might like. What offence I should have given by the suggestion I can't conceive. The notion that I should disinherit you is yours, not mine. I said only that I would not contribute to this course of folly, neither do I see reason to alter this view. The notion that I will not pay your next two quarters is yours, not mine. I stated distinctly the contrary. . . . You appear to have got into the hands of some bad advisers who think it their business to represent your father as a tyrant and yourself as a martyr. Judge calmly. Is it so? Just let us look at things quietly.

34

I have no objection to your taking up drawing as an amusement—I said so long ago. But as to the wild scheme of making it a profession with no knowledge whatever how far it may answer and to the neglect and ruin of every other prospect, to this I will give no countenance at all—not for my sake but for yours. Why should your young friends be likely to wish you well more than your parents? Do they? I have had my say, I hope temperately. I am not aware that I wrote otherwise before . . . I have written a long letter to you about doctrinal difficulties, but it is quite in vain to send it now.'

Somewhat earlier, indeed, Canon Butler had asked Sam what specific objections he had against the Articles and Sam had replied with arguments based on the Pelagian position, which denied original sin. Canon Butler's reply to this was somewhat pathetic. He wrote, he said, 'partly that you may not conceive of us as a set of bigots, holding fast to the old-fashioned beliefs in which we were brought up, and mostly because you may perhaps be induced to keep this letter and look at it when you stumble upon it among old papers years hence, when it may bring with it a shade or two of more evenly balanced reflection'. He concluded, 'praying you most earnestly to believe that it is possible we may after all be right and your judgment immature'.

The long letter written more in sorrow than in anger ends with a long postscript, occasioned by a letter of Sam's to his sister Harrie. The bewildered Canon repeats that he is not forcing Sam into either the law or the Church, but that he cannot consent to his being a homœopathic doctor any more than an artist. As for farming, 'I told you when you were here that I did not think farming the life suited to you, but I will consent to it. That too must be learnt. Will you learn it? I too much fear you will say no. Just think how it was when I was ready to back your offer of the army or tutorship . . . I do not want to make your life miserable. Why should I? I don't think my conduct is like it. Nor probably will you think it if this correspondence comes into your hands after my death.' Sam replied promptly that he would learn farming, 'not that I care about being a farmer, but that I gratefully accept your offer to meet me on this proposition of my own. All I said about the army was that I should prefer it to the law. I never said I should like to be a soldier. You too accepted the idea rather on the ground of the wholesome discipline it would afford me than any other.' But if he were to consult his own wishes, he adds, he would be an artist.

One gets the impression as the letters proceed of an old tired bull being skilfully 'played' by a picador. The picador approaches and sticks his feathered darts into the bull, then quickly shifts his ground as the tormented beast rushes past. Then the poor bull, instead of charging again, complains of being ill-used. But with the Canon's next letter of 19 May, the combatants revert to the *status quo*, and the Canon takes Sam up on the observation that he does not care about being a farmer. 'I know you to be naturally unfitted for it. You throw away your education and will fall into a class not likely to be congenial to you.' Perhaps, after all, it would be better to revert to the idea of the tutorship? Or would he take any other schemes that have been proposed? The Canon is now very angry again and cannot resist saying that before he concludes his letter he wishes to make one further effort 'to make you see the sort of tone which your letters assume. I shall not go through every paragraph, but this tone runs throughout, in some places most offensively, as in talking of a letter of your father's as one "which no person at my age would receive without a determination to avoid the like for the future"—this is mere bombast. It is my duty

36

to tell you when I think you are going wrong and to check you as far as my power goes. Then why should you treat my just remonstrance as a letter from an equal?'

The fact is that Samuel Butler was already fighting the battle of sons against fathers, which for him came to have the biological significance of the new form of life struggling for survival against the strangling grip of the old. But it was not so simple as that. The situation was complicated by his wish to avoid a final break, not only because of the financial loss this would mean, but also because of his strong unconscious attachment to his family. To his father, his behaviour naturally seemed outrageous; but for all the Canon's apparent forbearance towards an intractable and exasperating son, he was deficient in fundamental sympathy and understanding. The only warmth that breaks through the perfectly reasonable tone of the letters is the warmth of anger. His father could no longer beat him physically, but he could and did browbeat him.

'He talks of writing', Canon Butler wrote to his wife, 'but it requires more than his powers to do this. He has not that in him that will be read. He is too bumptious and not sufficiently practical. . . . And at college he's a greater man than he would be elsewhere.' It is understandable that Sam's manner of life should appear to his father as aimless; 'desultory and speculative', the Canon called it; but as a writer—though he did not yet know that he was a writer—his instinct to keep himself free from professional entanglements was sound, and at the moment his greatest need was for leisure and freedom from moral pressure in which to discover his own mind. This need, obscurely felt, was at the root of his exasperating vacillation.

Two months later farming is out, and as soon as the law had been settled upon again, Sam wrote to his father in July: 'I am now under treaty to go in for a profession for which I have all along professed dislike. I see the time approaching for my adoption of it and no escape offering itself . . . for when I told my mother that I would go in for it, I expressed unwillingness as before . . . I know that the objection which you entertain for the profession which I would choose is founded on the opinion of amateurs, whereas the opinions that have led me to wish to adopt it are those of professional men—accordingly I cannot without the greatest reluctance adopt the law as a profession—at any rate without one more attempt at inducing you to allow me a chance at making my own bed before you insist on making it for me . . . I have heard you often say that you would never force a lad into a profession against his will, and feel that a grown man like myself cannot be so treated without injury to both himself and those who drive him.' He hopes, he says, that there are no expressions calculated to offend his father in his letter. He then returns to the suggestion of emigrating and asks whether his father will allow him to go to New Zealand. 'In that case, will you let me go at once—as soon, that is, as I can pack my things and go? I can scarcely believe that you will both keep me in the country and compel me to work at a profession which I hate. If you refuse me a chance at my own profession [i.e. painting] let me leave the country—if you wish to keep me in the country, give me a chance at my own profession.'

With this pistol held at his head, Canon Butler replied that his only object was 'to save you from ruining yourself', and he is going to Shrewsbury to consult William Lloyd on how this can be done. On 3 August he writes to say that he agrees to emigration and will continue Sam's allowance for twelve months and then advance capital, if needful. If after a year in New Zealand Sam can show any way in which he can make a livelihood, then 'I should be willing to do what might forward your views as far as I can afford it. I, however, must be the judge on the prospect of success. At present you know nothing of farming, neither do I in the least see any better opening in the colonies than at home. You mention New Zealand, to which I shall make no objection. It is, however, I believe about 5 months passage and takes near 12 months, therefore, to get an answer to a letter. . . . Would the Cape suit you? It's only 6 weeks, I believe, and communication any time much easier. Even Columbia is nearer than New Zealand. The artist scheme I utterly disapprove. It will throw you into very dangerous society. I have no doubt at the end of a year's trial you will draw well enough to be encouraged to go on, but this is not becoming a painter, and you may very easily learn to draw very nicely and yet come short of the excellence which alone would give station and responsibility to your career. Neither will it be clear whether you will or won't attain this for some considerable time. Meanwhile your society is cast in with a set of men who as a class do not bear the highest character for morality, you are thrown into the midst of the most serious temptations, and if it is possible that you *may* stand it is also possible that you may fall. I can't consent to it.'

It is this letter which, in Chapter XIV of *The Way of All Flesh*, became the basis of Theobald and Christina's objection to medicine, where we read that 'Medicine was a profession which subjected its students to ordeals and temptations which these fond parents shrank from on behalf of their boy; he would be thrown among companions and familiarized with details which might sully him; and, though he might stand, it was only too possible that he would fall.'

The Canon had, however, another proposition to make. 'Could you feel inclined to take up with diplomacy?' he asked. 'I would use every effort, and William Lloyd has kindly promised the same, to get you an appointment as *attaché* to some Embassy. You are quick at languages and know something of Italian and French. Of course, in the first instance, in a subordinate post.' But Italy and France? A fear crossed Canon Butler's mind. 'It must be, however, a *sine qua non*', he added, 'that if you take this line (and I'm not sure that it can be got for you) you should make it your profession and not a mere vehicle for seeing art and practising it as your object . . . I have purposely made no comment on the objectionable parts of your letter, though you say in effect that you'll take my money as long as you can't do without it.' Sam wrote, 'gratefully and gladly' accepting his father's consent to his emigrating. He has, he says, been reading the latest work on New Columbia, which seems to him to offer the best chances. He has begun packing already, and by leaving speedily he can get across the Rockies before October. By consenting to his emigration plan, he tells his father, he will rather have gained a son than lost one, and he anticipates great results on his character by the necessary hardships he may have to go through. 'What I shall do I cannot tell, but in a new country there is sure to be no lack of employment. . . . Don't fancy I rejoice at leaving England, quite the reverse. . . . Wednesday will be the 10th. Can I leave on the following Monday?'

Here the letters dealing with alternative careers end. Finally, New Zealand was agreed upon and Canon Butler said he would advance capital sufficient for Sam to set up as a sheep farmer. This new colony was chosen mainly because a body known as the Canterbury Association, whose president was the Archbishop of Canterbury, had acquired land in the centre of New Zealand for the purpose of founding a settlement on Church of England principles. These principles included selling land to prospective colonists at a profit, and then using this money partly in making roads and partly in forming a Religious and Educational Fund. It was only nine years since, in 1850, the first four ships known as the Canterbury Pilgrims—but very different in spirit from Chaucer's —had entered Lyttelton Harbour. Next year three thousand emigrants arrived, and the Canterbury Settlement was started.

On one of the last days of September 1859, Samuel Butler embarked at Gravesend on the *Roman Emperor*. A little boat took him out from Gravesend pier to the ship moored in the middle of the river. His account of his departure, in *A First Year in Canterbury Settlement*, reads like a scene by Frith. 'I was somewhat taken aback with the apparently inextricable confusion of everything on board; the slush upon the decks, the mustering of the passengers, the stowing away of baggage still left upon the decks, the rain and the gloomy sky. . . . Honest country agriculturists and their wives were looking as though they wondered what it would end in; some were sitting on their boxes and making a show of reading tracts which were being presented to them by a serious-looking gentleman in a white tie; but all day long they had perused the first page only, at least I saw none of them turn over the second. . . . By and by a couple of policemen made their appearance and arrested one of the party, a London cabman, for a debt. He had a large family, and a subscription was soon started to pay the sum he owed. Subsequently a much larger subscription would have been made in order to have him taken away by anybody or anything.

'Little by little the confusion subsided. The emigration commissioner left; at six we were at last allowed some victuals. Unpacking my books and arranging them in my cabin filled up the remainder of the evening, save the time devoted to a couple of meditative pipes. The emigrants went to bed, and when, at about ten o'clock, I went up for a little time upon the poop, I heard no sound save for the clanging of the clocks from the various churches of Gravesend, the pattering of rain upon the decks, and the rushing of the river as it gurgled against the ship's side.'

That night, for the first time in his life, Sam did not say his prayers.

CHAPTER III

SHEEP FARMER

NOT ONLY DID BUTLER STOP SAYING HIS prayers as the distance between him and Langar increased, but he spent the voyage reading Gibbon's *Decline and Fall* and learning to play the concertina. Besides that, he organized the ship's choir, which performed Glorias and Te Deums. Towards the end of January 1860, after the usual experience of storms and calms common in the days of sailing ships, the *Roman Emperor* came into Port Lyttelton.

Port Lyttelton lies in the crater of an extinct volcano, the sides of which rise round it on the land side as a range of hills; behind these hills lie the Canterbury Plains. 'Oh, the heat!' wrote Butler in one of his first letters home. 'The clear transparent atmosphere, and the dust! How shall I describe everything—the little townlet, I cannot call it a town, nestling beneath the bare hills that we had been looking at so longingly all the morning—the scattered wooden boxes of houses, with ragged roods of scrubby ground between them—the tussocks of brown grass—the huge wide-leaved flax, with its now seedy stem sometimes fifteen or sixteen feet high, luxuriant and tropical-looking—the healthy clear-complexioned men, shaggy bearded, rowdy-hatted and independent, pictures of rude health and strength.' His first serious shock was when he discovered that beer cost sixpence a glass; but after dinner, he at once began to climb the hill behind the port. 'It is volcanic, brown, and dry; large intervals of crumbling soil, and then stiff wiry uncompromising-

43

looking tussocks of the very hardest grass; then perhaps
a flax bush, or, as we should have said, a flax plant; then
more crumbly, brown, dry soil, mixed with fine but dried
grass, and then more tussocks; volcanic rock everywhere
cropping out, sometimes red and tolerably soft, sometimes black and abominably hard. There was a great deal,
too, of a very uncomfortable prickly shrub, which they
call Irishman, and which I don't like the look of at all. . . .
So we continued to climb, panting and broiling in the
afternoon sun, and much admiring the lovely view
beneath.'

At Christchurch on the Avon, a larger town than
Lyttelton and more scattered, but with the same shaggy,
clear-complexioned men, wearing 'exceedingly rowdy
hats', the conversation was all of sheep, horses, dogs,
cattle, English grasses, paddocks and bush. Butler was
startled at hearing one man ask another whether he meant
to wash that year, and receive a negative reply. He soon
discovered, however, that a man's sheep are himself. As
he listened to the conversation, he was struck by un-
familiar expressions—'No fear!', 'Don't *you* believe it!',
'It is so.' He was amused too, by their use of 'hum'
without pronouncing the 'u', which, he noticed, stood for
either assent or dissent, 'or a general expression of com-
prehension without compromising the hummer's own
opinion. . . . In fact, if a man did not want to say anything
at all he said "hum-hum".'

He bought a horse, helped some friends to move into
their house, and scrubbed the floors of two rooms for
them. As he came to know the country better, it seemed
to him 'a sort of cross between the plains of Lombardy
and the fens of North Cambridgeshire'. At the club conversation continued 'purely horsy and sheepy'. He rode
further into the country and visited a farm, where he
found the owners, two brothers, dining off cold boiled

mutton, bread and cold tea without milk—then the usual
fare of New Zealand sheep-farmers. At another station
where he put up for the night, during one of his pros-
pecting expeditions into the interior, he found the men
all gentlemen and sons of gentlemen. 'One of them is a
Cambridge man who took a high second-class a year or
two before my time', he wrote to Langar. 'Four of them
shared a hut, with earth floor, and took turns at cooking
and washing up'—unheard-of occupations for gentlemen
in England. Under the bed Butler found a copy of *The
Idylls of the King*. Next morning, when he asked where he
should wash, his host 'gave rather a French shrug of the
shoulders, and said "The lake".' Altogether, observes
Butler approvingly, 'there is much nonsense in the old
country from which people here are free . . . but it does
not do to speak about Johann Sebastian Bach's fugues or
Pre-Raphaelite pictures.' He saw his first sheep killed—
'rather unpleasant, but I suppose I shall get as indifferent
to it as other people are by and by. . . . The same knife
killed the sheep and carved the mutton we had for
dinner.'

By June he had bought twenty acres on the banks of
a stream known as Forest Creek and was living there with
his man and two cadets, who worked for him in return for
food and lodging. After a few months spent at Forest
Creek, he discovered that the climate was not sufficiently
mild for sheep to survive there in winter, and early next
year took up a run of about 8,000 acres on a terrace overlooking the Rangitata and lying between that river and
its tributaries. This became his permanent home in New
Zealand, and he called it Mesopotamia, because of its
situation between the two rivers. 'Never was a freshman
at Cambridge more anxious to be mistaken for a third-
year man', he tells us, 'than I was anxious to become an
old chum, as the colonial dialect calls a settler.' Butler

came to be known as 'the small dark man with the penetrating eyes who took up a run at the back of beyond, carted a piano up there on a bullock dray and passed his solitary evenings playing Bach's fugues'. Sometimes, when he turned his bullocks loose at night to feed, they would wander off and he would be unable to find them in the morning. 'I used to try and throw my soul into the bullocks' souls, so as to divine if possible what they would be likely to have done, and would then ride off ten miles in the wrong direction', he wrote later in *Alps and Sanctuaries*. 'People used in those days to lose their bullocks sometimes for a week or a fortnight, when they were all the time hiding in a gully hard by the place where they were turned out. After some time I changed my tactics. On losing my bullocks I would go to the nearest accommodation house, and stand drinks. Someone would ere long, as a general rule, turn up who had seen the bullocks.'

Robert Booth, who worked for him, has described Mesopotamia when Butler had been living there for a year and had about three thousand sheep. 'The homestead was built upon a little plateau on the side of the downs, approached by a cutting from the flat, and was most comfortably situated and well sheltered, as it needed to be, the weather being often exceedingly severe in that elevated locality. Butler was a literary man, and his snug sitting-room was filled with books and easy chairs—a piano, also, upon which he was no mean performer. The station hands comprised a shepherd, a bullock-driver, hut-keeper, and two station hands employed in fencing-in paddocks, which with Cook, the overseer, Butler, and myself made up the total. At daybreak we all assembled in the common kitchen for breakfast, after which we separated for our different employments. At 12 noon we met again for dinner, and again at 7 p.m. for supper, which meal being over, Butler, Cook and I would repair

46

to the sitting-room, and round a glorious fire smoked or read or listened to Butler's piano. It was the most civilized experience I had had of up-country life since I left Highfield. . . .'

Next year, Butler was becoming pressed for money and wrote to his father on 31 May 1861: 'It is exceedingly distasteful to me to keep hammering at you for the remaining £1,000 [Canon Butler had just sent him £500] but I am compelled to do so. My mother, too, begs me not to; and I can see clearly that I am urging you to do something that you do not like. I have very little remembrance of what I wrote in the letter before last, but I fear I may have let fall expressions that I should decidedly repent at leisure.' Apparently his father had promised to let him have £3,000 by instalments over and above the £2,000 already sent out to New Zealand, and on the strength of this promise Butler had made large purchases. Since then the Canon had apparently become more cautious and the instalments were not reaching New Zealand as expected. There follows a long recapitulation of all the old misunderstandings. Butler reminds his father that he has never asked him for any money at all, but that since the money had been offered he had engaged himself up to within £200 of the whole amount. His tone, as usual, almost suggests that his father has been guilty of sharp practice. But his anxiety is understandable. 'I regret that I have lost one or two letters from home upon money matters; I have the one containing the original offer, and I have quite sufficient of subsequent ones to support what I am here stating; but I have not the whole connected chain, link by link.' Any subsequent change in his father's plans, he tells him, 'is not the less injurious to me for the excellence of the intentions which dictate it'. Besides, his sheep might get the scab—though that could not quite be laid at his father's door. As it is his flock is a fair one, rather above the average, 'but had I been able to command ten pound rams instead of three pound rams, my present lambing would be worth a great deal more than it is'. Also, had he had more money he could have built a better woolshed. 'If you send me out the remaining £1,000, as I earnestly request you to do, my entire outlay will have been £5,200. In eight or nine years time the net income from my sheep should be £400 per annum. Every year from date income rapidly increases while expenses remain nearly stationary. . . .' Nevertheless, Canon Butler did not send the remaining £1,000. Butler had received in all £4,400, with a loan of £600—not ungenerous of the Canon considering the relationship between father and son and the tone of righteous indignation adopted by the latter.

Sheep, however, did not occupy all Butler's thoughts. There were long periods of repose which gave him leisure for 'that mental exercise which I delight in', as he wrote to his cousin Philip Worsley in January 1861. While congratulating Philip on his engagement, he adds: 'I am not in love myself nor ever have been since certain spoony intervals as a boy. I have my ideal—and should I fall in with her shall recognize her at a glance, but as yet I have never done so. Still I can sympathize with those who have found the haven wherein their hearts can rest. My enemies doubt whether I am possessed of such an inconvenient piece of lumber at all. I believe, however, that it exists.' As for his religious opinions, 'a wider circle of ideas has resulted from travel, and an entire uprooting of all past habits has been accompanied with a hardly less entire change of opinions upon many subjects. . . . If anyone wishes to know my opinions upon a subject I can now content myself with stating them as clearly as I can, but I have ceased to regard it as a matter of personal con-

sideration to myself whether he agrees with me or no; for
I consider no man has a right to demand from another
that what appears to be satisfactory to himself should also
appear so to that other. . . . From Gibbon, whom I read
carefully on my voyage out and whom I continue constantly to snatch at, I fancy that I am imbibing a calm and
philosophic spirit of impartial and critical investigation.
Much as there is in Gibbon which we should alike con-
demn—for, however we may admire his sarcasms, it is
impossible not at times to feel that he would have acted
more nobly in suppressing them—he is a grand historian
and the impress of a mighty intellect is upon his work.'
Later, of course, Butler's sarcasms against Christianity
were to be as biting as any of Gibbon's. But he was still
very much preoccupied with the Gospels.

'I want a wife dreadfully up here', he confesses to his
aunt, Mrs Worsley, eight months later. 'What will you
all say if I marry a Maori? Unfortunately there are no
nice ones in this island. They all smoke, and carry eels
and are not in any way the charming, simple-minded
innocent creatures which one might have hoped. Can you
not imagine that a nice quiet wife—a good stay-at-home
helpmate—would be a very great boon to anyone situated
as I am? . . . My present cook, who has been with me
about a month, is the next best substitute for a woman
about this station that could easily be found. He can
actually starch collars, which I think proper to wear, even
in this out-of-the-way place.' He goes on: 'They will have
told you at home of my two huts, my paddocks, my
garden, which is now beautiful in a culinary point of
view, green peas coming into blossom, potatoes well up,
asparagus bed made and planted. . . . I have a few rose
trees, carnations and narcissus, a daffodil, some poppies,
stocks, sweet williams and larkspur—all in two little beds
on either side of the gate. The rest is chiefly potatoes and

other vegetables. I have three little pear trees, three peach trees, four plum trees and four cherry trees. . . . The only thing I really want is the intellectual society of clever men. . . .' He complains that the landscape is inclined to be colourless, the wild flowers few and ugly, the grass yellow; when it is fine the air is so clear and bright that everything is a dazzle. 'I don't know how it is, but the scenery is not really beautiful save in the gorges of the streams that run into the main rivers in the back country.' But through his backdoor he could see mountains of 12,000 and 11,000 feet, covered with glaciers and looking much the same winter or summer. 'I cannot compare the scenery with the Swiss or Italian. One reason may be the want of association with human labour or sympathies. . . . For my part, I never think about it when I am out looking for sheep, when at home I am thinking of music, of my studies (which are pretty considerable), or in the garden.' His chief study is still the New Testament. 'The subject has such intense and absorbing interest for me that it is no use. I must go on.'

A year later he is writing to his Cambridge friend Marriott: 'For the present I renounce Christianity altogether. You say people must have something to believe in. I can only say that I have not found my digestion impeded since I have left off believing in what does not appear to be supported by sufficient evidence. As for going to church, I have left it off this twelvemonth and more. . . . When I went last I made a few notes and on returning wrote a short account of what I had heard and felt. I wrote it without either exaggeration or humour, but tried to put down *bona fide* what passed within and without me.' His studies of the Greek Testament had forced him to the conclusion that Jesus Christ did not die upon the Cross. He also read Darwin's *Origin of Species*, became one of Darwin's most enthusiastic admirers, and in December 1862 contributed a dialogue on Darwinism to the Christchurch *Press*, a paper founded in 1861 by his friend Edward Fitzgerald and edited by Professor Sale. In this dialogue his opponent objects that Darwin's account of the ceaseless war of the different species upon each other and the survival of the fittest is 'very horrid', to which Butler replies that it is 'no more horrid than that you should eat roast mutton or boiled beef'. It is as though someone today should object that Marx's view of society as motivated by the ceaseless struggle of different classes for supremacy were horrid, and one should reply: 'No more horrid than that you should live upon dividends.' Later, Butler came to think Darwin's theory too mechanical, just as most economists today find Marx (who was largely based upon Darwin) mechanical.

At the time, the dialogue provoked a reply from Dr Abraham, Bishop of Wellington, who wrote an article to the *Press* called 'Barrel Organs', ridiculing Darwin. Butler replied to this under the initials 'A.M.' In March 1863 Darwin himself wrote to the *Press*, praising Butler's dialogue for the clear and accurate view it gave of his theory of evolution. The correspondence went on till May, and in the course of it the Bishop pointed out that Erasmus Darwin and Buffon had to some extent anticipated Charles Darwin. It was perhaps this that directed Butler's attention to these earlier writers on evolution, whom he came later to place above the author of *The Origin of Species* himself.

Of still greater interest, as the genesis of one of the leading ideas in *Erewhon*, is Butler's letter to the *Press* of 13 June 1863, the brilliant 'Darwin Among the Machines', signed 'Cellarius', which applies Darwin's theory to the different 'species' of machinery, and concludes by advocating that all the more advanced machines should be destroyed lest, by their continued evolution, they supersede the human race. What sort of creature, Butler asks, is man's next successor in the supremacy of the earth likely to be? 'We have often heard this debated; but it appears to us that we are ourselves creating our own successors; we are daily adding to the beauty and delicacy of their physical organization; we are daily giving them greater power and supplying by all sorts of ingenious contrivances that self-regulating, self-acting power which will be to them what intellect has been to the human race. In the course of ages we shall find ourselves the inferior race. Inferior in power, inferior in the moral quality of self-control, we shall look up to them as the acme of all that the best and wisest men can ever dare to aim at. No evil passions, no jealousy, no avarice, no impure desires will disturb the serene might of those glorious creatures. Sin, shame, and sorrow will have no place among them. Their minds will be in a state of perpetual calm, the contentment of a spirit that knows no wants, is disturbed by no regrets. Ambition will never torture them. Ingratitude will never cause them the uneasiness of a moment. . . . If they want "feeding" (by the use of which very word we betray our recognition of them as living organisms) they will be attended by patient slaves whose business and interest it will be to see that they shall want for nothing. If they are out of order they will be promptly attended to by physicians who are thoroughly acquainted with their constitutions; if they die—for even these glorious animals will not be exempt from that necessary and universal consummation—they will immediately enter into a new phase of existence; for what machine dies entirely in every part at one and the same instant?'

Such a passage is of still greater force in 1953, when machines have gained much of the ascendency over us forecast by Butler. For what in our civilization excites such admiration as the latest member of their species?

Just as Marx said that the capitalist class have brought into being the class that will supersede them, so, Butler argues, 'we are ourselves creating our successors—man will become to the machine what the horse and the dog are to man'. Two years later he attacked this view in another letter to the *Press*, 'Lucubratio Ebria', in which he put forward the contrary theory that machines and mechanical appliances should be regarded as mankind's extra limbs, and that it is because of these limbs that man differs not only from all other animals but from his own ancestors. Indeed, the two species among modern man, he says, are the rich and the poor. The rich can travel, the poor cannot, and 'he who can tack a portion of one of the P. and O. boats on to his identity is a man much more highly organized than the one who cannot. . . . We observe men for the most part (admitting, however, some few abnormal exceptions) to be deeply impressed by the superior organization of those who have money. It is wrong to attribute this respect to any unworthy motive, for the feeling is strictly legitimate and springs from some of the very highest impulses of our nature. It is the same sort of affectionate reverence which a dog feels for a man, and is not infrequently manifested in a similar manner.'

It is not surprising that a man who could write in this way soon became widely known in New Zealand. Butler had done well with his sheep, too. 'My sheep had bred; wool had kept high and so had sheep; runs which were pretty cheap when I reached New Zealand had gone up greatly in value', he writes. 'I had got hold of mine bit by bit and had pieced it into a compact, large, well-bounded, and, in all respects, desirable property.' He was however heavily involved with the merchants, and realized that if prices fell he might easily be cornered. In any case, the life of a grazier was utterly uncongenial to him. He there-

fore decided to sell, invest his money in New Zealand at
ten per cent, and go back to England. In four to five
years the £4,400 advanced by his father had become
£8,000. In every sense New Zealand had been the making
of Butler; the distance it put between him and his parents
enabled him to get hold of himself emotionally; the
healthy life developed him physically; solitude had helped
him to sort out his ideas, and material success had given
him self-confidence. He sold his run and moved into
Christchurch, where he became a regular contributor to
the *Press*. It was here, in the offices of the *Press*, that he
first met Charles Paine Pauli, the man who was to exercise
such a baleful influence on his life.

Pauli was the youngest son of Emilius Pauli, a merchant of Lübeck, who had settled in England; he was 'a
Winchester and Oxford man' and had a brother in New
Zealand known to Butler as the Resident Magistrate at
Kaiapoi. When Butler first met him he was working as
sub-editor of the *Press* at a salary of £150 a year. Pauli
was a great favourite with Fitzgerald, the editor, and it
seemed to be understood that he was going to marry
Fitzgerald's daughter. Indeed he charmed everyone, and
bewitched Butler. 'He was such a fine handsome fellow,
with such an attractive manner, that to me he seemed
everything I should like myself to be, but knew very well
that I was not', wrote Butler many years later. 'I knew
myself to be plebeian in appearance and believed myself
to be more plebeian in tastes than I probably in reality
was.'

Pauli was not slow to notice the impression he had
made. One evening in September 1863 he called at
Butler's hotel, quite unexpectedly, and stayed talking till
midnight. When he left, Butler was more impressed than
ever, and from then on, to quote Festing Jones, began
'one of those one-sided friendships . . . when the diffident,

poetical, shy man becomes devoted to the confident, showy, worldly man, as a dog to his master'. Pauli was a most efficient social machine; he was, in fact, Butler's *alter ego*. He saw Butler's weak points at once and used them for his own advantage, coldly and remorselessly. During the months while his affairs were being wound up Butler was constantly in Pauli's company. Pauli told him that he was unhappy in New Zealand, that the climate was bad for his health and that if he stayed there he would probably die. He said he wanted to return to England, consult English doctors, get called to the Bar, and then come back to New Zealand as a barrister. The only trouble was, he had no money—nothing beyond a reversion of £4,000 or £5,000 on the death of his parents, which he had already partly anticipated. Thereupon Butler, much moved by this story, offered to pay Pauli's passage back to England and to allow him £200 a year for three years till he could get called to the Bar. This was not so much a gesture of great generosity as melancholy evidence of the extent to which Butler had fallen under the spell of a charming swindler.

On 15 June 1864 the two friends sailed from Port Lyttelton in a small American barque of four hundred tons. A southerly gale nearly drove them on to the coast of North Island, where the settlers were still at war with the Maoris. The wind was so high that it broke the main yard clean in half, and had they been driven ashore they would in all probability have been killed and eaten, for the Maoris were still cannibals. Later Butler recorded in his *Notebooks* that a Maori chief, on being told that General Cameron was coming against him with big guns, replied: 'My big guns are night and storm.' On another occasion, the surveyor Cass told Butler that during a truce a Maori had said to him 'that he would shoot no more soldiers'. Cass said that he was very glad to hear it, but asked why. The Maori said that it did not pay; the powder cost him 13s. a pound, and if he shot a soldier the Queen could get another for a shilling. 'Now', he continued, 'it takes three years and a good deal of money to make a surveyor like you, and considering the price of powder, you are the kind of people whom I intend to shoot in future.'

But neither Butler nor Pauli were destined for the pot. Instead, the barque took them as far as Panama. Here they stayed two nights, in spite of a yellow fever epidemic, and watched cock-fighting in the streets. A miniature railway carried them, at exorbitantly high prices, across the Isthmus, and they re-embarked in a small steamer for St Thomas, where they boarded one of the finest paddle-steamers of the Royal Mail Company for Southampton. Among the passengers were many refugees from the Southern States of America, where the Civil War was still raging.

Throughout the voyage Pauli suffered acutely from his infected tongue and throat, though he allowed no one except Butler to know anything about it, and this stoicism only increased Butler's devotion. Though such a sentiment is most un-Erewhonian, it would have been better for Butler's peace of mind had he remembered the warning of his New Zealand friend William Sefton Moorhouse that 'very handsome, well-dressed gentlemanly men are seldom very good men'. But he felt supported and re-assured by Pauli's *savoir faire*. 'The main desire of my life', he wrote later, 'was to conceal how severely I had been wounded, and to get beyond the reach of those arrows that from time to time still reached me.' He felt that the mere fact of being Pauli's friend 'would buoy me up in passing through waters that to me were still deep and troubled, but which to him, I felt sure, were smooth and shallow as glass'. Unfortunately, it was Pauli himself who was smooth and shallow as glass. But when Butler looked at him he saw only all that he would like to have been.

They reached Southampton on 29 August 1864.

CHAPTER IV

PAULI

BY SEPTEMBER 1864 BUTLER AND PAULI were living in separate chambers at Clifford's Inn. Butler's rooms, and the staircase leading to them, dated from before the Fire. By present-day standards they had no conveniences; but they suited him admirably. The rather dry, legal atmosphere did not encourage family life. Clifford's Inn was a place for lawyers and bachelors with studious tastes, waited on by elderly women known as laundresses. It was a place for work and meditation, with the rich red brick of its seventeenth-century houses and the trees and central grass plot to relieve the severity of the brick. Butler had a sitting room, a bedroom, painting-room, pantry and a passage with cupboards in it on the second floor. The bedroom and painting-room looked east over Fetter Lane; the sitting-room looked west over the garden, dominated by the neo-Gothic towers of the Record Office. At first the rent was £23 a year; by 1898 it had risen to £36, including rates and taxes. Here Butler lived for the rest of his life. Today houses and gardens are gone, and on the site of Butler's rooms a block of offices, tiled white like a public lavatory, rears its blank back.

At first the two friends breakfasted and spent the evenings together. But it was not long before Pauli grew restive. He complained that the place was intolerable to him and that he must have 'a more airy situation'. So he moved into the West End, which accorded better with his tastes, though he still dropped in to lunch every day at Clifford's Inn, leaving immediately afterwards. 'From a very early period after his settling in London', writes Butler, 'the intimacy between us began to limit itself to this'—except, of course, that Pauli did not forget to collect his quarterly cheque. But when he had typhoid fever in 1866 he came back to Clifford's Inn to be looked after. In the autumn Butler took him to Dieppe for a month to recuperate, and at the end of this holiday Pauli said that, though he believed Butler had enjoyed himself, he had never been so miserable in his life. After that they never went out with one another again. Pauli still came to lunch, but he never bothered to conceal his boredom and became increasingly irritable in Butler's company. He was not interested in literature or music or painting or science or philosophy; he liked 'society' and Butler hated it. 'I was his host', Butler comments, 'and was bound to forbear, on that ground if on no other. I always hoped that, as time went on, and he saw how absolutely devoted to him I was, and what unbounded confidence I had in him, and how I forgave him over and over again for treatment that I should not have stood for a moment from anyone else— I always hoped that he would soften and deal as frankly and unreservedly with me as I with him; but, though for some fifteen years I hoped this, in the end I gave it up.' He did not give Pauli up, however, but continued to provide everything necessary to get him called to the Bar —books, fees, and all living expenses. Pauli was called to the Bar in 1867 and took chambers in Lincoln's Inn, in addition to his rooms in the West End. He told Butler to write to his office, if he had anything to say before they met again for lunch, but he was not to call. He also made it quite clear that Butler would not be welcome at his rooms, and when he moved he did not give him his new address, though he sometimes brought a friend to lunch.

Year by year, the more Butler did for him, the more Pauli kept him at arm's length. After he was called to the

Bar, Fitzgerald wrote from New Zealand urging him to return. He showed the letter to Butler, who said that he thought he ought to go, whereat Pauli burst into tears— 'a thing I had never seen him do', adds Butler, 'though I had done it often enough myself'. Altogether Pauli's behaviour was like that of a cruel mistress, who enjoys seeing just how far she can go in the exercise of her power. But some people are so wedded to those who hurt them most that in the end they cannot do without the familiar pain.

Since his return from New Zealand, Butler had worked hard. He devoted most of his time to painting, studying first under F. S. Cary in Streatham Street, Bloomsbury, and then at Heatherley's Art School in Newman Street. He worked at painting doggedly for seven hours a day; he also finished a pamphlet, begun in New Zealand, critically examining the Evangelical accounts of the Resurrection, and wrote some more of the essays which were to form the basis of *Erewhon*. He also kept up his music, practising in the evenings. Except for his fellow students at Heatherley's, Pauli, and his family when he visited Langar or Kenilworth, or went to Wales to stay with his brother and his wife, he saw practically no one. After one of these visits to Langar, he painted his best known and most delightful picture, 'Family Prayers', now at St John's College, Cambridge. Of this he said, justly: 'If I had gone on doing things out of my own head instead of making studies, I should have been all right.' Though Canon Butler can have taken no pleasure in such a work as 'Family Prayers', which is set in the dining-room at Langar, Butler was still painfully anxious to justify his choice of a career in his father's eyes. 'I wish the next time you are in London you would call at Heatherley's and ask old Heatherley what he thinks of me. He never flatters and will I am sure say very little and commit himself to nothing, but I think he will say enough to satisfy you that he sees no reason why I should not arrive at excellence: he looks very absurd and at first I thought him very affected in his manner and dress—his get-up being dishevelled or what he thinks "artistic", but the more I see of him the better I like him; it is a funny place too, and would amuse you.'

But he was driving himself too hard and this, combined with the humiliation of his dog-like devotion to Pauli, brought on a swollen tumour in his neck and noises in his head—danger signals which were, from that time onwards, to manifest themselves whenever he was in low health. The noises usually came on when he was on the point of going to sleep, and the first few times they occurred he got out of bed and went into his sitting-room, thinking that something had crashed to the floor. These symptoms, which began in 1866, had now increased to such an extent that the homœopathic specialist he consulted advised him to give up his work for five months and go abroad. He took the doctor's advice to the extent of going abroad in November 1869, travelling through Belgium, Switzerland and Italy to Menton, where he stayed from the middle of December till the following March, spending most of the time sketching and walking in the mountains. The tumour in his neck continued to grow and the noises in his head to increase, so he returned home at the end of March. 'Neither symptom', he says, 'became materially better until the death of my father.'

Next year he went abroad again, and while staying in Venice in the spring he met an elderly Russian baroness, 'plain, quiet, and not, at first sight, attractive'. They talked much together, and when he was leaving she said: '*Et maintenant, monsieur, vous allez créer*'—meaning that he had been looking long enough at other people's work and should now do something of his own. 'This sank into me and pained me: for I knew I had done nothing as yet, nor had I any definite notion of what I wanted to do. All was vague aspiration, admiration, and despair; nor did I know yet, though I was fully thirty-four years old, that the study of other men's works—except by the way—is the surest manner of killing the power to do things for oneself. . . . I had not yet, for all my education, got to know that doing is the sole parent of doing; and creating a little the only way of learning how to create more. . . . Still, I went home resolved to do at any rate something in literature, if not in painting.' With this resolve, Butler began looking over his old newspaper articles and the outcome was *Erewhon*. It was Sir Frederick Napier Broome, who had had a sheep-run near Butler's and who called on him by chance before taking up his appointment as Governor of Western Australia, who administered the 'final shove'. As they talked of old times, Broome mentioned Butler's articles and suggested that they would make a book. So Butler set to work on Sundays and in the evenings, recasting 'Darwin Among the Machines' and 'Lucubratio Ebria', which became 'The Book of the Machines', Chapters XXIII-V of *Erewhon*; 'The World of the Unborn', 'The Musical Banks' and 'An Erewhonian Trial' were also developed from some other articles he had written since his return from New Zealand.

The intermittent wrangling with his father over money now began again. His father had written asking his consent, as part owner, to the sale of the Whitehall fields to Shrewsbury School as building ground. Before consenting, Butler this time made enquiries about the value of the property and as a result realized that he had been 'bamboozled' by his father and his aunt when they asked his consent to the sale of the Whitehall Manor in 1857. Accordingly, on the advice of his Cambridge friend,

Creswell Peele, now a solicitor at Shrewsbury, he threat-
ened proceedings to try and get the original sale upset,
and a long and angry correspondence with his father
ensued, which he subsequently destroyed. 'If my mother
had not at the time become so ill as to be obviously
dying', he wrote later, 'I should have gone through with
the matter. But I could not go to law with relations among
whom was my own father, with the knowledge how bitterly such a course would be felt by my mother.' Butler
said that he would consent to the proposed sale of Whitehall fields to the school, provided his interest in his
grandfather's will was enlarged so as to become an absolute instead of a contingent reversion. As it was, unless
his father and his aunt would agree to cut off the entail,
he could not realize his share of the property until after
both their deaths. Canon Butler showed no willingness
to die at the moment, and while he lived his son remained,
as far as his inheritance was concerned, dependent on his
good will. But the Canon could not see why Butler
wanted to anticipate his inheritance. Was it, he asked,
that he was thinking of getting married? If so, and 'if, as
I have no reason to doubt, the lady is such as we can
fairly approve', there might be other ways in which he
could help him. This only annoyed Butler still more. He
replied that he was not in need of his father's help and
that he was not thinking of getting married, but 'a man
who can at any time lay his hand upon £6,000 more than
he had before is in a very much stronger position by the
mere possession of the power, even though he never uses
it—as I *believe* would be the case with myself'.

As a matter of fact, he was worse than married, for he
could no longer support Pauli out of his income, however
frugally he lived. His capital, some £8,000, was invested
in New Zealand at ten per cent; he now determined to
recall it. But the money was lent to Moorhouse on mort-

gage and, for all he knew, by suddenly calling it in he might put Moorhouse in a very difficult position. Butler tormented himself for years afterwards for having 'broken faith' with Moorhouse, 'one of the very finest and best men whom it was my lot to cross'. Unfortunately, no safe investment would yield anything like the interest he had been getting in New Zealand. While he himself could live on a much lower rate of interest, supplemented by what he hoped to make as a painter, it would not be enough to support Pauli, whose demands upon him seemed to increase in proportion to his growing dislike.

In 1873, Henry Hoare, of Hoare's Bank, the old college friend who had paid for the printing and production of *Erewhon*, started various companies which promised to pay high rates of interest. Among these were a patent steam-engine company, a gas-meter company, a company for pressing jute in India, and one for making hemlock bark in Canada, which was to pay at least sixty per cent and revolutionize the leather trade. Butler was unfortunate enough not only to invest his own money in the Canada Tanning Extract Company, but to get several of his friends, including Pauli, Pauli's brother, Heatherley and Jason Smith (another college friend) to do the same. So promising did the Canada company look at first that he gave Pauli back the assignments of his interest in his reversion—the only security he possessed for all the sums he had up to then advanced to him. Meanwhile both Butler and Pauli became directors of the company, and sat back with the expectation of making their fortune.

Their disappointment was not long deferred. Within two years, Hoare, whose income was between £40,000 and £50,000 a year, went bankrupt as a result of delirious speculation, and Butler found most of his capital gone. He still hoped to save at least part of what he had invested, however, and it was agreed that he should go over to Montreal to investigate matters on the spot. As before in New Zealand, when faced with practical problems he showed great energy and good sense. He soon discovered that the company could never hope to succeed, for their extract of bark, though it made excellent leather, gave it such a disagreeable odour that no one would buy it, and week by week barrel after unsaleable barrel of leather went on accumulating. Butler advised his co-directors to issue no more contracts for bark till they had found or created a market. Though this seems to have been no more than common sense, his advice made no impression on the board in London, and this, for the first time, shook his high opinion of Pauli's worldly wisdom. Then the company's representatives in Canada bitterly resented his being put over them. The resident manager, Foley, complained that 'the works statements are examined to a farthing by him'. As Foley had been juggling with the accounts, he had reason to fear Butler's scrutiny of them, and in his anger he grew abusive: 'He is to get to the bottom of it if it cost him his life', Foley wrote to Bradley, the foreman. 'It should cost him a good kicking; he wants to be snubbed.' Foley became so obstructive that Butler had to dismiss him, with the result that he went to law with the company. Butler was cross-examined in court for hours together, and Foley's counsel tried to get his evidence set aside on the grounds that he was an atheist.

Butler did not like Canada, and was depressed by its commercial and suburban atmosphere. When a Montrealler told him that he had a yearning to get away from civilization, Butler replied that 'we are all of us given to discontent and seldom knew when we had got what we wanted'. In the Natural History Museum at Montreal he came upon plaster casts of the Antinous and the Dis-

cobolus stowed away in a lumber-room among dried
skins, snakes, insects and stuffed owls. 'Ah', said Butler,
'you have some antiques here. Why don't you put them
where people can see them?' 'Well, sir', said the cus-
todian, who prided himself on a family business connection with Spurgeon, the Baptist, 'you see, they are rather
vulgar.' This experience gave rise to the famous 'Psalm
of Montreal', with its despairing refrain:

Stowed away in a Montreal lumber room
The Discobolus standeth and turneth his face to the wall;
Dusty, cobweb-covered, maimed and set at naught,
Beauty crieth in an attic and no man regardeth:
>> O God! O Montreal!

. . . .

And I turned to the man of skins and said unto him 'O thou
man of skins,
Wherefore hast thou done thus to shame the beauty of the
Discobolus?'
But the Lord had hardened the heart of the man of skins,
And he answered, 'My brother-in-law is haberdasher to Mr
Spurgeon.'
>> O God! O Montreal!

'The Discobolus is put there because he is vulgar,
He has neither vest nor pants with which to cover his limbs;
I, Sir, am a person of most respectable connections—
My brother-in-law is haberdasher to Mr Spurgeon.'
>> O God! O Montreal!

Butler was in Canada, with the exception of two short
visits to England to consult the board, from June 1874
to November 1875. During this time the company's
affairs went from bad to worse, for the board in London
continued to issue large contracts. The climax came when
Foley tried to get Butler arrested on the charge of con-

spiring against him and perjuring himself by his evidence. Butler hurriedly left for England and finally Foley was arrested instead. When the company smashed, Butler discovered that he had only £2,000 left of his original capital, and this he and Pauli set themselves to eat up bit by bit. Though he was 'ruined', the experience was valuable to him, Jones remarks caustically, as it showed him something of the ways of business men, of which he would have otherwise been ignorant. It also showed Butler that Pauli was not a superior being.

'I kept on writing, first *Life and Habit*, and then *Evolution Old and New*, and painting as well as I could, but though I wrote, so far as I can judge, better and better, I painted worse and worse. I was assiduous at dear old Mr Heatherley's School—the very last thing to help me—but people said my work was "jaded", and I have little doubt that it was so. The Academy would hang me no more, and by degrees I resigned myself to the conviction that literature was my strongest card. If I had known as much as I do now I should have known that such books as *Life and Habit* and *Evolution Old and New* could never possibly pay their expenses. To write them was to run my head against a stone wall.'

At Christmas 1875 Butler told Pauli that he ought to let him know more freely how he was doing at the Bar, for he had kept nothing from him, and he expected Pauli to be equally frank about his own affairs. For reply Pauli burst into tears and said that he was just covering his expenses. He promised in the course of the year to be more explicit, but begged Butler not to question him further. By next Christmas Butler's funds were still lower, so he once more asked Pauli how he stood. Pauli again burst into tears and again promised to be more open in the future, and meanwhile continued to take Butler's money. Christmas 1877 came. 'I was oppressed at all

6

times with a sense of the utter iniquity of the treatment I was receiving, but my book; my foreign trip in the autumn to the Canton Ticino; my friendship with H. F. Jones, which was now ripening into intimacy; my own sanguine temperament; and lastly the fact that the time during which Pauli and I were actually in one another's company was limited to his lunching with me from 1.20 to 2.10 three times a week, enabled me to bear it.' It is therefore all the more surprising to read the dedication of *Life and Habit* to Pauli, 'in acknowledgement of his invaluable criticism of the proof-sheets of this and my previous books and in recognition of an old and well-tried friendship'. If Butler's account of their 'friendship' is true, nothing could be more ironical. But perhaps it is not the whole truth.

By Christmas 1878 their relations had assumed the character of a macabre comedy. Butler spoke again, and Pauli burst into tears and told him nothing. On one occasion, indeed, Pauli did admit that he ought to have said more in the way of thanks, but that his pride prevented him; to which Butler gently replied: 'Pauli, that is not well said. Your pride never hinders you from receiving an obligation, and if it were of the right sort it would not hinder you from acknowledging it.' 'I know', said Pauli melodramatically, 'I shall die without ever having said what I ought to have said, and if I do, I shall suffer the agonies of the damned.'

As a matter of fact, he was doing pretty well. He conducted all the complicated negotiations attendant upon Sir Erasmus Wilson's removal of Cleopatra's Needle from Alexandria to London and its erection on the Embankment. Butler, however, knew nothing about this and continued to pay him an allowance.

In October 1879 Butler wrote to his father to say that the time was approaching when he would be absolutely

without means. This must have come as an unpleasant
shock to the Canon who, nevertheless, promised to do
what he could, provided he knew all the facts. Not unnaturally, he suspected blackmail, or some other discreditable entanglement. He was not far wrong. 'Pray let
no false shame hinder you from making a clean breast of
it', he wrote. Butler at once took violent exception to the
tone of his father's letter and refused to disclose his
private affairs. The Canon replied, not unreasonably: 'Do
not look out for points to cavil at. I wanted and still want
to know what would set you free from your present entanglements . . . if you catch at phrases you may find
matter for offence in an invitation to dinner. . . . I repeat
I am willing to help you if you will deal openly and send
your address. I will send you £50 at once, but to help you
further I must know all.' Butler had written asking his
father to keep his confidence and not to pass on what he
told him to his sister May. His father objected that, as he
lived with May and as there was no one else to whom he
could 'pour out his worries and anxieties', he could not
consent to anything that would put a barrier between
their free confidence. Butler thereupon sent his father's
letters to Peele at Shrewsbury and tried to get him to tell
the Canon that he had demurred to certain passages in
them on Peele's advice. He then told his father to deal
direct with Peele.

The Canon's incomprehension when he heard about
Pauli is understandable. 'But still he lives upon you', he
wrote in amazement on 28 October 1879, 'and though
perhaps not earning as largely as I supposed [he had
made independent enquiries and discovered that Pauli's
income was about £1,000 a year], still he is earning something and more, I imagine, than yourself. I am not
writing to upbraid you, but am asking you to break
through your reticence and to clear Mr Pauli of the

appearance of somewhat mean conduct, if he can be cleared. I am disposed to think that you can put some more favourable construction on all this, and that I have misapprehended something, but the only way is to give me a plain statement of the real facts.' Butler replied: 'I have sent your letter to Mr Peele who will advise me into how much detail I ought to go—I mean can rightly and properly go.' To Peele he wrote that his father's intention was 'to get damaging matter against my friend out of me under the pretext of doing justice to him. My father's letter is full of exaggeration and mis-statements, but I cannot enter upon a harassing correspondence with him such as a detailed answer to his letter would entail. He has refused to help me to help my friend over the next twelve months. . . . He wants to cross-examine me as to my expenditure for fifteen years. Each question that I answer leads to others, and all goes to my sister. If you think well to see my father and write to him, pray do so; in conversation he is better than by letter.' Peele replied that if Canon Butler was mistaken in his view of the case, the best course would be for Butler to give him an account as short as possible of the real facts—which was all the Canon had asked for originally.

So Butler sent his father a letter of twenty pages, marked 'Private and Confidential', giving the whole history of his relationship with Pauli. 'The story as you put it', he told his father, 'wears a very ugly appearance; if it were true, it would reflect strongly upon Pauli, and hardly less so indirectly upon myself. There is, however, so little truth in it, not only this, but such small appearance of truth, that I wonder you should have thought it worthy of any credence.' He helped Pauli, he said, because he 'had got him into a very deep hole' by inducing him to invest in Hoare's companies. He had pulled Pauli out of this hole 'in such a manner that it

would take a good deal stronger man than either he or
you to have resisted me. . . . Pauli hoped and hopes to
repay me whatever he had from me. I know Pauli very
well, and have always observed him, and found those who
know him to consider him a man of scrupulous integrity
in money matters, nor has anything occurred to shake my
confidence in him.' Poor Butler! By virtue of some extraordinary hold he had over him, Pauli had so far managed
to extract from him £3,500. 'Of course he knew I was
running very short, and was, I take it, as unhappy on
this score as his worst enemy could desire. It was never
contemplated that anything I then did—very easily—
very gladly—and with a perfect right to do it—should
be raked up against him years afterwards, exaggerated,
distorted, put into juxtaposition with calumnious stories
almost wholly without foundation, canvassed by yourself
with a sister whose ways of looking at things are widely
different from my own, and go afterwards I know not
where, nor in what shape.'

On receipt of this Canon Butler observed with remarkable self-control that Sam's letter had cleared Pauli
'of a great deal of that which seemed to me unsatisfactory
in his conduct', but that he did not 'quite understand his
continuing to accept it [the allowance] knowing that you
are now without funds, and with the purpose not merely
of enabling him to live but to make such appearance as
might impress others with the notion that he was doing
more than he really was. . . . I may add that I never
received one word of explanation from Mr Peele, beyond
the paper which I had from him through Mr How
stating that you wanted £1,060 this year and £405 per
annum afterwards.' Finally, the Canon agreed to allow
Sam £300 a year, provided he undertook to do no more
for Pauli and to deduct any sums he earned by writing
or otherwise. At the same time he said he would only

leave him a life interest in the estates at Shrewsbury. Butler replied that his father had dealt him 'almost the heaviest and most far-reaching blow which a father can inflict upon a son'. Pauli 'behaved well' when he heard that Butler could not give him any more money. But next time he came to lunch he put on an old coat and coughed a good deal.

Alarming reports now began to reach Canon Butler about the life his other son, Tom, was leading in Brussels. In the autumn of 1880 he therefore went across to Belgium to investigate. He 'did not like the hours Tom kept', he wrote, but, apart from that, he could not discover 'anything tangible'. The following January Tom visited his father at Shrewsbury, where the Canon had retired since giving up his living at Langar, bringing with him a Belgian woman, Barbe Kuster, whom he lodged, unknown to his family, at an hotel in the town. He had not been at his father's house for long before a telegram arrived from Brussels saying that his son Harry was dangerously ill, and he left at once for Belgium, accompanied by Barbe. 'While Tom was in the drawing-room at my father's', records Butler, in his account of the whole affair in a long note to his General Correspondence, 'after all the blinds were drawn down for the night and the curtains drawn, she had come into the garden and had tapped quietly at the window to call Tom out, and her footsteps were noticed next morning, but were not supposed to have anything to do with my brother. I can't say whether it was then that Barbe Kuster gave him the telegram . . . which she had no doubt prepared before she left Brussels, and left with a confederate to be forwarded at the proper moment, but at any rate shortly afterwards the telegram was produced and obviously believed by my brother to be genuine. There followed enquiries from my father and May about Harry's health, and by and by my sister-in-law told the whole story to my father and asked his protection.'

It is all very exciting and Victorian—the 'bad woman' rapping at the window at night and the footsteps in the snow. Curiously enough there had recently been an Anglo-Belgian *cause célèbre* in which a Belgian *cocotte* had proposed to a young Englishman that they should murder his father. The woman never intended that the father should be murdered and only wanted compromising evidence against the son in order to blackmail them both. 'I imagine', says Butler, 'that Barbe Kuster had laid some hardly less nefarious scheme before my brother and, not intending that it should ever be carried out, had prepared the telegram which she had arranged should be sent as soon as she considered that my brother had been sufficiently compromised.' At any rate, Tom, as Canon Butler wrote to Sam, after the whole story had come out, with his 'profligacy and falsehood and utter folly', had practically ruined both himself and his family. 'I don't care to go further into it than to say his recklessness has pledged him to an abandoned woman for 60,000 francs and 10,000 more, and has suffered her to tear up her receipts for what portion he had already paid her and burn them. The business is sound but brought to the verge of ruin and bankruptcy by this wickedness, and he has mortgaged his expectancy on Kenilworth. It is absolutely necessary to stop this, and by Belgian law a guardian can be appointed, and that I hope will be shortly done, but it requires an application by six of his family relations. . . . The evil has been going on for eleven years, beginning with that wretched Miss Adams about whom you know and who was two years (I now learn) at Brussels.' To Tom he wrote: 'There is nothing short of God's help that can bring you through it and without prayer it is impossible you should be brought through it.

73

Therefore pray you must. These wretched women must be neither seen nor spoken to nor written to again.' Tom wrote his reply roaring with laughter: 'Father, I have sinned, and am no more worthy to be called thy son. I cannot hope that you will forgive me but I trust that God can and will', and so on, says Butler, for three or four pages. The fact is, that under the Victorian code repression was so severe that when sex did manifest itself it took ugly and secretive forms, and it became a most potent instrument of blackmail.

Canon Butler was very well off, but he now had Tom's wife and family on his hands, and his exasperation with his 'infidel' son, whom he was now also called upon to support, exploded in the letter of 30 May 1881. 'Dear Sam, I this morning desired Messrs Burton & Co to pay £150 to your account as before, and you will receive the same sum next December. After that I shall pay you £125 for the two next half years and after that, if I live, £100. My income is reduced and I have to contribute to your unhappy brother's family to enable them to live. And this summer I shall have to borrow £150 to pay you. You will not therefore be surprised that I shall expect you to do something for your maintenance.' Butler replied: 'My dear Father, I have been endeavouring to answer your letter of the 30 May in a way agreeable on the one hand to my own sense of self-respect, and on the other to what is expected from a son towards his father. On the whole I conclude I shall best succeed in this by confining myself to the acknowledgement of your letter and to saying that I have noted its contents and taken steps accordingly.'

The only way in which Butler could increase his income was by going into business. He therefore proposed to build houses on the Whitehall estate, if his father would lease him the land. To this proposal his father replied on

3 June: 'I have kept your letter a day to wonder at it! I do not know what you suppose my income to be, but I allowed you £300 a year, a very serious sum out of it, and in reducing that sum, which I am now compelled to do, I have shown more consideration for you than you did for me, for I proposed to give you a year to turn round in, and you gave me no time at all when you first declared yourself with a debt of £360. [This was actually Pauli's debt to Butler's cousin, Reginald Worsley]. I have never had a sign of gratitude for all I have done for you and you talk magnificently of what is due to yourself as if you were treating me with the greatest generosity in not using bad language. This is simply absurd.' As for leasing the Whitehall estate to him, the Canon wrote that he could not get the present tenants out till August twelvemonth and that he had no intention of doing so then. 'I cannot afford to lose the rent and do not think your security as good as theirs, or that our relations would be improved by more money transactions. Your note seems quite insensible to the kindness you have received or the inconvenience to which I am, and have been, and shall be put in my endeavour to make things easy for you. I think if you had an offer of entering business it was your duty to have accepted it rather than live in idleness on me. I gather you will now do this.'

Butler was disgusted by the 'coarseness' of his father's letter. True, he reflected, he had failed to make money by either his painting or his books so far; but surely he had made his mark, and this should lead to money before long. His father knew very well that he was working to the extreme limit of his tether. 'If he had had any goodwill towards me he would have said what he had to say in a less brutally offensive manner. But he had got me down and the fun of kicking me was too great to be neglected.' He contented himself with the thought that his father was nearly seventy-five, and could not last for ever.

Then Canon Butler suddenly did what Sam had been asking him to do for years and cut the entail of the Whitehall estate. Butler was now independent of his father; he could raise money on the estate and had no further need of an allowance. With the assurance of £6,000 to draw upon, he wrote to T. M. How at Shrewsbury: 'I am sorry to say that the relations between me and my father have suddenly and unexpectedly become such that they cannot be continued on their present footing. He has written upbraiding me with "ingratitude" and "preferring to live in idleness upon him" rather than work. I trust that both accusations are unfounded. I have answered my father's letter in three lines dealing solely with the business part of it, but I cannot have a recurrence of such letters, and have decided on the step I mean to take; I shall be very glad, however, to consult you personally as to the least undesirable manner of taking it. I wish to see you, then, partly on necessary business of my own, and partly as an old friend of my father's in whom I know him to have confidence.' Butler then went down to Shrewsbury and put up at the George Inn, enquiring through How whether his father would be prepared to see him. On having How's assurance that he would, he called upon his father at Wilderhope House.

The interview lasted about twenty minutes. Canon Butler began by saying that Sam had been over hasty in taking offence at 'certain very innocent expressions' of his own, but he was willing to overlook that and to assist him to the extent named in his letter, which was as much as his income would allow. Butler said this was what unfortunately he could not assent to. His father had accused him of idleness and ingratitude and so the allowance must stop. He exonerated himself from the charge of ingratitude and reminded his father that he had repelled all his advances. The Canon admitted this, and added that Butler's life had been practically one of idleness. 'You are now forty-seven', he said [he was only forty-five]. 'Nothing to which you have set your hand has ever prospered with you.' Butler said that at any rate he was writing his Italian book (*Alps and Sanctuaries*). The Canon tossed his head and said that that book ought to have come out before. 'Then seeing that he was unyielding and not disposed to look at my view of the matter, I said I was afraid I must close the interview. He demurred at this, and said that he did not think I could live without some assistance, and would still go back to the offer as per his last letter. I said: "I can have no more allowance, and I can have no more such letters as those two." He replied promptly, "If you don't have the allowance you will have no letters at all." I was beginning to say that it was not necessary that all communication should cease because the allowance did so, but I felt how hollow it all was and stopped in the middle.

'I then said I was sorry I had come there, for I found we were only irritating one another, which for my part I was most anxious to avoid. He was calmer then and I pointed out to him that the result of my coming to him for assistance had been more disastrous to me than almost any terms I could have made with others would have been—but I said this in as little offensive a way as I could. He cut me short here; he was very sorry—if I chose to take his offer, well; if not, it was no fault of his. I bowed and left him, saying something to the effect that this could not be done. As I got to the door I turned round and said, "It is not likely that you and I shall meet again." He replied "Probably not" in a tone which said distinctly "and so much the better for me", and so we parted. . . . I was quite quiet the whole time—exactly in the same form as I was at Mr How's.'[1]

After leaving his father, Butler felt some compunction and tried to write to him and apologize for having left him so abruptly. But he could not bring himself to do it, in case his father should think that he only wanted money. So he contented himself with writing to How and asked him if he would kindly find an opportunity of saying to Canon Butler that he hoped all intercourse between them was not at an end, and that if he thought his father would be glad for him to do so he would go down to Wilderhope in the autumn. How replied: 'Canon Butler will receive you and do his best to make things easy for you.' On 23 June Butler told How that he had had a perfectly kind and genial letter from his father, and that he was going down to Shrewsbury in a fortnight or three weeks' time for a few days. By the autumn friendly relations had been re-established and Butler was sending his father the illustrations for *Alps and Sanctuaries*. As for Tom, when How applied to him for £100 a year he had agreed to contribute towards his family's maintenance, Tom replied merely: 'War to the bitter death.' In another letter he said that in a few weeks he would be setting off from Brussels for a distant country and 'should never be heard of more'. Soon afterwards he cancelled an order to pay his dividends to his wife and instructed Sam, whom he addressed as 'Dear Sir', to hold them for him until further notice. At the same time he sent his wife and children cards decorated with forget-me-nots. According to his wife Etta, he was 'still in absolute slavery to more than one person, as he has been for years—he lives in a hell than which I think there can be no worse, and I am powerless to help him.' In fact the doctor had insisted on their living apart, and had told Etta that Tom would not

[1] General Correspondence.

live very long, inferring that he had contracted a disreputable disease.

There is a strange parallel between Sam and his bad brother: both had reacted violently against their early religious environment and had ruined themselves by their attachment to parasites. Tom, Butler tells us, hated his father 'with a fury which it would he hard to surpass' —a feeling that was reciprocated by the Canon, who said to Butler at this time: 'I don't care about knowing where he is, so long as we hear of his death.' For his part, Butler had always regarded his brother as 'an impossible person'.

At the end of 1883 Tom disappeared altogether. 'I quite see and have long feared that he might cause very great annoyance by being lost sight of and leaving no trace', wrote Canon Butler. 'The greatest risk is that he may have been stabbed in a brawl or got into some difficulties and be in hiding.' Two years later news came through the British Consul in Ajaccio that Tom had died in Corsica.

Butler now raised £5,000-£6,000 on his share in the Whitehall estate and, on the advice of Festing Jones, invested in small house property. He borrowed money at four and a half per cent and bought long leasehold household houses to pay, so he was assured, eight per cent if well bought and well managed. Reginald Worsley, an architect and builder, was to choose the houses and to be advised by Thurgood, a well-known auctioneer in Chancery Lane. The plan was as follows. Property was to be bought for, say, £6,000 in all; this was to yield a profit of £210 net after paying interest. This property was then to be mortgaged for, say, £3,000 which should, it was planned, yield £105 more. It was a complicated scheme and did not, in practice, work out quite so well, for the houses were a continual source of worry to Butler and in the end did little more than pay the interest on the mortgages. 'If Jason Smith had not from time to time tided me over difficulties', Butler admitted, 'I doubt whether I should have weathered all storms till my father died.' At any rate, it saved him, he says, from having to go to his father for help.

After allowing a little time to elapse, for appearance's sake, Pauli let Butler know once more that he was still very much in need of money. He did not actually ask for it, but he gave the impression that he was in difficulties. So Butler said he would allow him £200 a year without any condition, but on the understanding (implied, though not expressed) that without it he would be practically bankrupt and unable to carry on his profession. 'I would never have forgiven myself', says Butler, ' if he had been wrecked while I was able, at whatever cost, to help him.' Investing in house property led to Butler's keeping accounts by double entry, and from this it appears that Pauli had from him more than £3,000 from 1881 until his death in 1897. Pauli asked that those sums should be put down in a superintendence account, as though they were paid to him as manager of Butler's property. Though Butler says that he had by this time fully recognized that anything worthy of the name of friendship between Pauli and himself 'was not to be', Pauli still lunched with him three times a week, staying, as usual, just long enough to finish his lunch. Their conversation was perfectly friendly and genial. 'Nevertheless I could see that it was an effort to him to be in my company at all, and knew perfectly well that the whole thing was a sham—on my part an endeavour to deny that my passionate devotion to him for so many years in times gone by was spent in force, and on his part to satisfy himself that the intimacy between us was still so close as to warrant his taking money from me.'

Every quarter, when Butler gave Pauli his cheque, Pauli would smile apologetically and say 'Oh, thank you'. But no other allusion to money matters was ever made between them until Butler had once more reduced himself to bankruptcy. Until that recurring point was reached again, one suspects that Butler rather enjoyed the grim little comedy of these lunches. They had become, perhaps, a subtle form of revenge.

Butler now had to borrow again and cut Pauli down to £100 a year, on the understanding that he could borrow the other £100 from his brother, and then Butler would repay Captain Pauli on the death of his father. 'A second time we ate and ate and ate down to the bone, and in the autumn of 1886 I saw that by March 1887 my complete ruin was inevitable.' And so, no doubt, it would have been, had not Canon Butler died on 29 December 1886. Curiously enough, on the day after the Canon died, Pauli's father also died, and he came into his reversion. But he let Butler know that after all his debts had been paid there would be nothing left for him.

Butler had long feared that when he came into his own inheritance Pauli would expect more money still, 'and once or twice I said to him laughingly that I knew he would expect this, and knew also that I should not be able to do it'. Not a very pleasant joke, perhaps; but it contributed to the revenge. Nevertheless, he let Pauli have his £200 a year and repaid Captain Pauli (with five per cent interest) the arrears of the allowance that for the last few years he was supposed to have advanced, but it was to Pauli that he repaid them. In spite of this, Pauli still dropped the hint that he was 'd——d hard up', but 'I turned a deaf ear and laughingly said that I was very sorry I could do nothing to help him.' It was one of Butler's nightmares that Pauli was married and that at his death he would find himself responsible for his wife and family. But by this time Pauli had become such a wreck that every winter seemed likely to be his last, and Butler confesses that his obviously wretched health was one of the greatest holds he had upon him—a most un-Erewhonian sentiment.

But there was nothing to be done but 'so to behave towards him at all times that I might never be haunted by the remembrance of any unkind word, should it turn out that I was the survivor'. And clearly Pauli could not last much longer. Each winter he had increasingly severe attacks of bronchitis, and became so *distrait* in Butler's company that 'I felt sure that he had something on his mind. And I left it to him to speak, and he never spoke.' When a great friend of Pauli's, who 'adored' him, a man of very considerable means but almost out of his mind for many years with excessive drinking, died and only left Pauli £200, Pauli spoke 'as a man bitterly disappointed, but determined to take his disappointment like a gentleman'.

Christmas 1897 was, however, not to be celebrated by Pauli, for he had a worse attack of bronchitis than ever and was taken to a nursing home. Butler went off to spend his Christmas at Boulogne, and there he received a note from Pauli, written by one of the nurses, to say that he was weak but progressing and that Butler was on no account to attempt to see him. On his return to Clifford's Inn, Butler was reading *The Times* after breakfast on 30 December when he came upon an announcement of Pauli's death. He got in touch at once with the undertaker, who informed him that the funeral was to be on 1 January. The mourners assembled in the Westminster Bridge Road close to the Necropolis Station and a special train took them down to Brookwood cemetery. Among the mourners Butler noticed some men whose looks did not please him, especially one who announced himself as Pauli's executor. Butler got into a carriage with Edwin

Lascelles, one of Pauli's best friends, and 'a most respectable looking man' whom he took to be an undertaker. Butler asked Lascelles where Pauli lived and was told Belgrave Mansions, Grosvenor Gardens. Presently the respectable looking man in the corner said to Lascelles: 'I think, sir, you must be Mr Lascelles; if so I have a letter for you from Mr Swinburne—I am Mr Swinburne's valet.'[1] Lascelles read the letter, and observed: 'I wonder what made Mr Pauli take to living there.' 'Mr Swinburne persuaded him', said the valet, 'for he lived there and wanted to have him near him. Besides the rooms were very cheap. He only paid £120 a year for them, which was less than he had been paying in Bruton Street.' Butler asked Lascelles, 'Have you any idea how much Pauli made by his profession?' 'I do not know how he has been doing of late years', said Lascelles, 'but many years ago—perhaps twenty, but I cannot be certain—he told me he was earning about £700 a year. During the last few years, owing to illness, he had not been making more than £500 or £600. . . .' At the last he had been unable to take anything but grapes and champagne. Oh yes, Mr Swinburne had seen to it that he wanted nothing. 'He used to like having me about him', added the valet; 'I would sit by his bedside and read the paper to him every afternoon.'

After the funeral at Brookwood, the mourners partook of a sumptuous luncheon that had been sent down from London by Swinburne, and Butler had the grim satisfaction of reflecting that for once in his life he was making a hearty meal at what was very nearly Pauli's expense. Presently he heard the unpleasant-looking executor say to someone close by: 'He has left his brother, Colonel Pauli, a thousand pounds.' At that, Butler's reserve broke down for the first time, and he began to

---

[1] This is not, of course, Swinburne the poet.

7

realize how thoroughly he had been duped. Taking Lascelles aside, he said that he was in great doubt what to do; it seemed that Pauli was leaving money behind him and 'he had had between £6,000 or £7,000, first and last, from me; ought I to tell the executor or no?' Lascelles thought that Butler should put in a claim, if he had any means of substantiating it. When the first shock was over Butler recovered his equilibrium and realized that to say anything at all would be both useless and undignified. But he could not help asking Lascelles: 'Did he ever borrow money from *you*?' 'No, never, not so much as a five pound note', was the rejoinder.

On the return journey, Butler again found himself in the same carriage as Lascelles, and they were joined by the executor, Sam Bircham, a man named Preston, with whom Pauli used to go yachting, and Ainslie, the solicitor of the estate. Butler had a strong feeling that these men got into the same carriage with the intention of 'exploiting' him. The executor, who struck Butler as 'a very third-rate person', asked him if he knew anything about Colonel Pauli, and Butler said that he believed him to be 'a good simple-minded fellow', at which they all laughed. 'Well', said the executor, 'he has taken £1,000 under his brother's will.' 'I am very much relieved to hear it', said Butler with dignity. Then they all talked a little more about Pauli, his age, his health and so on, and Butler answered all their questions genially. At Waterloo they all shook hands and parted.

A few days later Butler wrote to Swinburne, in an attempt to get some kind of acknowledgement that he was under no further liability to Pauli, for he had an uneasy feeling that he might have been made responsible for £1,000 which Pauli had borrowed from Swinburne. He also asked if Pauli had left any kind of message for him. Swinburne replied that there was no message, told him what he had already heard from the valet, adding, 'He was blessed with excellent friends and was much attached to you', and asked if Butler would like any little memento. Butler replied: 'There is not the slightest chance of my forgetting Pauli so long as I can remember anything, and I wish for no other memorial of him than that which will abide within myself.'

Ainslie, the solicitor, then wrote to Butler, returning a will dated 1864 which had been made almost entirely in Pauli's favour, and which Pauli had kept, though he knew that Butler had made a later will, doubtless with the idea of trying to have the later one upset on some pretext had Butler died first. Ainslie added that he had some books and mementoes at his office and perhaps Butler would like to call and take his choice. Butler went to see Ainslie, whose first question was whether he knew a certain man named 'X'—the rich man who 'adored' Pauli. Butler said that he had only seen him once coming up some stairs as he was going down them many years ago. He then told Ainslie all he had done for Pauli, and when he heard that Swinburne had been 'helping' him too, he realized for the first time why Pauli would never give him his home address; it would have been most awkward if the two benefactors had ever met. Swinburne had been very surprised when he got Butler's letter saying that Pauli had lunched with him three times a week for twenty years. 'Butler? Butler?' he said, 'Why have I never heard of Butler for this twenty years past?'

Ainslie then said that Pauli's gross estate amounted to £9,000, and that, besides the legacy to his brother, £300 was to go to an old servant, £50 to his clerk and, after debts and estate duty had been paid, the balance went to a distant cousin.

'And how', said Butler, 'did he become possessed of this sum?'

'Heaven only knows', said Ainslie; 'I thought perhaps you might be able to tell me.'

Before leaving, Butler told Ainslie that he could tell Swinburne as much or as little of what he had said as he thought fit.

'It will be better to say nothing', said Ainslie. 'Pauli was on a high pedestal in the opinion of Swinburne and all his set. It would shock them terribly if they were to know what you have told me.'

Swinburne thought so highly of Pauli that he believed he had written *Erewhon* and, in his generosity, had allowed Butler to put his name to it.

After leaving Ainslie, Butler could not help wondering at the large sum Pauli had managed to amass, till it occurred to him that perhaps the answer lay hidden in the assumed casualness of tone with which the solicitor had asked him whether he had known 'X'. In fact, it began to look as though Ainslie suspected that the greater part of Pauli's fortune had come from that source. Butler then remembered Pauli laughing to him about the shifts by which 'X' was continually trying to evade income tax; also, during the winding up of his estate it was found that large sums of between £40,000 and £50,000 had disappeared. Pauli had said that he believed that 'X' must have been blackmailed for years. Indeed, for several years before his death he had been paralysed and under the care of two men to each of whom he left £4,000, as well as quantities of jewellery, for which he had had a passion. One of these men, according to Pauli, was a blackguard; the other was 'a decent fellow enough', had he not shared 'X's' weakness for drink. Pauli was, of course, far too adroit to adopt crudely criminal ways of getting money out of his friends and may, Butler thinks, have dealt with 'X' after some such fashion as this. He had doubtless complained, too, of being 'd——d hard up'

86

and 'X' may have said that he would like to do something
for him, beyond the odd sums he doubtless 'borrowed'
at different times—say, £10,000 in his will. Pauli may
have then pointed out that if 'X' did this, not only would
it all go in paying legacy duty, but a friend to whom he
owed several thousand pounds would expect to be repaid
when the will was made public. Much better give him
the money by deed or gift; he would then invest it and
give 'X' a formal acknowledgement that he was holding
it in trust for him during his lifetime. Then, if 'X' made
Pauli his sole executor, leaving him £200 for appearance's
sake, he could destroy all traces of the transaction. The
fact that Pauli had left £9,000 instead of £10,000 could
be attributed to his having eaten up £1,000 or so of his
capital during the last years of his life. Money to Pauli,
says Butler, 'was like cream to a cat—it had to be given
to him, he would never steal it', just as he never actually
told a lie. He never told Butler in so many words that he
would be bankrupt if Butler did not continue his allowance. He only burst into tears if he was questioned and
looked ill and down at heel and coughed, knowing that
Butler could never resist such appeals.

Butler comforted himself with the notion that Pauli,
though he cared nothing for him at least feared and
respected him. Had he cut off Pauli's allowance, and had
Pauli then died as the result of one of his winter attacks
of bronchitis, he would have been haunted by the fear
that he had been the cause of it to his dying day. Whereas
now, he said, his conscience was absolutely clear of all
offence towards him. 'I can laugh at the way in which
Pauli hoodwinked me; and, as I said to Ainslie, though
he left me nothing in his will, he has, in effect, left me
from £200-£210 a year, clear of all outgoings, for the
luncheons must be taken into account. We both laughed
somewhat heartily when I took in the luncheons.'

Butler's long account of his relationship with Pauli, written after his friend's death, is very nearly all we have to go upon, since he returned all Pauli's letters to him and there are no letters of his to Pauli. For all its protestations of goodwill and forgiveness—indeed, because of them—it is a sour document, all the more devastating for the considered quietness of its tone. (In this respect it might be compared with Oscar Wilde's long and bitterly reproachful letter to Lord Alfred Douglas, *Epistola: in Carcere et Vinculis*, though that has all the pity and terror of a tragedy, which Butler was careful to avoid.) Jones inevitably drew upon Butler's account in the *Memoir*; but when this appeared in 1919 it provoked letters of protest from Pauli's surviving friends. Sam Bircham wrote to the *Times Literary Supplement* of his lifelong friendship with Pauli, which began at Oxford in 1857: 'I never found him otherwise than loyal, true and sincere. We all loved him.' Edwin Lascelles also wrote to the *Times Literary Supplement:* 'In common with Mr Bircham and many other friends, I considered him the soul of honour and uprightness. I sometimes dined with him at his club when Mr Butler was also his guest, in regard to whom he invariably expressed himself in terms of affection and consideration.'

Both Swinburne's and Lascelles' letters conflict with Butler's assertion that Pauli cared nothing for him and that he never had any sort of return for his hospitality.[1] One can only conclude either that Pauli was not as bad as Butler painted him, or that Butler was an ideal victim who derived satisfaction from humiliating himself to a stronger and more worldly nature, and after Pauli's death revenged himself by humiliating him in the eyes of pos-

---

[1] On the other hand Swinburne's assertion in his letter to Butler after Pauli's death may have been simply due to kindness, for when he got Butler's letter he said that he had not heard of him for twenty years.

terity. Nevertheless Butler was uncertain whether he was doing right in leaving an account of their relationship at all, and warned future readers that it was an *ex parte* statement, since Pauli's version could never be known. But at the head of it he set La Rochefoucauld's maxim that it is less shameful to be deceived by one's friends than to distrust them.

CHAPTER V

ELIZA MARY ANN SAVAGE

I T WAS WHILE HE WAS WORKING AS A STUDENT at Heatherley's School of Art, 47 Newman Street, Oxford Street, that Butler first met Miss Savage in the late 1860's. He won her heart one day by silently holding out a basket of cherries as he passed her in the street. Up to then, he says, she had systematically snubbed him. 'One day when I was going to the gallery, a very hot day, I remember, I met you on the shady side of Berners Street, quietly eating cherries out of a basket', she tells him in one of her letters. 'Like your Italian friends you were perfectly silent with content,[1] and you handed the basket to me as I was passing, without saying a word. I pulled out a handful, and went on my way rejoicing without saying a word either. I had not before perceived you to be different from anybody else. As I went away to France a day or two after that, and did not see you again for months, the recollection of you as you were eating cherries in Berners Street abode with me, and pleased me greatly . . . '

They were both studying painting—Butler with a laborious determination to paint like Giovanni Bellini— but their common interest was literature. John Butler Yeats (the father of W. B. Yeats), who was their fellow student at Heatherley's in 1867-8, has left a charming account of both of them in his *Essays: Irish and American* (1918). The students, he says, called each other by their surnames, without the prefix of Mr, but Butler was

---

[1] See *Alps and Sanctuaries*, ch. 3.

always *Mr* Butler. Yeats, who was the younger man, while drawn to him by his essential kindness and good nature—'there is nothing so winning', he says, 'as a look of helpful kindness in a mocking face'—found Butler at the same time a little schoolmasterish and intimidating. It was difficult to behave in a Bohemian way when he was there. 'Butler was an Englishman through and through, and an Englishman of "class", with the superior manner of the public school and university man', writes Yeats. 'He had thick eyebrows and grey eyes—or were they light hazel? These eyes would sometimes look tired as he plied his hopeless task of learning to paint;[1] but the discovery of any mental slavery or insincerity among our band of students would bring a dangerous light into them, and he would say things that perhaps hurt very much men who were absolutely sincere, however mistaken. Then Butler . . . would humble himself and make apologies that were not always accepted, and in the grey eyes, like a little fire on a cold hearth, I would see a melting kindness that it must have been hard to resist. Good nature was fundamental in his character and was, I think, the source of most of his writings and opinions.' At this time Butler was still an ardent Darwinian and would ask his fellow students if they had read 'the book', meaning *The Origin of Species*, and if they had not he would offer to lend it to them. He used to shock people, too, by asking them if they believed in God.

Towards women Butler was always 'kindly and

[1] Not so hopeless, as is shown by 'Family Prayers' and the 'Self Portrait' at St John's College, Cambridge, 'Mr Heatherley's Holiday' at the Tate Gallery, the portrait of Alfred and the illustrations to *Alps and Sanctuaries*. Butler is describing his own work, a little sardonically, in *The Way of All Flesh* when he writes that old Mr Pontifex 'could play as much as he could draw, not very well according to professional standards, but much better than could have been expected'. Mr Pontifex's drawings were 'so unaffectedly painstaking that they might have passed for the work of some good early master'.

fatherly and innocent'. At Heatherley's they called him
'The Incarnate Bachelor'. He soon discovered that Miss
Savage laughed easily, but as usual he was cautious. She
was not very young, and she was lame—'fair', says Yeats,
'with a roundish face and light blue eyes that were very
sensitive and full of light; a small head, her features
charmingly mobile and harmonious'. She was about
Butler's age—that is, about thirty—and she radiated
friendliness and good humour. Butler was charmed by
her wit and grace of mind, but he was not attracted by her
lame, dumpy person which, as she grew older, got increasingly dumpier and dowdier. The only existing
photograph of her, taken about this time, shows a
pleasant, broad, sensible, rather masculine face, which
doubtless depended for its charm on its vivacity and intelligence. From the time that Butler began sending her
Erewhon in the spring of 1871, Eliza Savage was, and
continued to be, his best critic. She considered him a born
novelist; but it is doubtful whether he had more than one
novel in him, the history of his own development.

As their friendship grew, with its letters—on her side
some of the best in English—occasional teas together at
Clifford's Inn, or meetings at the offices of the *Woman's
Gazette* or at one of the ladies' clubs she managed, Butler
began to reproach himself for not being able to return
Miss Savage's obvious devotion in the way that he supposed she wanted him to return it—by marrying her.
And as he had a horror of marriage, or of committing
himself irrevocably in any direction, or of allowing anyone
to have any claims upon him, he began to resent Miss
Savage.

She lived in Beaumont Street, off the Marylebone
High Street, with her parents. Her father was Humphrey
Savage, the architect of St Luke's, Chelsea. She was
attached to her father, disliked her mother, was poor and

moved mostly in the company of aging spinsters, dreary New Women, and 'dear good silly little lady artists'. She probably had no delusions about Butler's feelings for her, but had she lost his friendship she would have lost everything. Butler has been much blamed for his treatment of Miss Savage; but he cannot be blamed for not being in love with her. There was the constant strain of being friendly, yet not too friendly, in case, as he said, he 'encouraged hopes, which I made it plain from the first could not be realized'. His relationship with the 'little lame lady' was the reverse of his relationship with Pauli.

In September 1871, during one of his yearly visits to Italy, Butler first met Isabella Zanetti, the daughter of the keeper of the Hotel d'Italia at Arona, Maggiore. 'I have never seen any woman comparable to her', he confided to his *Notebooks*, 'and kept out of her way on purpose, after leaving Arona, as the only thing to be done, for we had become thick.' Festing Jones, who saw Isabella seven years later, describes her as 'a magnificently beautiful woman of whom he had often spoken to me'. But, once again, Butler was afraid of compromising himself. Had he seen more of her, it might have meant marriage —and what on earth would he have done with an Italian wife in Clifford's Inn? There would, too, have been the annoyance and expense of children. He dared not go back to Arona for seven years.

Instead, on his return to London he began his regular visits to Lucie Dumas, the young Frenchwoman he picked up one evening at the Angel, Islington. 'I have a little needlewoman', he told J. B. Yeats, 'a good little thing. I have given her a sewing machine. I go to see her.' As he made this confession, says Yeats, 'he retired backwards, bowing his head several times as in mockery of himself, and acknowledgment of a sad necessity from which even he was not exempt.' He went to see her once a week, and later shared her favours with Festing Jones. 'Madame', Jones tells us, had had predecessors, but during the twenty years of her intimacy with Butler she had no rivals—'none of the predecessors had known how to retain his friendship as she retained it.'[1] Such a working arrangement had obvious advantages—it preserved him from the unwelcome attentions of the World of the Unborn, and he was able to keep his rooms to himself and order his time as best suited his work. Butler knew that he could never do with domesticity. 'Madame' could not become importunate, because she did not know either his name or his address—at least, not for fifteen years. His more passionate friendships were with young men. When his friends married, Butler was inclined to drop them. 'About this time', reads an entry dated 1873 in a chronological record of his life, 'McCulloch got married and began so far as I am concerned to cease to exist.' Jones, of course, never married, and his friendship with the painter, Gogin, just managed to survive the latter's marriage. His cousin, Reggie Worsley, was married, but not for long, and delighted Butler by saying that 'the time just after his divorce was that which he enjoyed most'. 'I don't know why', says Edward Overton in *The Way of All Flesh*, 'but I never have heard that any young man to whom I became attached was going to be married without hating his intended instinctively, though I had never seen her.'

Meanwhile, he was painting hard, both at Heatherley's and at home; his evenings and Sundays he devoted to *Erewhon*. He wrote it with difficulty. 'It seemed to me

[1] Alfred Cathie, Butler's clerk and valet, told Malcolm Muggeridge, when the latter interviewed him in his old age, that Butler visited her every Wednesday, Jones every Tuesday. 'She was a fine woman', he said, 'dark, large, not a regular street-walker, but receiving gentlemen in her room . . . He and Jones paid her a pound a week each, including their holidays.' (*The Earnest Atheist*, p. 168)

that it would never get long enough', he observes in one of his autobiographical notes. 'Having so little experience of writing, I was unaware of the way in which new ideas crowd in through the very process of expressing old ones —like new shoots which grow the more vigorously the more the old ones are pruned. I had not written, and therefore did not know that I could write.' In *Erewhon* may be seen at its clearest the intricate and ambivalent pattern followed by Butler's mind. The fascination of the book consists in his ability to surrender himself to ideas as other people surrender themselves to emotions, though it was one of his main tenets that any idea followed logically to its conclusion becomes absurd, and his favourite motto was *surtout point de zèle*. He could change from one side to the other several times in a single argument. *Erewhon* contains most of Butler's main ideas— morality seen in terms of well-being and good looks; the treatment of crime as sickness and, conversely, the treatment of sickness as crime; the calamity of being born and, still worse, being chosen as a parent by one of the unborn; the false currency of religious and ethical ideas, represented by the valueless coinage of the Musical Banks; and, most prophetic of all, the sense of the growing power of machinery over human life, with the ultimate danger of humanity degenerating into the parasites of machines.[1] Though stated in an extreme and paradoxical form, many of Butler's ideas have since passed into general acceptance.

Erewhon concludes with a satire on the methods of British colonization. Higgs, on his return to England, draws up the prospectus of a company whereby the conversion of the Erewhonians to Christianity can be made

---

[1] This view has been most powerfully expressed in our own day by Lewis Mumford, particularly in his *Art and Technics*, where the full effects of the mechanization of the mind is explored.

into a most profitable undertaking. To begin with, he says, it would be necessary to send a light gunboat to Erewhon, 'for we must protect ourselves'. It would then be explained to the Erewhonians that large fortunes could be made by emigrating to Queensland. But should any of them 'resist emigration' and attack the servants of the Erewhonian Evangelization Company, 'our course would be even simpler, for the Erewhonians have no gunpowder, and would be so surprised with its effects that we should be able to capture as many as we chose. In this case we should be able to engage them on more advantageous terms. But even though we were to meet with no violence, I doubt not that a cargo of seven or eight hundred Erewhonians could be induced, when they were once aboard the vessel, to sign an agreement which should be mutually advantageous both to us and them.' Once in Queensland, they would receive the benefit of religious instruction from the owners of the sugar plantations. 'As soon as they could be spared from work in the plantations, they would be assembled for praise and be thoroughly grounded in the Church Catechism.' The Erewhonians would thus, Butler concludes, be made 'not only into good Christians but into a source of considerable profit to the shareholders'—an irresistible combination to the Victorians. Butler modestly disclaims the merit of originality in this scheme and quotes from *The Times* of January 1872 a report of the Marquis of Normanby's tour of inspection of the Queensland sugar plantations with their Polynesian workers. 'His Excellency pointed out the advantage of giving them religious instruction. It would tend to set at rest an uneasy feeling, which at present existed in the country, to know that they were inclined to retain the Polynesians, and teach them religion.'

Butler sent *Erewhon* to Chapman and Hall, where

Meredith read it and turned it down. 'I should probably have condemned his *Diana of the Crossways*, or indeed any other of his books', Butler observes, 'had it been submitted to myself. No wonder if his work repels me that mine should repel him.' He then went off to Italy. On his return he sent the book to Trubners. He had to pay their reader's fee of a guinea, but this time the report was favourable, and Trubners agreed to publish *Erewhon* at Butler's expense. The money for its printing and production was put up by an old Cambridge friend, Henry Hoare. So miraculously swift, compared to modern conditions, was book production in those days that proofs reached him a few weeks later, early in February 1871. 'It reads very well', he wrote to Miss Savage, 'and the type is excellent; even Pauli, who had been the most freezing critic hitherto (in so far as he could be got to listen to a passage here and there), thawed a little as he read: the fact is, he is frightened out of his wits about it, and expects my father to cut me off with a shilling, but he does not say this because he knows I should fly at him if he advised me to let my father's will enter into the matter at all.' Nevertheless, Butler issued the book anonymously and suppressed one or two passages on Pauli's advice. Pauli, a 'man of the world', did not see the sense of irritating Canon Butler more than necessary— as long, that is, as he was drawing money from Butler.

'*Erewhon* is out and will be advertised to-morrow', he writes to Miss Savage on 29 March; 'I have your copy— the sample copy, i.e. the first issued. I have written your name in it to make sure; also an inscription in which there is bad grammar and bad writing. Shall you be coming to Crane Court? If so, please call and you shall have it; otherwise I will take it to Miss Johnson's.' Miss Johnson was the bedridden 'dear good silly little chirrupy lady artist', where they sometimes met for tea. He had inscribed this copy, which was sold in 1914 by Sydney Dobell for ten guineas: 'To Miss E. M. A. Savage, the first copy of *Erewhon* with the author's best thanks for many invaluable suggestions and corrections.' This was the nearest thing to a love letter Miss Savage ever had from him.

The opening chapters of *Erewhon* are very near to the descriptions of New Zealand in *A First Year in Canterbury Settlement*, which his father had compiled from his letters home and published in 1863, with revisions, a pious preface and an apology for his son's style. Butler always hated this book. 'On its being sent out to me when I was in New Zealand', he says, 'I opened two or three pages, and was so disgusted that I never touched it again from that day to this, but I cribbed a few sentences here and there from recollection.'

Erewhon was an immediate success, and Butler suffered a brief period of lionhood. As a 'lion' he was not a success; he always became aggressive and awkward whenever he met anyone with a 'name', fearing that they were going to snub him. When he met Rossetti, for instance, at Henry Wallis's rooms, Rossetti apparently played 'the silence trick'. Then Hoare and Marriott, another Cambridge friend, invited him to dinner to meet John Morley, having tactlessly prepared the way by recommending Morley as a stylist upon whom, they said, Butler should model himself. 'Marriott gave a splendid feed', Butler recorded in a note of 1887, 'which I regret to say I have never to this day returned, and Morley and I were put to sit in the middle of the table side by side, and there was to be a feast of reason and a flow of soul—a part of the program that did not come off. Morley talked a good deal, and so, I have no doubt, did I . . . all I remember is that I disliked and distrusted Morley.'

98

As his uncle Philip Worsley was fond of telling him, the book owed its success in great measure to its having appeared anonymously. 'The reviewers did not know but what the book might have been written by a somebody whom it might not turn out well to have cut up, and whom it might turn out very well to have praised.' The reviewers, in fact, thought it was by Lord Lytton. They compared the earlier chapters to *Robinson Crusoe* and the later chapters to *Gulliver*. It was all very flattering. But it came out that the book was by Butler, and the demand dropped from fifty copies a week to two or three.

On 6 June 1872 his elder sister Harrie wrote from Ventnor to tell him how pained and grieved about *Erewhon* everyone was at Langar. 'I want to tell you a little about it, and say how I think you may help a little in the matter. . . . My Mother's feeling has always been tender for you. My father's reserve is such that one cannot always tell how acutely he feels things. I am sure he is really unhappy now. Your suggestion "send him to Wales" does not meet the point at all and sounds so little understanding, *more* than that, that Mamma and May would not like him to see it.' If only he would write, she says, and show that he feels for them, 'I think that Langar will look a little brighter and that you will be glad to hope it should do so'. At the foot of the letter Butler wrote: 'In consequence I wrote to my father what I intended to be a conciliatory and apologetic letter. It was dated 8 June. I have destroyed it.'

Canon Butler's reply was very much in the character of Theobald. He would, he said, take Sam's advice and not read *Erewhon*. 'I write as shortly as possible because I was unwilling to discuss a subject on which I might easily say that which would irritate you and might widen a breach I would far sooner bridge. And I conceived that in the first flush of what you consider a great success it was not likely that you would listen to the regrets of others. . . . If one holds religious belief with any reality, don't you think it natural that one should feel something a great deal stronger than a mere passing regret that those dear to us do not feel with us? If there is anything whatever in it there is everything in it. As for expecting us to feel any vanity or triumph in your success it is wholly impossible. We should heartily rejoice to find it as ephemeral as I am yet disposed to hope and believe it may be. (He was quite right here, but at the same time he was only wanting to say something unpleasant.—S.B.) I don't greatly care whether you put your name to the book or not, I quite believe you withheld it for our sakes but the pain is in your having written it, not in its being found out. . . . It will probably prove an injury to yourself in many ways. Partly by diverting your attention from such degree of drawing as you attained to (I had already, as he knew, exhibited more than once at the Academy— S.B., 16 June 1901). And if you fancy that your name will be found in the "front rank of the writers of your time and country" is not that a little strong? (This is just enough—S.B.).' Since his visits would be painful, the Canon concludes, he does not wish him to come down to Langar for the present. He signs himself, 'Your affectionate father, if you will let me be so'. Canon Butler wrote at the same time about *Erewhon* to William Longman, who told Butler years later that he had heard he and his father did not get on, but the Canon's letter convinced him that Butler 'had just cause for complaint'.

Butler sent his father's letter to Miss Savage, with the comment, 'but it doesn't matter, for whatever I said would have been wrong'. He also wrote to Charles Darwin. He had no intention, he says, in 'The Book of the Machines', of being disrespectful to *The Origin of Species*, 'a book for which I can never be sufficiently

grateful, though I am well aware how utterly incapable I
am of forming any opinion on a scientific subject which
is worth a moment's consideration.' He had, he goes on,
first written 'Darwin Among the Machines' in New
Zealand 'for mere fun', then he developed it and introduced it into *Erewhon* 'with the intention of implying
"See how easy it is to be plausible, and what absurd propositions can be defended by a little ingenuity and dis-
tortion and departure from strictly scientific methods".
. . . However, you have a position which nothing can
shake, and I know very well that any appearance
of ridicule would do your theories no harm whatever. . . .'

Perhaps Butler protests a little too much, but at this
time his relations with Darwin were still friendly. He
had previously sent him his pamphlet, *The Evidence for
the Resurrection of Jesus Christ . . . Critically Examined*, and
Darwin had been much interested. Now, after the publication of *Erewhon*, came an invitation to spend the week-
end at Down, and shortly afterwards he procured for the
great man some drawings of dogs by Arthur May, a
student at Heatherley's, which appeared next year in *The
Expression of the Emotions in Animals*.

In June 1872 Miss Savage reviewed *Erewhon* in *The
Drawing Room Gazette*, to which Butler had already contributed some notices of performances of Handel and
Bach at the Exeter Hall. She began by citing Chamfort
to the effect that 'what generally makes the success of a
book is the affinity between the mediocrity of the ideas of
the author and the mediocrity of the ideas of the public'.
Erewhon, however, was an instance to the contrary, for,
though it was 'a satire sharp and caustic enough', it was
'tempered throughout by fun so irresistible that we laugh
while we wince'. Poor Miss Savage had many occasions
for wincing during her friendship with Butler. Never, she

says, has the character of a prig been so amusingly set forth. 'There are touches here and there in this character that would make Molière writhe with envy.' At the very beginning of the review she indicates that though Butler was in advance of his time in many of his ideas, the public might be induced to swallow the ideas by the wit —a recipe afterwards adopted by Bernard Shaw, who always acknowledged his great indebtedness to Butler. Popular as *Erewhon* was, twenty-seven years after publication it had only sold 3,842 copies and made a profit of £62 10s. 10d.

Foreseeing disappointment and frustration, Miss Savage began urging Butler to write a novel, to which he replied: 'How about this for a subject? A hero, young, harum-scarum, with a keen sense of fun and few scruples, allows himself to be converted and reconverted at intervals of six months or so, for the sum of £100 on each occasion, from the Church of Rome to Methodism and back again by each of two elderly maiden relatives who have a deep interest in the soul of the hero and the confusion of one another. Also he hangs an awful threat over his father (who is a respectable country parson and has forbidden him the house on account of his notorious wild oats and loose conversation) to the effect that he will go down to the village inn the night before the next Communion Sunday and take the sacrament *coram populo*. The threat shall hang like a sword of Damocles over his father's head . . . But I am very doubtful about a novel at all: I know I should regard it as I did *Erewhon*, i.e. as a mere peg on which to hang anything that I had a mind to say. The result would be what you complain about in *Middlemarch*. . . .' We do not know what Miss Savage thought about *Middlemarch*, which appeared in the same year as *Erewhon*, but she had sent it to Butler as an example of the kind of intellectual novel that was finding favour with the public. Butler, however, found it 'a long-winded piece of studied brag'.

On 12 June he wrote to Miss Savage: 'It is all very well, but I cannot settle down to writing a novel and trying to amuse people when there is work wants doing which I believe I am just the man to do. I shall never be quiet till I have carried out the scheme that is in my head.' This was *The Fair Haven*, the stated purpose of which is to defend 'the Miraculous Element in our Lord's Ministry upon Earth, both as against Rationalistic Impugners and certain Orthodox Defenders'. It purported to be written by 'the late John Pickard Owen'. But Owen had the same sort of ambivalent attitude to things as his author, for the introductory memoir traces his transition from religious faith to unbelief and back again to faith, though under the strain of these spiritual crises his mind finally gives way. Owen's mental collapse is hastened by his conviction that in order to combat unbelief effectively it is necessary to enter thoroughly and sympathetically into all the doubts and difficulties of unbelievers, and in a matter of faith this is a very dangerous proceeding. In the end, he is only able to defend his faith by rejecting the results of his own rational analysis in a manner which gives full play to Butler's irony.

But *The Fair Haven* was by no means a hoax. The intense seriousness of Butler's feelings can be seen in the early pamphlet, which dealt with what half the world for nearly two thousand years had considered, or professed to consider, the most important event in history. From an analysis of the Gospels, Butler had come to the conclusion that there was really no evidence of Jesus Christ's having died on the Cross. This being so, he could not have risen from the dead, and when he appeared to his disciples he must have done so in the flesh. Butler argues that Jesus recovered under the care of Joseph of Arimathea, who had begged his body of Pilate, and that he was, therefore, during his lifetime, the only man who realized the full imposture of Christianity. It was a theme to which Butler returned, in the last year of his life, in *Erewhon Revisited*, when Higgs goes back to Erewhon to find himself deified as the Sunchild after his ascent to heaven in a balloon. Butler seems to have reached his conclusions independently, from a close study of the Greek Testament; he had heard of Strauss and the German rationalists, he says, but not knowing German had not read their works, nor was there any mention of them in any English book he had come across. In any case, Strauss had dealt very cursorily in his *Life of Jesus* with the survival theory, though in 1865 an English translation of his more popular *New Life of Jesus* had appeared, and Butler discusses this in *The Fair Haven*.

Butler thought that anyone who read the Gospels at all critically must be driven to the same conclusion as himself. It was all so obvious. Yet vested interests were such, he argued, that no one would admit it, for if Jesus did not die on the Cross, then the whole gloomy and oppressive edifice of the Christian Church fell to the ground. It was not merely that he was gathering ammunition against his father, though it was certain that *The Fair Haven* would get him into even greater disgrace at Langar. Its prefatory Memoir is in the nature of a semi-satirical self-portrait and Butler wrote it to see what he could do in the way of narrative and character drawing. Owen's mother, with her fantastic day-dreaming, is to some extent a preliminary sketch for Christina in *The Way of All Flesh*.

He was at work on the book while on holiday in Switzerland in August 1872. He made it a rule to do a couple of pages a day and he usually did them while resting in the open air. But he did not enjoy his holiday.

'You are quite right', he wrote to Miss Savage, 'I do not idle well. I will try to mend', and from Grindelwald he wrote in September: 'I am coming home shortly. I have done no work, and am sick of doing nothing; besides, I am better—really—and I want to finish my book and get back to painting. You ask me about Rossetti. I dislike his face, and his manner, and his work, and I hate his poetry, and his friends. He is wrapped up in self-conceit and lives upon adulation. I spent a whole evening in his company at W. H. Wallis's—W. B. Scott being the only other except Wallis, Rossetti and myself. I was oppressed by the sultry reticence of Rossetti's manner which seemed to me assumed to conceal the fact that he had nothing worth saying to say. I liked W. B. Scott well enough—the other two were horrid.' He had an equally healthy dislike for Burne-Jones's work—no words could express it, he said.

Early next year he was laid up as the result of a fall from a bus, which injured his foot. The bus, according to its custom, jerked forward violently just as Butler was preparing to get off, and he slipped down the narrow, winding stairs—narrower and more winding in the horse-buses of the 1870's than today. He sent Miss Savage *The Fair Haven* as he wrote it and the Memoir made her sure that he would write a wonderful novel. 'The moral of this is', she wrote to him, 'that I want a novel—ever so many novels.' But he only returned the compliment and told her that she was letting her great talents go to waste. 'I do not know what I shall write next', he tells her. 'I do not want to write anything in particular and shall paint until an idea strikes me which I must work out or die, like *The Fair Haven*. I shall do nothing well unless *con amore*, and under diabolical inspiration. I should hope, however, that attacks on *The Fair Haven* will give me an opportunity for excusing myself and, if so, I shall endeavour that the excuse may be worse than the fault it is intended to excuse. If I do write a novel I will send you the plot to hack and rearrange for me before I do it.' The crowning irony of the situation was that *The Fair Haven* was not only *not* attacked, but taken up and expanded from the pulpit by grateful clergymen.

In March 1873 his mother fell seriously ill at Menton, where she was staying with the Canon and May. 'She constantly mentions you', his father wrote to him on the 21st. 'If I say with anxiety and distress I must also say with the deepest affection and love. . . . I think she would like you to know that she finds prayer an inexplicable comfort and that her faith is able to support her in the sufferings which she endures. If she should rally I should move her as soon as she was able to bear it. If otherwise, God's will be done. She has been a blessing and a comfort to me for 42 years.' Fortunately prayers were supplemented by injections of morphia, which brought the poor woman comfort more explicable. On receipt of this, Butler wrote to May to let him know at once if his mother was in danger. The letter is a strange one coming from the author of *The Way of All Flesh*. 'I could not think of myself as going about my daily affairs and my mother lying perhaps at the point of death, without a sight of the one whom I am very sure that she loves not the least of her children. It would be intolerable to me to think of this, yet I know and deeply regret that my presence could not be without its embarrassments. I find nothing so depressing to myself as the sight of suffering in others; but how much more so when the sufferer is the one whom we naturally desire to save from suffering. You will say, then why have you written *Erewhon*? The mistake was in not keeping it more quiet, and then in thinking that the very success which the book has met with would make my father and mother proud of my having written it. . . . I thought my father and mother would be proud of my having met with the approbation of the most intelligent classes of my countrymen, and that not in half measure, but in whole measure. I am sorry I was mistaken. But had I known my mother's health was failing at the time I would have kept it back. Whatever else I do, I will do my utmost to do without it reaching the ears of those whom it will pain; but I cannot hold my tongue. Pray thank father for his letter, and assure him that I will endeavour to cause no anxiety which I can avoid, either to him or to any of you.'

In reality, Butler wanted his family's recognition, and throughout his life continued to let them know when he won any praise for his work. He did his best to preserve friendly relations with them, but neither of his sisters had much sense of humour, and he could not resist teasing them occasionally. Mrs Garnett describes May Butler as a type to be met with in the novels of Charlotte M. Yonge—'the perfect churchwoman: spiritual, intellectual, devoted; strong in her faithful following of duty, sweet-tempered, serene and cheerful from an active and disciplined life'. Needless to say, these were not qualities to appeal to her 'infidel' brother. The day after this letter to his sister, Butler wrote to Miss Savage: 'My mother is ill—very ill. It is not likely that she will recover—

I had rather
It had been my father.

I am pained about it. She is at Menton, and though my father writes as if he had no hope, they clearly do not want me to come, which is as well, for though in such a case I should travel, yet the less I am on my feet the better—I ought to keep them up. What pains me is that I cannot begin to regain the affection now which alas! I have long ceased to feel. I have finished *Middlemarch*—it is very bad indeed. I am sorry for your little troubles; I wish I could think that you had none others—but it is a bad world. Why don't *you* write a story?'

At the beginning of April, he went over to Menton. His mother died on the ninth and was buried among the cypresses in the cemetery that overlooks the little town, with its pink and yellow houses and steep cobbled streets clambering up the mountain side, its avenue of shaggy date-palms along the front and its wide bay of unbelievably blue sea. At the beginning of April Menton is at its most beautiful. The light is dazzling, the air perfumed with flowers and tingling with brine. But Canon Butler and his sisters were there to cast an English clerical blight over everything, and his father told Butler that his mother had been killed by *Erewhon*. He therefore left hurriedly on the day after the funeral.

There is every reason to think that the description of Ernest's visit to his dying mother at Battersby in *The Way of All Flesh* is based upon this visit to Menton. 'The poor woman raised herself in bed as he came towards her, and weeping as she flung her arms around him, cried "Oh, I knew he would come, I knew, I knew he would come". Ernest broke down and wept as he had not done for years. . . . His mother fell into a comatose state which lasted a couple of days, and in the end went away so peacefully that it was like the blending of sea and sky in mid-ocean upon a soft hazy day when none can say where the earth ends or the heavens begin. Indeed she died to the realities of life with less pain than she had waked from many of its illusions. "She has been the comfort and mainstay of my life for more than thirty years", said Theobald as soon as all was over, "but one could not wish it prolonged", and he buried his face in his handkerchief to conceal his want of emotion.'

So Fanny Butler lies at Menton, in the same graveyard as Aubrey Beardsley, an odd assortment of Russian grand dukes and Spurgeon the Baptist.

While he was at Menton, Butler received a letter from Darwin, forwarded from London, about *The Fair Haven*. 'It has interested me greatly and is extremely curious', wrote the great biologist. 'If I had not known that you had written it I should not even have suspected that the author was not orthodox, within the wide stated limits. I should have thought that he was a conscientious man like Blanco White, whose autobiography you no doubt know. It will be a curious problem whether the orthodox will have so good a scent as to detect your heresy. . . .' But what struck him most, Darwin went on to say, was the dramatic power, 'the way in which you earnestly and thoroughly assume the character and think the thoughts of the man you pretend to be. Hence I conclude that you could write a really good novel. . . . Your book must have cost you much labour, and I heartily hope it will be widely distributed; but it is not light reading.' Leslie Stephen, he adds, was lunching with him and knew that Butler was the author. Stephen does not seem to have reviewed *The Fair Haven*, though he wrote to Butler very appreciatively, and when his *Free-thinking and Plain-speaking* appeared later this year Butler reviewed it for *The Examiner*. In his reply to Darwin of 15 April, Butler says that 'had I known how ill my poor mother was, I could not have brought out or even written my book at such a time'. He will, he says, 'try a novel pure and simple with little purpose next, but I am still in the flesh, and however much the spirit may be willing, I fear that the cloven hoof will show itself ever and anon'. The novel without a purpose turned out to be *The Way of All*

Flesh, where the cloven hoof not only showed itself but proceeded to kick both his parents, politely but exceedingly hard.

On his return to Clifford's Inn there was a letter from Miss Savage anxiously asking about his health and whether *The Fair Haven* had been reviewed yet. 'You should have heard me discoursing about it yesterday. I said it was a sweet book (so it is) and most convincing—it had been lent to me by a religious friend, in hopes that it would do me good, and it *had* done me good. . . . I hope you have heard better news of your mother, and that you are yourself happier altogether than when I saw you.' The ladies at the Berners Street Club teased Miss Savage about Butler. Most of them were of the 'emancipated' sort who found marriage 'degrading'.

In May Miss Savage wrote to say that she had been to the Academy, 'though I have not a new bonnet and scarcely dare look my friends in the face when the old one is on my head'. She went, it would seem, to do propaganda for *Erewhon*. 'Such devotion is not often met with', she adds, 'and I don't expect that you will ever appreciate the greatness of my sacrifice. . . . However, as you are going to be a great novelist it would not be a bad exercise for you to try to fathom my feelings under the circumstances.' Lame and dowdy, limping slowly with the aid of the stick he had given her, Miss Savage had made her way among the expensively dressed ladies and gentlemen on the opening day to do some small service for Butler, who did not need to be a great novelist to be perfectly aware of what this must have cost her. He only wished she would not do it! He was only too sensible of the growing warmth of her attachment, and it made him very uneasy.

His father wrote to him on notepaper edged with half an inch of funereal black, enclosing mementoes of his mother—'a little locket which you could wear with your watch' and an owl seal, 'the owl I gave her at her marriage and she constantly used it to seal with'. Canon Butler also sent the long letter addressed to 'My Two Dear Boys', which Mrs Butler had written in 1841, when she did not expect to recover from her last confinement. This letter came just in time for Butler to incorporate it in his novel. He was still working hard at his most ambitious, but singularly dreary, picture 'Mr Heatherley's Holiday'. His evenings were now given up to writing, instead of music, and before going on a three weeks' outing to Dieppe in June he promised Miss Savage the first chapter of *Ernest Pontifex* (the original title of *The Way of All Flesh*) on his return. ' "Never have I been so calm, so soothed, so filled with blessed Peace",' she wrote in August 1873, quoting from *The Fair Haven*, 'as this morning when the first instalment of your novel came. If it goes on as it begins it will be a perfect novel, or nearly so as may be.' On 9 November she wrote begging him to take care of himself. 'If you knew the treasure we possess in Butler, you would take care of him; you would indeed.' Frightened by the warmth of her concern, perhaps, he did not reply until 20 December, when he sent her a matter-of-fact note: 'My cold is better, and having done no work for a fortnight, I am rested, and am not now overworked. The lump on my neck is smaller, and I don't get deaf immediately that anyone has bored me for more than five minutes—in fact I am rested, but I am pulled down.' When, in March 1874, Hoare's companies smashed and he bought back his friends' shares—an act of quixotic generosity, since he was himpractically ruined in the *débâcle*—Miss Savage exclaimed: 'I don't think there is anyone quite so good as you are. When I know of someone who is, I will tell you. . . . But I am grieved when I think that you will still be worried and overworked and interrupted with business matters.'

But he had no time now to attend to Miss Savage, and hardly time to give her the news of himself she craved, until in April she wrote: 'I am quite shocked when I think of the way in which you break your word. Did you not say you would let me know how you are? . . . I have been very unhappy lately. I have not slept for two nights, and Thursday and today I have had no appetite, and you know how *gourmande* I am. Yesterday I saw you at your window and felt dreadfully inclined to rush in and ask your advice, but common sense prevailed and I went on my way. I wish I had not common sense, for then I should have told you all about the matter, and that would have relieved me very much.' At the beginning of June he wrote to tell her that he was off to Canada, and she replied rather forlornly: 'I was going to pay you a visit on Monday and bring you a bundle of paint rags, but I shall not see you now, you will be too busy, and you shall have the rags when you come back, but I am dreadfully cross at being disappointed of the little (I mean *great*) pleasure I was promising myself.' The substitution of 'great' for 'little' was an expression of what she really felt tactfully disguised beneath a mutual joke about his sisters' epistolary style.

In Canada his business worries did not prevent Butler from indulging his passion for long walks, and he made daily excursions into the country surrounding Montreal after office hours, and even visited Niagara. On a magnificent evening on Montreal Mountain he wrote a passage which later became part of *Life and Habit*, which was occupying his mind now just as much as The Canada Tanning Extract Company:

It is one against legion when a man tries to differ

from his own past selves. He must yield or die, if he
wants to differ widely, so as to lack natural instincts,
such as hunger or thirst, and not to gratify them. It
is more righteous in a man that he should eat strange
food, and that his cheek should so much as lank not,
than that he should starve if the strange food be at
his command. His past selves are living in him at this
moment with the accumulated life of centuries. 'Do
this, this, this, which we, too, have done and found
our profit in it', cry the souls of his forefathers within
him. Faint are the far ones, coming and going as the
sound of bells wafted to a high mountain; loud and
clear are the near ones, urgent as an alarm of fire.

A passage in which a Biblical strain is crossed, characteristically, with memories of *Antony and Cleopatra*, when
Octavius contrasts the aging Antony's 'lascivious wassails'
in Egypt with his earlier fortitude as a soldier, when he
drank 'the stale of horses' and ate 'strange flesh, which
some did die to look on . . . that thy cheek so much as
lankt not'.

Butler returned to London in June to consult the
Directors and left again for Canada on 5 August. Before
leaving he wrote a hurried note to Miss Savage: 'It is all
I shall do to get away by Wednesday; but if you are able
to come and bid me goodbye, say from 5.30 to 6 tomorrow, Monday, please do so.' The novel, he says, is going
ahead, 'but it must be quite innocent, for I am now recon-
ciled to my father, and must be careful not to go beyond
scepticism of the mildest kind. I shall have to change the
scheme, but shall try to keep the earlier chapters.'

In Canada again, Butler began to enjoy the work of
investigation. 'I don't see how a man could be much
luckier', he writes, 'than to run right against such a
position at the very moment that he wanted it, and to

jump without apprenticeship or training into a post such as many try for in vain all their lives long. . . . I go to bed early and get up early. I am much better than I was three months ago, and am sure to get better and better, as I did in New Zealand. A year or two here will do me no harm, and will be a cheap price to pay, if I can save the company and return to a modest competence again, as before all these companies were started.' Miss Savage was rather doubtful about the good luck. It seemed to her that Butler protested too much. 'However, whatever luck you may have I think you have rather more than your share,' she replied naughtily. 'I thought so after that last time I saw you, and you told me what you had been doing buying back other people's shares in the company. You have great and varied talents, genius, I should say, and you have so much capacity for so many kinds of enjoyment. You were born with a sweet temper, an un-selfish disposition, and a natural inclination to deal righteously with your fellow creatures and power of mind enough to cultivate the inclination, and yet you want to be rich. I call you a most unreasonable man. Let the poor stupid disagreeable people have the money (I think they very often do); they want it, poor things. When you get that modest competence you speak of, I shall look upon you as defrauding somebody or other.' Her father is very ill, she says, but her mother does not allow her to do much for him. 'I am very fond of my father. I wish I were as fond of my mother, but I suppose that would be too much of good luck.'

In November 1874 Butler wrote to say that he was still alive, but that he had fallen among thieves. 'Well, I believe I may also say that the thieves have fallen among *me*.' As we have seen, Foley, the manager, had tried to intimidate him, storming and threatening, but Butler remained so cool that in the end he had to give it up. He has been reading *Wilhelm Meister* and it seems to him the worst book he has ever read. 'No Englishman could have written such a book. I cannot remember a single good page or idea, and the priggishness is the finest of its kind that I can call to mind. Is it all a practical joke?' Meanwhile Miss Savage was counting up the weeks between his letters, as, she tells him, 'the pricks on the calendar on my wall will testify'. She says that she is in two minds whether to wish him success with the Company, for then he will stay in Canada, or failure, in which case he will return home. She now made him write to her two or three times before she would answer, and he heard nothing from her between August and December. 'I was never placed in a more difficult position', he observed at the end of his life. 'To write was to encourage false hopes— not to write was to be grossly unkind.' He sent her a copy of 'The Psalm of Montreal' and she read it, she told him, at the Club to Miss Drew in the dressing-room among the damp waterproofs and goloshes.

Butler came home in June 1875 to report to the Board of Directors and left for Canada again in August. On the way out he travelled with Lord Houghton, the former Monckton Milnes and biographer of Keats, from whom he won 26s. at whist on different nights. He accompanied the chants and hymns of the Sunday services on the piano and 'old Lord Houghton warbled "Rock of Ages" in a very edifying manner', though Mrs Eustace Smith, who was also on board with her husband, assured Butler that Lord Houghton was ' "the most horrid old reprobate—oh, *horrid, horrid*, I assure you", so I liked hearing him sing "Rock of Ages".' This time Miss Savage did not write at all, and when Butler called upon her on his return in December she was out after inviting him to come. But she was soon writing again, telling him that she had seen him at a concert, passing on invitations to tea with her spinster friends, teasing him for his lack of taste in food, advising him that 'at Dumas's in Princes Street, Leicester Square, nearly opposite the violin shop, you will get all sorts of good things in the way of pork-pies, and such-like dainties'. The coincidence of the name is curious. Had Miss Savage known about Lucie Dumas, she would have taken as poor a view of Butler's relationship with her as she took of Towneley's visits to Miss Snow in *The Way of All Flesh*. It will be recalled that Ernest, not without some mixture of motives, was about to give pretty Miss Snow a little Bible talk in her bedroom at Ashpit Place when footsteps were heard bounding up the stairs and the handsome Towneley burst into the room with, 'I'm come before my time' and 'What *you* here, Pontifex! well, upon my word!' Ernest felt deeply humiliated, as he contrasted himself with his hero, and beat a hurried retreat to his room. As Towneley's 'hearty laugh' came to him through Miss Snow's door, he kicked his Bible into a corner and, with no longer any doubts in his mind about what he really wanted, burst into Miss Maitland's room. Miss Maitland resented this boisterous approach, ran out of the house to fetch a policeman, and poor Ernest was charged with criminal assault. 'If the better part of valour is discretion', comments Butler, 'how much more is not discretion the better part of vice?'

When she read this episode, Miss Savage objected, 'Your Towneley, too, must be toned down—a coarse creature with vicious propensities which he indulges in a slum'. But then she felt the whole 'grand catastrophe' to be unconvincing: 'Ernest, poor fellow, according to the impression I receive of him, couldn't have frightened a mouse.' Miss Savage doubtless guessed that Towneley's escapades were based upon Butler's own experience, and it would be illuminating to know how Towneley appeared before he was 'toned down'. But when, after his return from Canada in 1876, Butler's work for the Canada Tanning Extract Company continued to interrupt what Miss Savage considered to be his real work—that is, writing—she wrote to him, 'I wish you did not know right from wrong' (i.e. in business matters), and Butler, with his guilty conscience, interpreted it as a declaration of passion. This observation continued to haunt him for the rest of his life, as may be seen from the unhappy sonnets—unhappy in more senses than one—he wrote about their relationship in old age.

> She said she wished I knew not wrong from right;
> It was not that; I knew, and would have chosen
> Wrong if I could, but, in my own despite,
> Power to choose wrong in my chilled veins was frozen.
> 'Tis said that if a woman woo, no man
> Should leave her till she have prevailed; and, true,
> A man will yield for pity, if he can,
> But if the flesh rebels what can he do?
> I could not. Hence I grieve my whole life long
> The wrong I did, in that I did no wrong.

The identification of love-making with wrong-doing is very English. That he should have taken her up like this is enough to show how uncomfortable their relationship had become.

Not long after this, Bernard Shaw was writing plays in which determined young women, rampant vehicles of the Life Force, regularly take the initiative with more timid intellectual young men. Butler was never enchanted with the Life Force, like John Tanner, but then its vehicle in this case was widely different from the irresistible Ann Whitefield in *Man and Superman*. When he met the Life Force embodied in Isabella, he turned tail and fled. 'My books', he told his sister, 'are to me much the most important thing in life. They are, in fact,

"me" much more than anything else.' Much as he enjoyed reading Miss Savage's letters, they had to be
answered, and a man whose time is taken up with writing
books, Festing Jones reminds us, not without a sly relish
of the situation, does not want to write letters: he wants
to get on with his work. If Butler had married Miss
Savage, he would not have had to answer her letters; but
there would have been even more serious interruptions.
'I fear that even if Miss Savage had had the beauty of
Isabella', Jones concludes, 'intimate relations would still
have led to boredom.'

Meanwhile, the bright witty letters continued, frustration showing itself now and then in the teasing tone,
sudden bursts of annoyance, sudden little jabs, quickly
covered up by a flood of affection that can no longer hide
itself beneath the surface glitter of the mutual jokes
against parents or Christianity. But as Butler so rightly
says, 'there is no bore like a brilliant bore', and her playful brilliance nearly teased him to death. 'She rarely left
my rooms without my head, for the time being, being all
wrong and my neck swelling.' In December 1875 she
wrote to him playfully: '*There is one thing*, though, that I
must tell you, and that is, that if you become surrounded
by a circle of adoring spinsters (of which I see symptoms)
I shall drop your acquaintance.' Upon which Butler
commented after her death: 'Who, I wonder, was it that
was doing her utmost so to surround me, and boring me
beyond endurance in spite of all my admiration, respect,
gratitude, and compunction at my own inability to re-
quite her affection for me in the only way that would
have satisfied her? If ever man gave woman her answer
unequivocally and at the beginning, I gave mine to Miss
Savage—but it was no use. She would not be checked
and I had not either the heart to check her—or—well,
never mind. I would if I could, but I could not.'

He proposed, however, that they should collaborate in a book, a proposal which Miss Savage rejected. At the end of April 1876 he writes to tell her that he has 'two things (I cannot call them pictures)' in the Academy. They were a water colour, 'A Girl's Head', and an oil, 'Don Quixote'. This was the last time the Academy hung any of Butler's work. He had previously exhibited 'Miss Atcheson' in 1869, 'A Reverie' in 1871, 'A Child's Head' and 'Mr. Heatherley's Holiday' in 1874. This year he sold his 'Don Quixote' for fifteen guineas and when he went away to Switzerland he realized how utterly worn out he was. 'I don't think I ever was so fairly done up before', he writes to Miss Savage in June from Faido. 'I have had the worst three years I ever had since the horrors of childhood and boyhood.' In reply Miss Savage said that for her part she was feeling 'much puffed up just now', having received a commission to do a short book on art needlework in the Home Help Series. She has not made his kettle-holder yet, but after reading her book he will be able to make one for himself.

Butler did not enjoy his holiday this summer: 'Either I had been working too hard, or worrying because I cannot paint, or the food did not agree with me, but I have got pretty much into the state in which I was when I left London. I never felt how badly I paint more than now—and after all these years. I ought to have done what I am doing now five years ago. I was on the right track then, only I did not know it.' Butler blamed Heatherley's conventional teaching for putting him on the wrong track. Returning now to his more personal naïve style, he did 'some very decent water colours' at Fusio. Ten years before he had done the Douanier Rousseau-like 'Family Prayers' and that charming painting of a corner of his sitting-room at Clifford's Inn, both now at St John's College, Cambridge. At Fusio he made friends with

Spartaco Vela, the son of the Italian sculptor, and some other Italian painters, and did many of the sketches which appear in *Alps and Sanctuaries*. His method was to make 'a careful outline' on thin whity-brown paper called Cap paper. He then traced this drawing on to the canvas or paper on which he was going to paint. The *Alps and Sanctuaries* illustrations, however, were redrawn in charcoal from the original sketches, and Gogin put in the figures. At Piora he wrote the pathetically revealing passage in praise of grace, which appears in *Life and Habit*:

> Grace! the old Pagan ideal whose charm even unlovely Paul could not withstand; but, as the legend tells us, his soul fainted within him, his heart misgave him, and, standing alone on the seashore at dusk, he troubled deaf heaven with his bootless cries, his thin voice pleading for grace after the flesh.
>
> The waves came in one after another, the sea-gulls cried together after their kind, the wind rustled among the dried canes upon the sandbanks, and there came a voice from heaven saying, 'Let My grace be sufficient for thee!' Whereon, failing of the thing itself, he stole the word and strove to crush its meaning to the measure of his own limitations. But the true grace, with her groves and high places, and troops of young men and maidens crowned with flowers, and singing of love and youth and wine—the true grace he drove out into the wilderness—high up, it may be, into Piora, and into such-like places.

This passage leads up to his credo near the close of Chapter II:

> Above all things, let no unwary reader do me the injustice of believing in *me*. In that I write at all I am among the damned. If he must believe in anything, let

him believe in the music of Handel, the painting of Giovanni Bellini and in the thirteenth chapter of St Paul's First Epistle to the Corinthians [i.e. in praise of charity].

In that I write at all I am among the damned! Here we have the intellectual man's hatred of intellectualism— a state of mind which regularly overcomes English writers in Italy. It found expression most violently in Byron and D. H. Lawrence, more gently and reasonably in E. M. Forster, most urbanely in Norman Douglas and Aldous Huxley. All the knowledge we need, Butler came to think, is inbred, and the more unconscious it is the better. 'If the reader hesitates, let him go down into the streets and look in the shop-windows at the photographs of eminent men, whether literary, artistic, or scientific, and note the work which the consciousness of knowledge has wrought on nine out of every ten of them.' But he dared not go back to Isabella at Arona. Instead 'Madame' and Pauli and 'the little lame lady' awaited him beneath the dirty white skies of London, among the swarming crowds in their mud-coloured clothes and the endless dreary streets of mean houses. And there was his father and the anxiety and wrangling about money. In August 1876 he went to Langar for the last time, for in the autumn Canon Butler gave up the living and retired with May to Wilderhope House, Shrewsbury—'a house with a mocking name', Butler called it. Before visiting him at Shrewsbury, Butler wrote warning his father, somewhat prematurely as it turned out, that however much he may have lost in the Canada Tanning Extract Company, he would not accept any further help from him. 'I have always felt, no matter who might say what, I have made what you originally gave me do me and do me hand-somely [even his style lost its balance when he wrote to his father]—without further burdening my friends, and it is so strongly my wish that this should continue to be the case that I am sure you will not again allude to the matter. . . .'

Life and Habit was now taking definite shape. 'The theory frightens me', he wrote to Miss Savage in the autumn of 1876, 'it is so far-reaching and subversive— it oppresses me, and I take panic that there cannot really be any solid truth in it; but I have been putting down everything that it seems to me can be urged against it, with as much force as if I were a hostile reviewer, and I really cannot see that I have a leg to stand upon when I pose as an objector. Still, do what I can, I am oppressed and frightened.' And well he might be! Unfortunately *Erewhon* had not disposed people to take him seriously as a scientific writer. He was regarded, rather, as a man whose work carried the implication (as he had himself written to Darwin), 'See how easy it is to be plausible, and what absurd propositions can be defended by a little ingenuity and departure from strictly scientific methods.' Nor was that all. 'I am well aware', he had also written to Darwin, 'how utterly incapable I am of forming any opinion on a scientific subject worth a moment's con- sideration.' He had already attacked the foundations of Christian belief in *The Fair Haven*; now, in *Life and Habit* (1878) and the books that followed it, *Evolution Old and New* (1879), *Unconscious Memory* (1880) and *Luck or Cunning?* (1887), he attacked Darwin and the whole body of scientific orthodoxy.

It was only after his death that what Bernard Shaw, in the preface to *Major Barbara*, called 'the extraordinarily fresh, free and future-piercing' nature of Butler's theories came to be partly recognized. But only partly; because, as Shaw adds, when he produced plays in which Butler's ideas had an obvious share, he was 'met with nothing but vague cacklings about Ibsen and Nietzsche'. As a matter of fact, Butler's scientific books were far more revolutionary than even he realized, for here he is on the verge of the whole vast subject of social psychology—a subject whose importance has only been recognized in our time. It is, therefore, as pioneer works in psychology that *Life and Habit*, *Unconscious Memory* and *Luck or Cunning?* deserve revaluation today. Butler thought he was simply attacking Darwin's theory of evolution; in reality he was on the track of something far more original. No wonder his own theory frightened him as being 'so far-reaching and subversive', for he realized that the intellect was only the servant of far more powerful unconscious forces than man had yet begun to explore.

By 1877 Butler was getting more and more anxious about the future. 'If *Life and Habit* fails as *The Fair Haven* did I do not know what will happen—and I have a great and ever present source of oppression of which I cannot tell you or anyone else', he wrote to Miss Savage in February. But he continued working at *Life and Habit*, and painting. He did 'The Last Days of Carey Street'— a painting of a group of costermongers having tea on a barrow in front of an advertisement hoarding with the tower of St Clement Dane's in the background lit up by the rising sun. This picture was rejected by the Academy and seems to have disappeared, which is a pity, as it sounds both original and amusing. 'I have made "The Messiah" the central advertisement', he tells Miss Savage, 'between "Nabob Pickles" and "Three Millions of Money". . . of course I copied the advert. from nature.'

Butler now began working regularly at the British Museum Reading Room. He went there every Monday, Wednesday and Friday from 10 to 1, and liked it so much that he wondered why he had never been there before. 'I sit at letter B (B for Butler) or if I cannot get there at letter C', he told Miss Savage, adding, 'My father was very snappish and crusty all the time that I was at Shrewsbury. My younger sister, who alone lives with him, is no friend to me; she makes matters worse between my father and me.' 'I'm glad you like the Museum', replied Miss Savage, 'I always told you it was delightful: I shall begin to go there again next week because it is open till 6 o'clock. I never hardly go till the afternoon, so as you go away early I shall get you to leave your place for me—only you must sit at letter G. I am miserable anywhere else—and facing the south-west. . . . I am not well—in fact I am ill and should go to the doctor, only he always jeers at me in an unfeeling way.' By this time the malignant cancer of which she finally died had probably made its appearance, though she never complained of more than a cold or neuralgia. Earlier in the year she had been turned out of a cab in quite an eighteenth-century manner, when going out to dine. 'No harm done, except to my best gown', she wrote, 'which suffered from my having to put my arms round the neck of a damp policeman, who helped to pull me out. At first they tried to pull me out by the hair of my head, but I did not like that; so the dye of the policeman's coat has come off on one of the sleeves of my best gown—and all the frillings and grillings round my arms being made of tulle (a material as you know, principally composed of starch) hung down in sticky lumps. . . . My little misfortune seemed to put everyone into good spirits; and as the accident happened at the very door of the house I was going to, the thing could not have been better managed if it had been planned beforehand.' This letter may have provided Butler and Jones with some amusement, but it was a disaster to Miss Savage, who could not afford another evening gown.

In May, Butler went off to Piedmont. In fact had he

not taken this yearly holiday of two months in the summer, he says, he would not have lived through the next nine and a half years until his father's death left him comfortably off. But he had to borrow money to do it. When he came back Miss Savage did not reply to his note informing her of his return. In September he infuriated her with an extraordinary piece of *gaucherie*. He suggested that perhaps she was not writing to him so often now because he had told her that he was keeping her letters, whereas some years ago he had hurt her by saying that he burnt them. Her letters, he said, are so good that he cannot imagine why he had ever destroyed any of them. 'Perhaps it is because I have lost them that I imagine that they were written with greater care than any that I have received since.' He suggests a compromise. 'I will keep your letters, but put them together and address them to yourself, so that on my death they may be returned to you.' Miss Savage replied next day:

With Care! This Side Up!

Dear Mr Butler, It must be confessed that I am a most unreasonable person. What! I leave off writing 'with care' when I hear that you don't keep my letters, and I don't write at all when you tell me that you do! . . . And now, my dear Mr Butler, let me give you a little good advice. If you wish to make yourself agreeable to the female sex, never hint to a woman that she writes or has written 'with care'. Nothing enrages her so much, and it is only the exceptional sweetness of my disposition that enables me, with some effort, I confess, to forgive you this little blunder on your part.

As a matter of fact, I don't care what becomes of my letters. Keep them, or burn them as you please, only for goodness sake don't label them to be returned to me at your death. If you do, I shall never write to you without thinking of your death, and that I cannot bear to think of. Besides, you assume that I shall live the longest, which is flattering to my vital forces, but suppose I die first? What will become of my letters then? Pray let every contingency be prepared for and provided against while we are arranging the matter. . . . I am longing dreadfully to read some more of your book. When may I have some?

On another occasion he told her that Jones enjoyed her letters, too, and she had to tell him: 'You know, I don't *always* write to Mr Jones.' Sometimes two months went by before he wrote to her. 'I have had "write to Miss Savage" heading my agenda for the last seven days', he tells her, 'and I cannot believe that I should have let another day go by without writing.' 'You who are so capable of an exquisite refinement of cruelty . . .' she wrote to him, and she of all people should have known. But whenever she heard anyone praise his work, or saw a reference to it in the press, or noticed anyone taking his books out at Mudie's, she always wrote to tell him. When he told her that his father complained that he had only himself to blame if he did not make money by writing more popular stuff, she retorts: 'He is quite right about the magazines. Why don't you write twaddle? Why don't you be commonplace? I am not sure that I should not like you a great deal better myself if you were. If I were your near relative I am sure I should not like you at all. I can only just put up with your superiority as it is.' One wonders just how ironical Miss Savage intended to be. Again: 'There are many other reasons why I should like to hurl adjectives at you. I am beginning not to like you at all.' All the same, when she visits the Fisheries Exhibition she cannot help lingering in delight before a life-sized model of a sea-captain in yellow oilskins and sou'wester, because, she tells him, 'it was executed in that style of art which you so greatly admire in the Italian churches, and was so good a likeness of *you* that I think you must have sat for it.' Butler could not have been particularly glad to read this double thrust at Tabachetti and his own sanguine complexion. When Gogin painted him later he said that he had to 'cook' the colour of his face, for he could never have given him such a flaming complexion on canvas.

But something was always happening to prevent their meetings. Even when she set out to hear him lecture at the Working Men's College in December 1882, coming down stairs at the club she stepped on a chestnut, 'which cut short my career by causing me to take a somersault down the stairs. The consequences of this performance were not serious, but they were unpleasant in the extreme, and it was an hour before it would have been wise for me to venture into the street, and I had a splitting headache. . . . Tell me, too, how you are, for you have neglected me horribly for weeks past.' Butler excused himself, when he was editing their correspondence, by the reflection: 'She very well knew she had only got to whip me up with a scrap of any kind [Miss Savage usually wrote to him on odd scraps of paper] when she thought I had been too long without writing, and also . . . if I answered her letters at once I should be written to again immediately; and these years from 1881 till the death of my father were the most harassing and arduous of my whole life. . . . I was in a very bad way as regards Pauli, my houses, the failure of my books, and my relations with my people. I often wonder how I got through it all as well as I did. Moreover I had not the faintest idea that Miss Savage was stricken with mortal disease.'

In addition, poor Miss Savage was constantly unwell

with such colds that she could neither speak, nor see, nor hear, and neuralgia confined her to her room for a fortnight at a time. Butler tells her that he has been overdoing it, too: his head is all wrong, the tumour on his neck is beginning to swell: 'I am well enough, but low, and as usual clinging to ledges of precipices with bright green slopes of grassy pasture always well in sight, and always eluding me, especially when I think I am closest to it.' He has broken a rib on one of his Sunday country walks with Jones and Reggie Worsley. He was climbing over a stile when he slipped and fell against a homœopathic medicine bottle in his watch-pocket. Jones was always falling ill, too, and soon after Butler's accident with the medicine bottle he developed scarlet fever and Butler had to sit up with him all night, sleeping on an arm-chair with his broken rib, just as he had sat up with Pauli. In an Erewhonian court neither of them would have got off without a long term of imprisonment on the dual charge of ill-health and bad luck.

All this time Butler did his best to preserve good relations with Shrewsbury. But when in March 1878 he sent his father the good reviews of *Life and Habit*, his father replied: 'Dear Sam, I return the papers which must no doubt be very gratifying to you. I have purposely refrained from reading any of your books except *Canterbury*, and could feel more sympathy in any artistic success you might attain than in this.' Butler always kept his father posted with news of his books, painting and music, and before his death the Canon was writing to congratulate him on good reviews. He also wrote kindly to his sisters about subjects which he thought would interest them. To May he wrote at the end of March 1878: 'I believe the most interesting piece of intelligence I can send is that I saw an open cowslip in a boy's hand—root, flower and all on Sunday last. I had myself seen some buds very nearly open, and last Sunday fortnight found some buds just beginning to show. I was not, however, fortunate enough to find a head actually in flower. I dined out the other day and took in a very pretty young lady to dinner, and sat opposite a very nice quiet gentlemanly man to whom I vented now and again conservative opinions which I imagined were well received. When the others were gone I asked my hostess who it was that I had taken in to dinner—and was told Miss Cobden (Cobden's daughter). I then asked who had sat opposite me. "Mr Chamberlain, M.P. for Birmingham" was the reply. . . . I am sorry you should think in sending those reviews to my father I was "forcing differences upon him". This was not my intention, but rather to show him that disinterested third parties considered us in more substantial agreement than he was perhaps aware of— and this I believe to be true; indeed I am more and more sure of it every year.' Butler used to say that whenever his sister had anything particularly unpleasant to say to him in a letter, she always began by telling him which flowers were out in the garden. May had evidently written recommending him to read the poems of Sydney Dobell, and he now replied: 'As a general rule I distrust energetic joyous temperaments, and as you know I am no lover of poetry. . . .'

In the autumn of 1878 he was in Italy again, and this time he visited Isabella at Arona. 'I wanted to show her to Jones, and to see her again as I might now safely do', he tells us in the *Notebooks*. 'I saw her at the hotel door leaning against the side of the house as I came up from the quay, looking much older, and as usual very sad when her face was in repose. It made me feel very unhappy, but I went on and she woke up from her dreaming as she saw strangers coming. She knew me at once and gave me one of her frank, gracious smiles as she put out her hand. I was awkward and said that I had often been on the point of coming. She caught me up in a moment, "and this time", she said with the same genial smile, "you have come, and we are glad to see you. . . ." '

In Chapter XXI of *Erewhon Revisited* Higgs meets Yram again after twenty years, and the scene of their meeting is so real and described in such circumstantial detail that it looks very much as if it were founded on actual experience—and, if on experience, on what but Butler's meeting after seven years with Isabella? The details of the scene, with its wine and brilliant sunlight, are obviously taken from Italy. It is not quite clear from *Erewhon* whether Higgs and Yram had actually been lovers, but it now transpires in the sequel that he had made love to her on the night before he left the prison at Coldharbour and that a son had been born of their union. *Erewhon Revisited* is an account of this second visit written by Higg's other son by Arowhena. Of Yram we read: 'He told me he had never seen anyone to compare with her except my mother'—the identical phrase used to describe Isabella in the *Notebooks*.

At his second meeting with Yram, Higgs is very much distressed: 'He could only bow his head and cover his face with his hands. Yram said: "We are old friends; take your hands from your face and let me see you. There! That is well." She took his right hand between both hers, looked at him with eyes full of kindness, and said softly: "You are not much changed, but you look haggard, worn, and ill. . . . Remember, you are among friends, who will see that no harm befalls you. . ." As she spoke she took the wine out of her basket and poured him out a glass, but rather to give him some little thing to distract his attention than because she expected him to drink it—which he could not do. She never asked him whether he found her altered, or turned the conversation

BUTLER AGED 30

' THE BEST SET '
Butler, aged 18, standing

BUTLER AGED 33
From a drawing by James Ferguson

BUTLER   ETTA   TOM   CANON BUTLER
HARRIE   MRS BUTLER   MAY

From a photograph taken about 1865

PAULI

MISS SAVAGE

FESTING JONES AND BUTLER, 1890

CANON BUTLER

BUTLER AND FAESCH AT GADSHILL, 1894

ever such a little on to herself; all was for him; to soothe and comfort him, not in words alone, but in look, manner and voice.' But Higgs says: 'I fear to do as much harm now as I did before, and with as little wish to do any harm at all.'

Isabella remained Butler's ideal of womanly beauty, and he went to see her after that whenever he was in Italy. Later she moved to Florence, where she opened an hotel of her own.

Between 1880 and 1883, Butler was rewriting *The Way of All Flesh*, which had been interrupted by *The Fair Haven*, and the books on evolution. In July 1883 he wrote to Miss Savage: 'I am more doubtful about it, in reality, than about any book that I have ever done. I never wrote a book yet about which I felt so uncertain whether it was good or not. I have no doubt about *The Fair Haven*, *Life and Habit*, and *Alps and Sanctuaries* being good, but this may for aught I feel clearly about it be very good or very bad.' He left instalments of the revised manuscript for Miss Savage in the men's cloakroom just outside the door of the Reading Room at the Museum, where Miss Savage used to leave her umbrella instead of climbing up to the Ladies. 'A lady I know was quite shocked', she told Butler, 'when she saw me one day getting my umbrella there and said the authorities would not like my doing so. I told her that although no doubt the indiscriminate association of male and female umbrellas might in a general way be productive of evil, yet my umbrella having become imbued with my personal qualities, she might be trusted to conduct herself with the most perfect propriety. At all events I should wait for the authorities or the male umbrellas to complain of her before altering my ways.' Then in November 1883 she read the whole manuscript of *The Way of All Flesh* straight through in bed one night, not finishing it until 4.45 the next morning, when smarting eyes and a headache produced some tart criticism. She cannot abide Towneley, she says, and Ernest gets more and more priggish as the book goes on, 'especially in the treatment of his children, which is ultra-priggish'. Butler replied in a brief note: 'I have no doubt Ernest becomes priggish—for as I have told you I am very priggish myself—everyone is more or less. For the rest we can talk about it when we meet.' After the next reading, however, Miss Savage wrote: 'I think it is almost perfect this time and I have not a single fault to find except with the spelling now and then. . . . There are no end of sweet bits. I wish I could remember them all. . . . It was very nicely put too, where you say that as a man has to run his chance for parents, so parents ought not to grumble at having to run their chance for children. . . . You know there is a good bit that I have never seen before, and all the first part is very much cut down and altered since I saw it long ago. The style is delightful, and it reads as smooth as cream.' Butler replied: 'My own idea is that the first volume is the best of the three, the second the next best and the third the worst, but then they have been rewritten just in this order; the first having been ten years in hand, the second five and the third only one, but I don't suppose I shall be able to do very much more to it—at any rate not till I have put it by and forgotten it for some time, and then I must begin again with the third volume.' But he never did. After Miss Savage's death he put the manuscript away and did not touch it again, and it was not published until after his own death, in 1903.

The Way of All Flesh did not come into its own until after the 1914-18 war, when the generation that suffered most from the war turned against their elders, who were responsible for it. It became a classic of the 1920's—*the* classic in fact—and was, in a sense, the ancestor of

Joyce's *A Portrait of the Artist as a Young Man* and all the other novels written by sensitive and misunderstood young men and women. In the political 1930's it still had a vogue among the Left Wing because of its sensible, matter-of-fact, realistic temper, and a certain nostalgia for working-class life that runs through it. Ernest marries a working-class girl, opens an old clothes shop at the Elephant and Castle, and generally severs connections with his own class—until he comes into his money. For, of course, Butler's ideal has all along been the gentleman of independent means who is at ease with himself and the world because he does not have to worry about money. Butler was anything but a Socialist, but he was a firm believer in economic determination in some respects.

Of Aunt Alethea in *The Way of All Flesh*, we are told that she did for Ernest 'the one thing anyone can do for anyone else . . . making a will in his favour and dying there and then'. Overton, the narrator and an elder incarnation of Butler, is in love with Alethea, but he says that it is impossible for him to explain 'how it was that she and I never married. We two knew exceedingly well, and that must suffice for the reader.' As a woman, charming and witty as she is, Alethea is necessarily incomplete, a little dried and arid. She irritated Miss Savage, who probably noticed in her certain parallels to herself. 'You make her like that most odious of women, Mrs John Stuart Mill', she wrote, 'who, though capable of surpassing Shelley, preferred to efface herself for the greater comfort of Mr John Stuart Mill! At least that is what he was so extraordinarily simple-minded as to be taught to believe!' They both realized, of course, that Butler required her to efface herself emotionally for *his* greater comfort.

When he visited his family at Shrewsbury in May 1883 he found them 'as cold as stones'. He was feeling run-down and low in health and wanted their sympathy; but they looked upon him with suspicion and when he said he was going abroad, the disapproving silence with which his remark was received, inferred, plainly enough, that they thought he had no business to spend money on foreign holidays when he was so hard up. May pressed the tumour on his neck, 'to find out whether it was a fatty tumour or a cancer', although he had told her that any kind of pressure upon it 'not only hurt me but set up cerebral disturbance. She never did anything more callous to me than this.'

In December his father became so ill that Butler went down to stay at Wilderhope House again. 'I have been caged here a fortnight with Charlotte,[1] or rather two Charlottes, and I am sure I must have an angelic temper to have avoided a row', he writes to Miss Savage on the 18th. 'Every time my father has rallied they have flown at me. Every time he has sunk they have toadied'— because presumably they knew that on his father's death he would be rich. But Canon Butler refused to die, and Butler had to come back to Clifford's Inn with hopes deferred. Still, there had been several gratifyingly unpleasant incidents to record in his notebook. His relations had tried to 'scratch' him about his books and paintings, and when he had cashed a cheque of his father's for £100 —£85 in notes and £15 in gold—and he gave Harrie the seventeen £5 notes, she objected that he had only given her sixteen. Butler counted them again and Harrie said that there were still only sixteen. 'Nothing that I can say', he notes, 'can give any adequate idea of her tone and manner.' In danger of losing his temper for the first time during his visit, Butler took the notes and laid them out in fours on the table, so that his sister had to admit

---

[1] The name under which Butler's sisters appear in *The Way of All Flesh*.

that he was right, but she made no apology 'and I believe still thinks I took one and put it back when she found me out.' Butler had left town so hurriedly that he had come away without enough money to pay his fare back, so he asked May to cash him a cheque. Harrie said she would do it, and when Butler gave her the cheque she looked at it suspiciously and said, 'Very well then, I will give you five pounds if this is all right.' His father, how-ever, was perfectly civil, though 'he never even pretended to care two straws about me. He never said anything to me except the merest commonplaces. . . . When he felt better what he turned to instinctively was shaving water and the *Daily Telegraph*. . . . He has made up his mind to get well, that is clear,' Butler concludes gloomily. 'I cannot say that I had a very pleasant jour-ney home.'

Canon Butler did not die till three years later, but poor Miss Savage had only just over another year to live. Four months before she died, she began to knit socks and kettle-holders for Butler, writing to him in October 1884: 'Here is a kettle-holder, and I can only say that a man who is equal to the control of two kettle-holders fills me with awe, and I shall begin to be afraid of you.' 'The kettle-holder is beautiful', replied Butler; 'it is like a filleted sole. . . . It is not at all too thick and fits my kettle to per-fection. I have been lifting my kettle on and off the fire with it, and then hanging the kettle-holder on its nail again, all day.' Apart from this, he was working at a cantata with Jones, *Narcissus*. The correspondence about the kettle-holder, the socks, the cantata, the health of their respective cats and the effect of changes in the weather on Canon Butler continues for a few months longer. In his last letter to Miss Savage Butler complains that he is overworked and low and that he has lost his friend Mr Tylor. 'Curious—as soon as I get a really useful friend able and willing to back me—he, poor man, as soon as he comes "to know me well" "is sure to die". Those people have died who ought not to have died, and those people who ought to have died have not died, and there is no sense of propriety in them.' Still, 'Jones's and my minuets and fugues etc. will be out next week. You must come and fetch your copy. . . .'

But Miss Savage never visited Clifford's Inn again, and the joke about the inappropriate deaths of his friends must have seemed to him singularly inappropriate when, a week later, he received a note from a Mr Gwynne Bird, telling him that she had been obliged to undergo a painful operation, 'and as a consequence is incapacitated for writing. She seemed cheerful, and wished me to tell you she was getting on well.' Four days later, Mr Gwynne Bird wrote again. 'It is with very great regret that I have to inform you of the death of my good friend Miss Savage. She died last night—her father was with her. I thought from your kind note that you also were a friend of hers. I have therefore thought it right to tell you.' The blow was sudden and totally unexpected. She had died from blood-poisoning after an operation for cancer. 'I received such a shock last night', he wrote to Harrie, 'that I hardly know how to write. I have lost my friend Miss Savage, whom you have often heard me speak of, and no words of mine can express how great this loss is. . . . I never knew any woman to approach her at once for brilliancy and goodness. . . . It is out of the question that I can ever replace her. . . . For the moment I am incapable of thinking of any other subject.' He then wrote to her father for the return of his letters so that he could place them with hers and make a book that should be a portrait of her drawn by her own hand. A few were returned to him at once, without comment; the rest followed after about two years. When they arrived, he was

pained to see 'how meagre and egotistical' they were. 'I
tore them up wholesale, but when I had torn till I was
tired, it struck me that I might want them when I came
to edit Miss Savage's letters.'

Butler was not asked to attend the funeral, but found
out that it was to be held in the cemetery of the parish of
St Marylebone at Finchley. Miss Savage's father, her
uncle, an old servant, and a few friends were there. 'It
was a lovely soft spring afternoon; during the whole time
of the funeral birds were singing and the sun was shining.
I felt that I was attending the funeral of incomparably
the best and most remarkable woman I had ever known.
Happy she rarely was. . . . I had already realized what till
death I doubt whether I had more than suspected. I
mean how much better woman she was than I was man—
and how far fuller measure of good things she had meted
out to me than I had meted to her in return. Therefore she haunts me, and always will haunt me, because I
never felt for her the love that if I had been a better man
I should have felt.'

She haunted him in retrospect, but had she been still
there he would not have behaved to her any differently.
Butler had always to find something or someone with
which to torture himself. His rooms were empty, so it
was only natural that he should people them with ghosts.
Among the dreary furniture of his sitting-room at
Clifford's Inn, with its dirty white panelling plastered
with photographs of Italian paintings, among the notebooks, the files of letters, the rolls of music on the little
upright piano, the gilt-edged account books, the little
white bust of Handel and the much-thumbed photograph
of Pauli on the mantelpiece, hung the kettle-holder made
for him by Miss Savage. 'I need hardly say', he wrote on
one of her letters in 1901, 'that the kettle-holder hangs
by its fetter on the wall beside the fire, and is not allowed

to be used by anyone but myself.' It is now in the Butler Collection at St John's College, Cambridge.

Butler never grew that carapace that other people cultivate to protect themselves from the world—the glossy surface of the worldly and successful that enables them to cannon off each other like billiard balls and run smoothly to their self-appointed pockets of office, club and home. He was too scrupulous, too honest, too sensitive to the feelings of others, too doubtful of his own, and too timid. In many of his photographs he looks both defiant and apprehensive. But by showing himself to us exactly as he was, in carpet slippers and shirt-sleeves (as he actually appears in a delightful photograph taken by Alfred, his 'servant and friend', and reproduced by Jones in the *Memoir*) he laid himself open to attack by those who are neither so scrupulous nor so honest with themselves. Just as he allowed himself to be exploited by Pauli, so he now tormented himself with the thought of all he might have done for Miss Savage, comparing his own 'egotism' with her 'selflessness'. He may have rejected Christianity, but Christ had not rejected him and still went on 'crucifying him in a quiet way' for the rest of his life.

CHAPTER VI

'JONES AND I'

BUTLER AND HENRY FESTING JONES FIRST MET in the rooms of Edward Algernon Hall, an old Cambridge friend of Jones's, in January 1876, after one of the Monday evening 'Pops' at the St James's Hall. Butler was sitting on the sofa with a piece of newspaper spread on his knees, eating his supper of bacon and bread, which had been in his pocket all through the concert, and talking about painting. Hall's people lived at Whatton, near Langar, and were well known to the Butlers. Jones, the son of Tom Jones, Q.C., was twenty-four at the time of this meeting, sixteen years younger than Butler and an upstanding young man of over six foot. He was articled to a firm of solicitors in the City and was living in rooms in Cork Street, off Bond Street, on an allowance from his mother.

Neither Butler nor Jones made much impression upon each other at this meeting, and their friendship did not really begin until a year later, when Jones formed the habit of dropping into Clifford's Inn on his way home from the City. Then he would sit quietly while Butler painted. Another year elapsed, and one day in 1878 Butler suggested, without really meaning it, that Jones should join him in Italy that summer. But he was surprised when a telegram arrived from Zurich accepting his invitation, and he said to himself: 'He is good-natured, he is exceedingly easy to get on with; if he wants to come, let him come, and if he bores me I will shunt him.' Jones accordingly joined Butler on the Sacro Monte at Varese.

He arrived late at night, and after he had had something
to eat, the two men sat together, watching the lights of
Varese and the lightning playing over the plains below.
Butler was still a little uneasy; he scarcely knew Jones,
and in any case he liked to be on his own abroad. 'But I
was comfortable', he says, 'I was smoking; I was in Italy,
and this would do very well for the moment.' Then Jones,
probably only in order to say something, asked Butler if
he knew anything about the stars. Butler, who disliked
astronomy, replied somewhat sharply, 'Certainly not!' So
Jones said no more. A moment or two later, Butler added
in a more conciliatory tone, 'I know the moon.' After
that there was not another awkward moment during the
whole three weeks they spent together.

Next morning, Butler took Jones up the Sacro Monte
to see the Chapels of the Mysteries, with their life-sized
terra-cotta figures, 'and I soon perceived', says Jones,
'that he enjoyed showing me these things as much as I
enjoyed seeing them'. He then took him to Arona to see
Isabella. From Fusio they walked over the mountains to
Faido, the town in the Ticino valley which had been
Butler's sketching headquarters on so many other visits.
He showed Jones the porch of the Rossura church and
explained that it was like Handel's music—'a diatonic
melody harmonized with common chords over a walking
bass. There were no cross rhythms in the porch of
Rossura church; no shifty diminished sevenths, saying
one thing and meaning another; no passionate aug-
mented sixths, tearing their hair; no extravagant modu-
lations to remote keys . . . it was a background for
Giovanni Bellini, not for Michael Angelo.' Jones was
more attracted to Butler the more he saw of him. He was
charmed by his kindness and courtesy, 'not only towards
me, but towards everyone we had anything to do with—
the other guests in the hotels, the landlords and their

families, the waiters, drivers, boatmen, porters and peasants'. Next Jones was struck by Butler's uncompromising sincerity. 'If a subject interested him, he took infinite pains to find out all he could about it at first hand; thought it over and formed an opinion of his own, without reference to what anyone else thought or said.' He was also struck by his gaiety, for Butler was at his happiest when travelling. 'A man's holiday', he would say, 'is his garden.' On his side, Butler found Jones 'easily pleased, very patient, more free than anyone whom I have ever met from affectation or bounce of any kind, very gentle in all his ways, and, in fact, in all respects singularly amiable'. But no one throws off old habits in a moment, and Jones still made some pretence of reading the dreadful books he had brought with him. One morning Butler came into his bedroom, took up a book on a table and said, 'There now, you have been reading that damned *Republic* again'. Also he wrote poetry, liked his mother and did not speak ill of his elder sister. Butler soon cured him of all that. 'He was so free from malice of any kind, so amusing, so ready to try and please, so easy to be pleased, that I condoned this, and, as I have said, before the end of our three weeks' trip I liked him very much, and thought exceedingly highly of him. . . . Still, I did not know that he was far and away, out and out, much *the* ablest man that I ever did see, or am ever likely to see.' Such a high opinion did Butler come to have of Jones (who, in time, grew to be almost a replica of himself) that he used to say that from that time onwards all his books abounded with passages suggested, if not more, by Jones.

If Jones was 'far and away, out and out' the ablest man Butler had ever met—though he had, after all, met Darwin—that was largely because he avoided anyone who had distinguished himself and limited his circle of friends and acquaintances to his inferiors. But, apart from the *Memoir*, it is difficult to see exactly where Jones's great ability lay. When he gave up the law, on the strength of Butler's allowance, his only discernible occupation was talking to Butler, travelling with Butler, going to concerts with him, singing to Alfred, and occasionally writing music. Though for years he took music lessons with Mlle Vaillant, whom Butler characteristically suspected of having matrimonial designs upon him when he visited her, and though both he and Butler took lessons in counterpoint from Rockstro, his music is never particularly distinguished. His principal role in life was to be a pensioned Boswell to Butler's Johnson, and to provide the older man with an object for his starved affections. As long as he never demanded anything more than this, it was doubtless a pleasant enough existence.[1]

But he had one defect, and it was a very serious one. He was always falling ill. Writing in 1884, Butler notes: 'I suppose he is about as well now as he ever is, but for the past two years he has been able to do very little—rheumatism, nervous exhaustion, eczema, impetigo, and a quick succession of carbuncles for nearly a twelvemonth being the chief evils.' Worst of all, his mother, who bullied him continually about money, did not die until 1900, only two years before Butler died himself. 'So it is with my cousin', writes Butler. 'All three of us, Jones, my cousin, and myself are depressed, over-driven, or at any rate over-weighted with worries, and only sustained by hope which had been deferred so long that we have begun to have little confidence that it will ever be any-

---

[1] Of course, Butler read all his books to Jones as he wrote them. 'He would say something *à propos*; then out would come my note-book and in would go Jones's remark.' When Alfred said: 'But you know, Sir, Jones is not so good as all that: no one ever was, or ever could be, such a perfect angel as you have made him out' Butler replied: 'My dear Alfred, I know that as well as you do, but all that I have said is true.'

thing more than hope.' What they were all hoping for—unless it was for their wealthier relations to die and leave them comfortably off—is not clear.

After their three weeks in Italy together in 1878, Butler and Jones continued to see a great deal of each other. Jones had gone back to live with his mother at Craven Hill Gardens, Bayswater, and used to make the journey into town and back three or four times a week to spend the evening at Clifford's Inn. 'I know of no one else from whom I could have stood such frequent visits', comments Butler. He introduced him to his cousin Reginald Worsley and Jones joined their Sunday outings. The first time he went with them was at the end of September, or early October 1878, when they walked from Westerham to Redhill. Both Butler and Worsley were still rather shy of Jones and still on their best behaviour, but by and by they ventured to be a little flippant and irreverent, and finding no signs of disapproval at length said exactly whatever they felt like saying. They told bawdy stories about the doings of their laundresses, little jokes against women, or God or Butler's father and sisters, and how a soldier whom Butler had met in a train in Wales had told him that he was not married 'because it was cheaper to buy milk than to keep the cow'. The *obiter dicta* of old Mrs Boss, Reggie Worsley's laundress, were a perpetual source of amusement to the three friends; she appears in *The Way of All Flesh* as Ernest's landlady, Mrs Jupp, and there is a special section in the *Notebooks* devoted to 'Bossiana'.

It was not till the end of 1878 that Butler and Jones discovered how much better they got on with one another than with anyone else. 'That is', says Butler, 'it took us three years to find each other out.' Of course, Jones's mother was jealous, and there were many unpleasant scenes at Craven Hill Gardens, till Jones decided to leave home and take lodgings in New Ormond Street. In 1881 he moved to Barnard's Inn, in order to live as near Butler as possible without actually living with him. Here, and at Clifford's Inn, they played a good deal of music together, chiefly Handel, though they had not by then begun their joint compositions—Jones, because Butler did not care for the sort of songs he had written already, and Butler partly because he did not think he could do it well enough to make it worth doing. At last, in the spring of 1883, the two friends were forced to spend several days apart from each other and Butler resolved to take the opportunity to write a minuet. Next time he met Jones at Heatherley's, where they both worked in the evenings, he played him the minuet on the piano. Jones was surprised and puzzled, not at the music, but that Butler should have written it. Next time Butler visited Jones, he found that he had written one or two pieces, and after that 'for ever so long had something new to play to me every time we met'. Butler also wrote two or three more short pieces, making four in all; 'then I was played out, and found I had too much on my hands and cut it.' The pieces Jones had written were, Butler says, very good, 'but still they were not exactly what I wanted'. It was not till he wrote a fugue that Butler was really pleased: 'this hit me off to a nicety'. Then Jones wrote the fugue which he afterwards used in the overture to *Narcissus*, and Butler liked this better than any fugue he had come across since Handel's time. But they were still consumed with a secret care because, says Butler, 'I had not written a song at all, and Jones had not done one which I unreservedly liked. . . . I kept on saying *more meo* that I was sure I could do it, and not doing it. "Do it", said Jones, "and bring it to me".' So he sat down at Jones's table and began sketching in a melody to some words of

Metastasio's, but was interrupted by someone coming into the room and he lost the idea.

All this while, Jones, like Butler, was in continual money difficulties and incessantly plagued by his nearest relations. He had not got on well in the law, and in 1881 he left the firm of solicitors he was working for, being disappointed in his expectation of a partnership. Luckily, Butler tells us, he had a quarrel with his father in the spring of that year and the money he borrowed on the Shrewsbury estate enabled him to give Jones legal work in connection with his house property, so that for a year or so after leaving his mother Jones was able to get on with very little (if any) assistance from her. But by June 1882, at the age of thirty-one, he was in difficulties again and had to get his mother to help him. His mother dribbled out money to him in ten and fifteen pounds at a time. Her letters were of the most parental description: 'Have you considered what your position would be if anything were to happen to myself? You surely do not expect your sisters to keep you?', and so forth. But hard as he tried, Jones was unable to get either clerkship, partnership, or work of any kind. One night, unable to sleep, he got up and composed a piece which he called 'A Letter from my Mother', and Butler said it seemed to say 'You've had one fifteen pounds' and to harp upon the subject throughout the whole composition. At last, in the autumn of 1883, Jones found a clerkship with a solicitor who struck Butler as 'one of the most disagreeable men in the profession'.

Then, on one of their Sunday walks in the spring of 1884, Butler said he would like to write a chorus about the Funds: 'The steadfast funds maintain their wonted state, While all the other markets fluctuate.' He hummed a little of it, and Jones said it would be nice to describe Mexican Railways, how they would run about and go up and down, and they talked about the way Handel would have treated several of the best known stocks. It was such fun that they decided to try their hand at a cantata. And this was the origin of *Narcissus*. Next Sunday, Butler told his cousin how they were getting on, 'and what shape the entire absence of plot had assumed'; and Reggie Worsley said: 'Oh, do have some shepherds, you should not do anything of this kind without shepherds.' Jones said: 'Yes, and let them call their flocks "tedious".' Then Jones and Butler hummed out the words of the song, 'I never knew her worth till now', an aria on the death of a rich aunt, and Butler set to work and wrote it down. Then they hummed, 'Shall I to Egypt's dusky bonds, A portion of my wealth confide?' Jones took the words home and next day the greater part were set. 'At last', says Butler, 'I had got what I had been wanting all these years. Before the introductory symphony was over I felt quite safe.'

Narcissus is a mock pastoral. The hero is in love with Amaryllis, who will not have anything to do with him when he loses his money. But she receives him with open arms on the death of his aunt. Meanwhile the other shepherds and shepherdesses come to London and speculate wildly on the Stock Exchange. Narcissus debates, in a duet with Amaryllis, as to how he shall invest his inherited wealth, and the nymph advises him sagely:

> Though jewelled monarchs plead for aid,
>   Your trusting hand restrain;
> Your loans will never be repaid,
>   So let them plead in vain.
> A maiden's words are little worth,
>   But, as you must invest,
> Of all securities on earth
>   The English Funds are best.

The Chorus repeats her advice and the cantata concludes
with a fugal chorus:

> How blest the prudent man, the maiden pure,
> Whose income is both ample and secure,
> Arising from Consolidated Three
> Per Cent Annuities, paid quarterly.

Butler did not begin his lessons in counterpoint with
Rockstro until three years later and, unfortunately, the
music of *Narcissus*—though astonishing for an untaught
amateur—is not so amusing as the libretto. It is, in fact,
intended to be serious and is only sometimes unintentionally amusing, for Butler shrank from poking fun at
his idol. The words, however, are an admirable parody
of Handel's librettist, but the joke is carried on for rather
too long.

A rehearsal of the work took place on 18 May 1886 in
Gogin's studio in King Henry's Road. Reggie Worsley
procured an orchestra for the occasion and helped to
copy the parts. There were three first violins, two second,
one tenor, one cello, and one double bass, one oboe, one
bassoon, one horn, and a pair of kettle-drums. Jones conducted. 'Everything went off quite smoothly', he says;
'the performers expressed themselves as much pleased
with the music and so did the few friends we had invited
to come and listen.' There was a good deal of discussion
going on then about additional accompaniments to the
Messiah, and Butler wrote a little verse to guard against
the danger of any future Mozart rescoring *Narcissus*:

> May he be cursed for evermore
> Who tampers with *Narcissus'* score;
> May he by poisonous snakes be bitten
> Who writes more parts than what we've written.
> We tried to make our music clear

For those who sing and those who hear,
Not lost and muddled up and drowned
In overdone orchestral sound;
So kindly leave the work alone
Or do it as we want it done.

Hitherto, remarks Jones, the musical societies of the country have adopted the former of the alternatives proposed in the concluding couplet. Parts of *Narcissus* were performed by the boys at Shrewsbury in 1887, and the whole work was sung right through again on 27 January 1892, with piano accompaniment and eight voices, at Mrs Beavington Atkinson's house in Kensington, where Jones used to join in weekly performances of madrigals and part-songs.

On 3 June Butler wrote to his sister: 'Jones and I went to a Philharmonic concert last night. We went to the shilling places behind the orchestra and sat close to the drums, so we could see each instrument and hear what it was about. I do wish people would not make their movements so long. We have resolved that all our movements shall be of reasonable length. I am afraid I liked our own music a great deal better than Beethoven's; but then, of course, if we had been devoted admirers of Beethoven we should have founded ourselves on him and imitated him.' This letter is expanded considerably into a deliciously absurd passage in the *Notebooks*. There we read that the concert began with Mozart's G Minor Symphony, which Butler and Jones 'liked fairly well—but if each movement had been half as long I should probably have felt cordially enough towards it, except of course in so far as that the spirit of the music is alien to that of the early Italian school with which alone I am in genuine sympathy and of which Handel is the climax. Then came a terribly long-winded recitative by Beethoven, and an air with a good deal of "Che farò" in it. . . . The Concerto for Violin and Orchestra (Op. 61) which followed was longer and more tedious still. I have not a single good word for it. . . . And finally there was a tiresome characteristic overture by Berlioz, which, if Jones could by any possibility have written anything so dreary, I should certainly have begged him not to publish.' He repeats that it was all too long, whereas 'Handel knew when to stop and when he meant stopping he stopped much as a horse stops, with little if any peroration'.

It is legitimate to dislike romantic music, and if one is particularly attached to the early Italian school one might not be in sympathy with Beethoven and Berlioz; it is another thing to dismiss their music as worthless. But then Butler's attitude to music was like his attitude to everything else: it arose from a determination not to allow himself to be emotionally exploited and had its roots in his mother's sofa talks with their appeals to his 'better nature'. He would not, therefore, let Beethoven or Berlioz get away with anything. Suspicious, he sat behind the drums, so that he could see and hear what each member of the orchestra was doing. Of course, in this position, he got a thoroughly distorted idea of the music and a full view of the conductor, of whom he also disapproved, because 'he had long yellowish hair and kept tossing his head to fling it back on to his shoulders, instead of keeping it short as Jones and I keep ours'. In Butler's view there was nothing to choose between the passionate, airy and exquisitely nervous melodies of Berlioz and the exhibitionism of the conductor with his long yellow hair. The *Gavottes, Minuets, Fugues, and other short pieces for the Piano* had appeared at the end of the previous year. The behaviour of Butler and Jones at concerts was similar to their behaviour at scientific lectures, when they would sit in the front row and ostentatiously unfold *The Sporting Times* and chuckle at the jokes.

Earlier in 1886 Butler had applied for the Slade Professorship of Fine Arts at Cambridge, which had fallen vacant on the death of Sidney Colvin. He did not get it, though he collected testimonials from G. R. Fortescue, Superintendent of the British Museum Reading Room, Dr Richard Garnett, Heatherley, Dr Kennedy, later Regius Professor of Greek at Cambridge, W. T. Marriott, and several R.A.'s. 'I have had a good many letters about my failure', he wrote to Harrie in March, 'I really believe a good many people believe I ought to have had it. . . .' He applied for it soon after his letter to the *Athenæum* of 20 February in which he claimed to have discovered two hitherto unrecognized portraits of Giovanni and Gentile Bellini among the onlookers in Gentile Bellini's 'St Mark preaching at Alexandria' in the Brera at Milan. There is, he pointed out, a close resemblance between the two heads side by side to the extreme left of this picture and the two male portrait heads in the Louvre, attributed in the seventeenth century to Giovanni Bellini. He was convinced that these were portraits of Giovanni and Gentile Bellini and were the work of Giovanni, though in his day they were attributed to Cariani. Since then, his view has been supported by Berenson. Butler discovered the same two heads in Carpaccio's 'Dispute of St Stephen', also in the Brera, among the bystanders to the right of the picture, and after that he continued to search for portraits of the Bellini brothers in Venice, and other likely places.

He also claimed to have discovered a Holbein water-colour drawing, 'La Danse', in the Museum at Basel. The Museum catalogue attributed it to Jerome Hess, but while copying it in 1884-5, Butler became convinced that it was in reality a Holbein, on the grounds both of the treatment of the drapery and its close similarity to a

Holbein drawing of the same subject in Berlin, of which the Basel Museum had a photograph. Holbein had made the Berlin drawing as a study for the decoration of a house in Basel known as the 'Haus zum Tanz'. The Basel water-colour, Butler pointed out, could not be by Hess, since the decorations on the 'Haus zum Tanz' had disappeared before Hess was born.[1]

'I am so glad you had a fine afternoon for your foundation-laying, and that the bishop was nice', he wrote to his sister in October 1886. 'I think bishops generally are rather nice. . . . I spent Tuesday and Wednesday copying Holbein in Basel and, leaving Wednesday night, got here on Thursday evening. I found my kittens well and strong, but as wild as little tigers through not having been habitually caressed. They spat and swore and altogether behaved abominably. Now, though only 48 hours have gone by, they are quite tame and very pretty.'

This year Butler began attending the Shrewsbury School dinners, and when he met Dr Kennedy he remarked that his candidature for the Slade Professorship had not come to very much. ' "No", said he [Dr Kennedy] drily and with the intake and outtake of breath which used to characterize him when I knew him years ago.' Why should he, Butler asked himself—knowing that he did not particularly like the sort of people who attended the Shrewsbury dinners, nor they him—why should he pay a guinea for a bad dinner, and eat and drink what it took him a whole day to recover from? It did not seem a very sensible thing to do. Yet he continued to do it, on the principle that 'the more I take the Ishmaelitish line, the more incumbent it is upon me to do the correctest of correct things occasionally.'

[1] He convinced the Curator of the Museum of his discovery and published his conclusions in the *Universal Review* for November 1889.

Canon Butler now died at last. When his expectant son arrived at Wilderhope House in December 1886, three weeks before the end, the nurses tried to rouse the old man into consciousness by saying, 'Mr Sam has arrived, Sir, he will come up and see you directly.' At this the Canon looked round, opening his eyes with a scared look, and said, 'Oh, then he'll tell us how long it will be before we shall all have to turn out.' Butler was standing by his bedside, but his father did not see him, and quickly became unconscious again. Only when Archdeacon Lloyd began in a loud professional voice to repeat some prayers for the dying did he open his eyes for a few seconds, 'but as he did so, there came an expression over his face as though he were saying to himself, "Oh no, it is not the Day of Judgment; it is only Tom Lloyd", and he became comatose again.' Butler was supporting his father's head between his hands when he died, which he did so peacefully that Butler turned to Archdeacon Lloyd and said: 'How gently do they that have riches enter into the kingdom of Heaven!' Soon after that Burd, the family doctor, was 'holding forth' and suggesting things for Butler to mention in the obituary article for the Shrewsbury papers and Butler said to him: 'You see, Dr Burd, one of the greatest feathers in my father's cap was one that I cannot refer to.' Dr Burd was surprised and asked his meaning. 'I mean', said Butler, 'that he was *my* father.' Dr Burd replied drily that he had not looked at the matter in that light hitherto.

'I have never been able to understand it', Butler remarks of his father, 'but the servants were genuinely fond of him, whereas the only person to whom he was really attached was the cat. . . . me he simply detested.' Writing to Jones from Wilderhope House on 3 January 1887, he says: 'I take only a life interest, and Tom's family have had decidedly the larger half though the division was

apparently equitable. I take £6,400 in money absolutely
and I take a life interest in realty with rental of £456 a
year valued (low) by my father at £14,204. Besides this,
I have £300 by the settlements—mortgaged as you know.
Roughly the estimate I have always made is about right
—and on the realization I ought to be good for £1,000
or £1,200 a year, but I have not yet got it into my head.'

Butler made no change in his way of life after his
father's death, except to buy a new wash-hand basin and
another pair of hair brushes. He was rather hard on his
brushes, Festing Jones tells us, 'because he had the habit
of brushing his hair every night one hundred strokes,
fifty each side'. He also engaged Alfred Emery Cathie as
his clerk and valet. Alfred was just over twenty-two and
the son of a friend of Butler's laundress, Mrs Doncaster;
he became the next best thing to a son for Butler. Jones
also benefited largely from the Canon's death, for Butler
now suggested that he should 'give up trying to succeed
as a solicitor' and should accept an allowance of £200 a
year in order that he might devote himself to him. As
soon as Mrs Jones heard this she stopped allowing her
son any money at all.

The death of Charles Darwin four years before, in
1882, was another load off Butler's mind, for Darwin
represented authority in the scientific world and had been
at Shrewsbury under Dr Butler. The story of their relations is a long and complicated one and falls into the
same emotional pattern as Butler's relationship with his
father. It takes us back to the earlier years of his career
as a writer. A note referring to November 1872 reads:
'My second visit to Charles Darwin at Down, when he
began treating me so rudely'. It is not clear in what way
Darwin had offended Butler, except that at first, it seems,
he treated him rather coldly. Next year, however, he took
offence at Darwin's letter to him about *The Fair Haven*.

'Very nice and kind', he comments. 'He told me he thought I should do well to turn my attention to novel-writing. All scientific people recommend me to do this.' Nevertheless, their relations remained superficially friendly, and Butler and Francis Darwin, Darwin's son, often met in London, either dining together or going to a concert. Before *Life and Habit* came out he wrote to Francis Darwin in November 1877 saying that he did not like the thought of Charles Darwin seeing the book, 'for it has resolved itself into a downright attack upon your father's view of evolution, and a defence of what I conceive to be Lamarck's. I neither intended nor wished this, but was simply driven into it.' Butler's objection to *The Origin of Species* was basically the metaphysical one that it had abolished mind from the universe and attributed everything to blind chance. He maintained on the other hand, as he wrote to Francis Darwin, that the origin and growth of the various forms of life were due to 'the continued personality between successive generations, and the *bona fide* character of the memory on the part of the offspring of its past existences in the persons of its forefathers'. This view has much in common with Jung's theory of the racial unconscious. Francis Darwin wrote to say that he had read *Life and Habit* with much interest, but Darwin himself did not write.

In February 1879 the German scientific journal *Kosmos* published an article on Erasmus Darwin by Dr Ernst Krause; in November an English translation appeared in book form with a preliminary essay on his grandfather by Charles Darwin. Meanwhile in May Butler's *Evolution Old and New*, 'a comparison of the theories of Buffon, Dr Erasmus Darwin, and Lamarck with that of Mr Charles Darwin', had appeared. Darwin sent a copy of the book to Krause with the remark that Butler 'was not worth much powder and shot'. Nevertheless, when Butler came to read the English edition of Krause's *Kosmos* article, he was struck by several passages which appeared to be taken directly from *Evolution Old and New*, and the last sentence, in particular, seemed to be directed at him. 'Erasmus Darwin's system was in itself a most significant first step in the path of knowledge which his grandson has opened up for us', wrote Krause, 'but the wish to revive it at the present day, as has actually been seriously attempted, shows a weakness of thought and a mental anachronism which no one can envy.' Not unnaturally, Butler was annoyed. How was it, he asked himself, that Krause could have written an article in February referring to a book which did not appear till the following May? The suspicion came to him that these passages must have been foisted into the English translation by Darwin. His suspicion was strengthened into a certainty after reading through the original German text in *Kosmos* and finding it to be shorter by six pages than the translation. It appeared certain, therefore, that the article had been altered in the light of *Evolution Old and New*. Butler wrote a formal letter to Darwin requesting an explanation. Darwin replied next day that before having his *Kosmos* article translated, Dr Krause had told him of his intention to alter it considerably and that it was this revised version that had appeared in English. Darwin apologized for not making this plain in the preface and promised to add a note to this effect to any future edition. As a matter of fact, Darwin had mentioned this in the first version of his prefatory essay, but had inadvertently cut it out when correcting the proofs.

This perfectly reasonable explanation should have satisfied Butler. But, with his 'sense of wrong', he was now convinced that Darwin had adopted an underhand method of revenging himself upon him. He thereupon committed the blunder of writing a letter to the *Athenæum* in which he said: 'It is doubtless a common practice for writers to take an opportunity of revising their works; but it is not common when a covert condemnation of an opponent has been interpolated into a revised edition, the revision of which has been concealed, to declare with every circumstance of distinctness that the condemnation was written prior to the book which might appear to have called it forth, and thus lead readers to suppose that it must be an unbiased opinion' (*Athenæum*, 31 January 1880).

Darwin then wrote two draft letters to the *Athenæum* in reply, restating what he had already written to Butler privately, but before sending them off he wrote to Huxley for advice as to whether he should publish them or no. 'Mr Butler has attacked me bitterly, in fact accusing me of lying, duplicity, and God knows what, because I unintentionally omitted to state that Krause had enlarged his *Kosmos* article before sending it for translation. . . . I should rather like to show that I had intended to state that Krause had enlarged his article. On the other hand a clever and unscrupulous man like Mr Butler would be sure to twist whatever I may say against me; and the longer the controversy lasts the more degrading it is to me.' Darwin had a hatred of any kind of controversy—he had had enough of it already—and if he had to write the simplest letter to the press it kept him awake all night. Huxley and his family, therefore, advised him not to reply. 'Oh Lord, what a relief your letter has been to me!' wrote Darwin. 'I feel like a man condemned to be hung who has just got a reprieve. I saw in the future no end of trouble. . . . The affair has annoyed and pained me to a silly extent; but it would be disagreeable to anyone to be publicly called in fact a liar. He seems to hint that I interpolated sentences in Krause's MS., but he could hardly have really thought so. Until quite recently he expressed great friendship for me, and said he had learnt all he knew about evolution from my books, and I have no idea what has made him so bitter against me.' There were many times in his life when Canon Butler had occasion to feel the same about his son. But once Butler had established a father-son relationship with Darwin, the fat was, psychologically speaking, in the fire, and, with his pervasive 'sense of wrong', he remained quite convinced for the rest of his life that Darwin had treated him like his father. It never occurred to him that perhaps both Darwin and his father were terrified of *him*. So he continued in books, articles and letters to attack Darwin bitterly, even after his death, projecting on to his unoffending head all the resentment he dared not express against Pauli and his father.

But he was not quite without recognition. In May 1887 Bernard Shaw's long and enthusiastic review of *Luck or Cunning?* appeared in the *Pall Mall Gazette*, under the title 'Darwin Denounced'. The first draft was much longer, but the editor cut it down for fear of offending the Darwinians. The review concluded with the following paragraph: 'Let it suffice to acknowledge his [Butler's] skilful terseness of expression, his frank disdain of affected suavity or imperturbability, his apparently but not really paradoxical humour, his racy epigrams and the geniality of his protest against "a purely automatic conception of the universe as of something that will work if a penny is dropped into the box".'

In September of the same year the Municipio of Varallo conferred upon Butler what he always said was the greatest honour he ever received. They gave him a public banquet in the loggia of the Albergo on the Sacro Monte. Butler made a speech in Italian in reply to the tributes. Jones was there, too, and before dinner they went with Dionigi Negri to inspect the figures in the Deposition Chapel. 'We had been told', Jones wrote to

Gogin, 'that two of the soldiers in the Chapel where Christ is taken in the Garden were made out of the statues of Adam and Eve when the present Adam and Eve in the first chapel were made, and we examined the chapel in the morning and made up our minds that the soldier with a moustache and real drapery was Adam and the other soldier with long hair and armour was Eve. Eve was bigger than Adam, which was wrong, and she had no breasts to speak of, but that might have been because neither Cain nor Abel were yet born. Her breast had been painted to represent armour in silver scales, which stopped short of her girdle, her intervening belly being painted blue like an ancient Briton. As we were going into the chapels before dinner we thought we might as well settle the Adam and Eve question for certain, so we went in and Dionigi groped the statues. I also pulled up their clothes and we found we had been quite wrong in the morning. It is Eve who has the moustache and the drapery hides her breasts; and it is Adam's stomach that is painted blue.'

They walked over the Col d'Olen to Gressony la Trinité and down the valley to Pont Saint Martin. 'Daniele was our guide the last two days', writes Jones, 'a charming young man who hates his sister.' They went on to Crea, where there is a sanctuary with figures by Tabachetti. Here they found one of the chapels turned into a studio by Cavaliero Antonio Brilla, an old Jewish sculptor, the image of Shylock, who was 'suitably engaged', says Jones, in modelling Christ for a wooden cross for the Cruxifixion chapel. 'It was the most rapid crucifixion on record. He assured us that he only began at eight that morning, and when we saw the figure at 11.15 it appeared on the point of uttering the last words "it is finished".' Then Jones went back to London and Butler went on to Chiavenna to paint. He has had three large photographs taken to supplement his sketches, he writes to Jones on 21 September, 'and if I cannot make three saleable pictures with these materials and without more expense than canvas and frames I ought to be kicked. . . . The *passero* [the Sparrow] is quite well and Carlo is very good to me. I have had no more love affairs.'

Butler was very happy in Italy, as readers of *Alps and Sanctuaries* do not need to be reminded. A postcard to Jones about his visit to Varese tells him: 'I found Giuseppe and Giorgio and Jacobino, Mino and the lot. Papa and Jacobino really are coming to London next month. Giuseppe better than ever; the Luzoatos and the other family not there, but another very nice mother and daughter instead. They were in the highest spirits and made a tremendous row, and the old woman and papa Diena danced and they all sang, and when I had gone to bed they came under my window and serenaded me with singing and mock musical instruments. The old lady implored me to stay. Why wouldn't I? To-night they really did mean *far fracasso* [make a noise] and I ought to be there. However I got away—but as for Giuseppe!'

He was back at Varallo again early in 1888, taking photographs in the clear frosty weather of the chapels for *Ex Voto*. The chapels were so dark inside that, although he used magnesium wire in some cases, he had usually to expose a plate for an hour or more, and during this time he was forced to contemplate the statues. 'In this way', comments Jones, 'he came to have a very intimate knowledge of them.' In the evenings he would sit talking to his landlord and Dionigi Negri at the Albergo della Posta, before a fire of peat and wood. At other times Dionigi would take him to the house of his uncle Zio Paolo, a baker in the Piazza, and they would all sit in the kitchen, in a semicircle round the fire: Butler in the middle, Dionigi on one side of him and Signor Cesare,

who had married Zio Paolo's daughter, on the other. On
each side of the fire sat the baker himself and Leonardo,
his young assistant, and well in the background, behind
the men, sat Leonardo's pretty sister and the maid,
darning stockings. Sometimes they listened to Leonardo's
musical box (a musical box cunningly concealed in the
binding of his photograph album) and when it played its
tunes they all exclaimed 'O bel!'

When Butler next wrote to Jones he said: 'You know
how much time Dionigi and Leonardo and Zio and
Fuselli are likely to leave me so neither you nor Alfred
will wonder if my letters are short. Give my love to Alfred
and tell him to light the stove in the sitting-room. . . .
Isn't he good? I'm glad you go and sit with him. Are not
he and I like Zio Paolo and Leonardo? I told them about
Alfred and showed them his portrait and they said he
was a *bel giovane.*'

On 26 January he wrote to Jones: 'I am all right but
have a sense as though I were getting rather confused
and somewhat over-ridden, and want badly to get back
to you and Alfred. . . . Leonino is delightful—and they
are all *very* good to me but I want to get home.' On the
way back he writes from Casale: 'Nice waiters gone—
new ones very nice too. . . . Tabachetti was buying land
and goods at Serralunga in 1601, 1606, 1608; he came
from Dinant, and his Calvary Chapel was finished before
1587—so I gather he got along quite nicely.'

One reason why Butler liked these chapels so much
was the artlessness of their unconscious humour. Looking
through the grating into the first of them on the Sacro
Monte at Varese, for example, he saw a representation of
the Annunciation. 'The Virgin had a real washing-stand,
with a basin and jug and piece of real soap. Her slippers
were disposed neatly under the bed, so also were her
shoes, and, if I remember rightly, there was everything

that Messrs Heal and Co would send for the furnishing of a lady's bedroom' (*Alps and Sanctuaries*). The aim of the original artists was, of course, to create as great an illusion of reality as possible, and Butler conjectures that had they been able to wind the figures up and set them going by clockwork, they would certainly have done so. These sanctuary chapels of Northern Italy, with their life-sized painted terra-cotta figures, sometimes horrifying in their grotesque realism, had an unending fascination for Butler, and he returned to them again and again over a period of thirty years. At Varallo, where he discovered the work of Gaudenzio Ferrari, Paracca and Tabachetti, he observed in *Ex Voto* that: 'All of them [the figures] have suffered more or less severely from decay. . . . Ages of winter damp have dimmed the glory even of the best preserved. In many cases the hair and beards, with excess of realism, were made of horse hair glued on, and the glue now shows unpleasantly; while the paint on many of the faces and dresses has blistered or peeled, leaving the figures with a diseased and mangy look. In other cases, they have been scraped and repainted, and this process has probably been repeated many times over, with inevitable loss of character; for the paint, unless very carefully removed, must clog up and conceal delicate modelling in many parts of the face and hands. The new paint has often been of a shiny, oleaginous character, and this will go far to vulgarize even a finely modelled figure, giving it something of the look of a Highlander outside a tobacconist's shop. I am glad to say that Professor Burlazzi, in repainting the Adam and Eve in the first chapel, has used dead colour, as was done by Tabachetti in his Journey to Calvary. As the figures have often become mangy, so the frescoes are with few exceptions injured by damp and mould.'

Nevertheless, enough remained of the originals to stir

Butler's enthusiasm, and they appeared to him, with their union of painting and sculpture as integral parts of a single design, the most daring works in the whole range of the history of art. Tabachetti at Varallo is certainly one of Butler's 'finds'; his Adam and Eve is an exquisite and original work. Butler's enthusiasm seems to have risen with each visit, until it reached its peak in the statement, 'Tabachetti's Journey to Calvary, with its forty life-size figures and nine horses, is of such superlative excellence as regards composition and dramatic power, to say nothing of the many admirable individual figures comprised in it, that it is not too much to call it the most astounding work that has ever been achieved in sculpture.' In comparison Michael Angelo's Medici chapel at Florence 'errs on the side of over-subtlety, refinement, and the exaggerated idealism from which there is but one step to the *barocco*'. He admits that Tabachetti does 'sometimes err on the side of over-downrightness. . . . Nevertheless, if I could have my choice whether to have created Michael Angelo's chapel or Tabachetti's, I should not for a moment hesitate about choosing Tabachetti's. . . .'—a judgment which recalls the easy dismissal of Beethoven and many other established reputations. The rather naïve literalness of Butler's mind was demonstrated when he had himself photographed inside one of the chapels standing beside Gaudenzio Ferrari's statue of Scotto, 'to show how real this statue looks even when compared with a living figure'. When Mrs Doncaster, his laundress, saw this photograph, she asked whether that was the lady Mr Butler was going to marry, mistaking Scotto's gaberdine for a petticoat. But the rich humour of this remark can only be relished by referring to the photograph itself in *Ex Voto*.

Tabachetti, as Butler established, was in reality a Flemish sculptor from Dinant whose real name was Jean de Wespin, though he was known in Flanders as Tabaguet. At Varallo he was responsible for the Journey to Calvary, the Adam and Eve, the Annunciation and Temptation Chapels. Butler also found evidence of his work in some of the figures in the Capture, Flagellation and Crowning with Thorns Chapels, and again in the chapels at Saas, the first village of importance on the Swiss side of the Monte Mora pass. 'The horses in the Saas chapels are all of Flemish breed, and have no affinity with the Arab type adopted by Gaudenzio Ferrari', he writes. 'Throughout the works, moreover, Northern influence is observable, but Northern influence modified by long sojourn in Italy.'

Another of Butler's 'finds' was a life-sized figure of Leonardo da Vinci in old age by Gaudenzio Ferrari in the Crucifixion Chapel at Varallo. This he claimed to be 'by far the most characteristic likeness of Leonardo that has come down to us. In his own drawings of himself he had made himself out such as he wanted others to think of him; here, if I mistake not, he has been rendered as others saw him . . . a searching, eager, harassed, and harassing, unquiet figure.'

In August 1888 Butler was again at Varallo. One very hot afternoon, he relates in *Ex Voto*, as he was trying to get a better photograph of Tabachetti's Adam and Eve, a young Italian of about twenty-four addressed him, cap in hand, 'with that exquisite courtesy and frankness for which the Italians are so justly distinguished. "Sir", said he, "I see you find it very difficult to get a good view of this chapel. I should like to help you, and believe it is in my power to do so. You see that wood? It is an excellent substitute for Paradise. You see this young lady?"—and he pointed to a comely peasant girl who was going the round of the chapels, but whom it was plain he was seeing for the first time—"she is not less beautiful than Eve herself. Persuade that young lady to go to the wood and

163   12

pose for you as Eve, and I will myself gladly pose as Adam." The girl laughed, looked down, and said, "It would not be at all proper" (*sarebbe poco conveniente*) and there the matter ended. I admired the impudence of the young man and the good-humour of the girl, and as I looked at the pair thought that they would have to get the serpent and not me to photograph them.'

Jones did not accompany Butler to Italy this year. He was recuperating in Normandy from the nervous exhaustion induced by Mlle Vaillant's attempts to marry him. ('As for Mlle Vaillant', notes Butler, 'she *hated* me and I always disliked and distrusted her.') From Normandy he wrote: 'I feel exactly what you felt in Brittany, viz. that it is not Italy and most of the people are horrid, revolutionary and rude. The waiter at Havre was delightful and we mashed one another a good deal.' Alfred wrote to him: 'Mr Butler and myself shall be very glad when you come back. I miss seeing you and your singing to me of an afternoon very much indeed.' It was during July 1888 that Butler did his charming painting of Alfred; in June *Narcissus* was published.

Next year Butler set to work on his *Life and Letters of Dr Samuel Butler*. One of his chief incentives for writing this was the thought of how much it would have annoyed his father. His father, as well as his cousin, Archdeacon Lloyd, had been, he tells us, repeatedly asked to write a memoir of Dr Butler by the Shrewsbury Archeological Society, but they would not do it. 'I am sure', says Butler, 'my father would have burned the whole correspondence had he known that my sisters would give it to me and that I should edit it. He had seen Stanley filch Dr Butler's laurels and put them upon Arnold's [Dr Arnold of Rugby] brow, but he said nothing.' Butler was intensely proud of his grandfather and resented it when *The Times* remarked that he was 'now chiefly remembered for his geography and Atlas'. His sisters gave him a very large box containing his grandfather's correspondence for nearly fifty years. 'I was much struck', he says, 'and indeed fascinated, by the character which I now for the first time began to understand.' The book was a pious labour; it occupied him intermittently for the next seven years; he published it in 1896 through John Murray at his own expense, like nearly all his other books, and it brought him congratulatory messages from Queen Victoria, Gladstone and the Fellows of St John's. Gladstone's postcard he framed over his mantelpiece. But he would have been disappointed if his book had not annoyed somebody. This time it was much resented by the still powerful followers of Dr Arnold. 'The fact is', he wrote to O. T. J. Alpers of New Zealand, 'I have never written on any subject unless I believed that the authorities on it were hopelessly wrong. The consequence is that I have throughout, I am thankful to say, been in a very solitary Ishmaelitish position.'

There are many photographs of both Butler and Jones in existence, but they were never taken standing together, for Jones, although he grew into almost a replica of Butler, was 6 ft. 2 in. and Butler was a small man. 'But you hardly noticed that', comments Desmond Mac-Carthy, who came to know him in the last years of his life. 'His slightly built frame was disguised in clothes of enviable bagginess and of a clumsy conventional cut, and he wore prodigiously roomy boots. But it was the hirsute, masculine vigour of the head which prevented you from thinking him a small man. . . . I had remembered him, it seemed, as even rather a heavy man.' His manner was that of a 'kind old gentleman, prepared to be a little shocked by any disregard of the proprieties. . . . He spoke softly and slowly, often with his head a little down, looking gravely over his spectacles and pouting his lips, and with a deliberate demureness so disarming that he was able to utter the most subversive sentiments without exciting more than a moment's astonishment.' Butler's appearance and manner were so correct, so courteous, that people thought that they must have misheard him. Jones had the same quiet, demure precision of utterance, the same deliberate politeness, and wore the same conventional black clothes 'They both seemed to declare, both in dress and behaviour, "I am determined to be quite respectable." Neither of them was anything of the kind.'[1] They must have looked like a pair of family doctors. But this elaborate disguise was, as Mr P. N. Furbank acutely remarks, merely the opposite of Oscar Wilde's flamboyant defiance.[2] Butler used to say that he was so much the *enfant terrible* of literature and science that it was imperative that his personal life should be above suspicion. He was 'respectable' in his appearance and conventional in his behaviour not only because he was afraid of being 'found out' but because he regarded social conventions as embodiments of the unconscious memory and cunning of the race. Yet, when he laughed, adds MacCarthy, 'the change in his expression was extraordinary. . . . The corners of his mouth went up in a wide semi-circle beneath his beard, his eyes sparkled with mockery, and suddenly before you . . . was the wild laughing face of an old faun.' This faun- or satyr-like expression developed as Butler grew older and is pronounced in the photographs of him in the company of Faesch.

Returning to England on the Dover-Calais boat, a friend of MacCarthy's, who had never met Butler but thought he recognized him from his photographs, went up and spoke to him. 'Yes', replied Butler, 'I *am* Mr Butler, and Jones is down below.'

[1] *Life and Letters.* Samuel Butler Number. October 1931.
[2] *Samuel Butler,* 1835–1902, p. 112–113.

CHAPTER VII

NAUSICAA AND HANS

BY THE SUMMER OF 1891, THE ORATORIO *Ulysses* was well under way, and Butler felt that he had better look up the *Odyssey* to make sure that he and Jones had not gone wrong in the story. Finding no readable prose translation, he went to the original and began translating it himself. But, while he was fascinated by its amazing interest and beauty, he had, nevertheless, 'an ever-present sense of a something wrong, of a something that was eluding me, and of a riddle which I could not read. The more I reflected upon the words so luminous and so transparent, the more I felt a darkness behind them that I must pierce before I could see the heart of the writer—and this was what I wanted; for art is only interesting in so far as it reveals an artist.'

It was during his translation of the *Odyssey* into what he called Tottenham Court Road English, in contrast to the Wardour Street English of Butcher and Lang,[1] that Butler stumbled upon the most far-reaching and exciting 'find' of his life. The Phæacian episode first aroused his suspicions. Here, he felt sure, the writer was drawing from life. Nausicaa, Queen Arete and Alcinous immediately seemed to him 'real people more or less travestied'. But it was not till he came to the Circe episode that it flashed upon him that he was reading the work, not of an old man, but of a young woman—'and of one who

---

[1] Perhaps it should be explained that Wardour Street was then a street of theatrical costumiers and that Butler took it to symbolize the pseudo-archaic language of Butcher and Lang's famous translation.

knew not much more about what men can and cannot do than I had found her to know about the milking of ewes in the cave of Polyphemus'. Everything that had puzzled him in the poem now became perfectly clear.

It had, indeed, long been felt that the *Odyssey* was as feminine in tone as the *Iliad* was masculine; but no one had ever gone so far as to suggest that it was actually written by a woman. To Butler, however, it began to appear, the more he pondered it, that the detailed descriptions of domestic matters and household management, the evident ignorance of seafaring and sheep-farming, together with what seemed to him to be sly digs at the men, all pointed to feminine authorship—to the hand of 'a fascinating brilliant girl, who naturally adopts for her patroness the bluestocking Minerva;[1] a man-hater, as clever girls often are, and determined to pay the author of the *Iliad* out for his treatment of her sex by insisting on its superior moral, not to say intellectual, capacity, and on the self-sufficient imbecility of man unless he has a woman always at his elbow to keep him tolerably straight and in his proper place.' And who was more likely to be the authoress than Nausicaa herself? Nausicaa appeared to him as a sort of ancient Jane Austen, with her slightly malicious wit; someone rather like Miss Savage, in fact, for he believed that what Jane Austen could do Miss Savage could have done. As for the alleged impossibility of a woman having written the poem, he observes that 'we have no reason to think that men found the use of their tongues sooner than women did, why then should we suppose that women lagged behind men in the use of the pen?' But there were, in fact, as he points out, many women poets in the earlier ages of Greek literature, though their works have not survived, and the writing of

[1] Butler used the Latin names of the gods and goddesses because they were better known than the original Greek ones.

epics had become quite a fashion among them. In *The Authoress of the Odyssey* Butler arrived at a real understanding of a woman for the first time in his life, and as the woman had been dead some two thousand five hundred years he felt quite safe in falling in love with her. One can feel him responding to the charm of Nausicaa as he writes, like old Paul standing among the dried canes on the sandbanks crying out for grace after the flesh.

But it was while he was revising his translation of the *Odyssey* itself that the most important part of his discovery came to him. In Book XIII Neptune turns the Phæacian ship that is bringing Ulysses back to Ithaca, into a rock at the entrance to the harbour of Scheria. It struck Butler that if an actual place was being described anywhere in the poem, this was the passage or one of the passages. Then, bearing in mind the tradition which associated the Cyclopes episode with the Lilybœan promontory, he went to the British Museum and looked up that neighbourhood on an Italian ordnance map and on Admiralty charts. 'And hardly had I got it in my hand', he writes, 'before I found the combination I wanted for Scheria lying right under Mt Eryx:—the land's end jutting into the sea—the two harbours one on either side of it—the narrow entrance between two marshes—the high mountain hard by—the rock at the entrance of one of the harbours—the absence of any river. . . . But this was not all. Not only was the rock of the right height, and so turned as to give the idea of a ship coming into port, but it bore the strange name of Malconsiglio, or Evil Counsel.' He thereupon wrote to Trapani to ask whether there was any tradition connected with the rock. The reply came that there was indeed a tradition that a Turkish pirate ship had been turned to stone as it entered Trapani harbour by the Madonna—clearly a Christianized version of the Odyssean story. The close combination of all these natural features with the topography of the *Odyssey* led on to the natural conclusion that both Scheria and Ithaca were taken from Trapani, and hence the voyage of Ulysses resolved itself into a circumnavigation of Sicily, beginning at Trapani and ending at Trapani.

It is only fairly recently that these theories have received any serious attention from classical scholars. Professor Benjamin Farrington, indeed, ranks them with those of Schliemann, also an amateur without academic qualifications, who discovered the site of Troy from a study of the topography of the *Iliad*, and he regards *The Authoress of the Odyssey* as the most important book on that poem that has ever been written. He points out that Butler gives the first plausible account of the peculiar weaknesses of the *Odyssey*, which have been remarked and glossed over by critics ever since Aristotle. 'With the insight of genius, Butler saw that if the original from which Ithaca was drawn could be found [for the Ithaca contradictorily described in the *Odyssey* bears no relation to the island of that name off the west coast of Greece] it would reveal to us, not the home of Odysseus, but that of the poet.'[1]

After writing of 'the frankness and spontaneity which are such an irresistible charm in the *Odyssey*', Butler points out that there are many mistakes which a young woman might make, but which a man would hardly fall into—'for example, making the wind whistle over the waves at the end of Book II; thinking that a lamb could live on two pulls a day at a ewe that has already been milked (IX, 244, 245 and 308, 309); believing a ship to have a rudder at both ends (IX, 483, 540); thinking that dry and well-seasoned timber can be cut from a growing tree (V, 240); making a hawk while still on the wing tear its prey, a thing no hawk can do (XV, 527). . . . It should, however, go without saying that much which is

[1] *Samuel Butler and the Odyssey*, 1929.

charming in a woman's work would be ridiculous in a man's, and this is eminently exemplified in the *Odyssey*.' After all, there is no reason why a literary man should know much about sheepfarming or seafaring, but whoever wrote the *Odyssey* seems to have had a horror of the sea.

Butler stated his conclusions in a letter to the *Athenæum* of 30 January 1892. The same evening he gave a lecture at the Working Men's College in Great Ormond Street on 'The Humour of Homer', during the course of which he said of the *Odyssey* that 'its interest centres mainly in the fact of a bald elderly gentleman, whose little remaining hair is red, being eaten out of house and home during his absence by a number of young men who are courting the supposed widow—a widow who, if she be fair and fat, can hardly be less than forty'. This description seemed sacrilegious to such people as Jane Harrison, the Miss Butchers and Dr Richard Garnett, who were all present at the lecture. But it is, after all, accurate enough and was aimed at bringing out the essential humanity of the poem.

In March 1892 Butler published his lecture as a pamphlet, and in April *The Spectator* reviewed it in three columns. 'We believe the article to be by a Miss Jane Harrison who wrote a book about Homer a dozen years ago or so in the affected Church style which so many people unfortunately mistake for culture', he wrote to his sister on 26 April. 'She was at my lecture, with the two Miss Butchers, who glared at me. . . . I am told she was scowling the whole lecture through. Of course I may be wrong—the review may be by Mr Gladstone, but we think Miss Harrison more likely. I think most people will see that it is by an angry woman who is determined to see nothing but bad, and who will not even deign to notice the topographical suggestions which she cannot contradict.' But, in 1895, when he met Jane Harrison in

Athens she told him that she had not written the *Spectator* review. Butler used to say that the Homeric scholars had been blind so long that they must have it that Homer was blind too. And though his theory of feminine authorship cannot be proved, any more than it can be disproved, he came very near to the view of the poem taken by one of its more recent translators—T. E. Lawrence, who saw it as 'a ladylike tale, which in parts stinks of unreality'. The author, says Lawrence, 'was out to construct an epic on the *Iliad*'s model, and it all smells forced'. Lawrence's feelings about the *Odyssey* were curiously ambivalent and oscillated between veneration and at times something near contempt. It was, he said, written in Wardour Street Greek and smelt of the literary coterie.

Now at fifty-six, Butler went to Sicily, in the furnace heat of August, to explore the country round Trapani in confirmation of this theories. Wherever he went, he found that local tradition supported him. The beach at Trapani corresponded exactly to the beach on which the Phæacians landed Ulysses, and nearby was the cave in which Ulysses hid his treasure. Meanwhile, in Thucydides, he found a reference to a Greek-speaking people living at Trapani about 1000 B.C. They had come from Troy and had brought the *Iliad* with them. 'By the way', he writes to Jones on 5 August 1892, 'I make no doubt I have got the exact place where Nausicaa washed her clothes and met Ulysses. It requires the sea to have come a little more inland than it does now, but there is irrefragable evidence that it did so come, and this being so the various required features are all found with such close fidelity that I do not see what more anyone can want. . . . I am, of course, delighted to have seen this place, in fact I should never have been happy till I had done so, but Sicily is nothing like so attractive as North Italy. It is terribly bare, arid, and brown, and the people ignorant, dirty and squalid. I mean the common people, for the upper classes are great swells. If I do not write now I know I shall not be able to do so, for I know the boys will be in directly.' These were three Italian students who had taken Butler round the Cyclopean walls at Erici and Cefalù. 'They knew all about them, and which are Phœnician, and which Pelasgic, and which mediæval, and they showed me the Phœnician marks and behaved beautifully all the morning.' The day before, he had slipped on the rough stones in the street and put his foot out of joint. It was pulled back into place again by a barber-surgeon, an operation which interested him nearly as much as the prehistoric remains, because Handel's father was a barber-surgeon. The doctor, when he came, ordered three weeks of absolute quiet in bed, but next day Butler was up again, hobbling about on crutches.

The Humour of Homer had been translated into Italian and was already well known at Trapani, and the whole time Butler remained in Sicily he was treated like royalty. 'My reception generally is overwhelming', he wrote, 'and quite equal to anything my vanity can desire.' His host, Emanuele Biaggini, who had written to him on the appearance of his essay, took him up Monte San Giuliano, the ancient Mount Eryx which is still sometimes called Monte Erice, and showed him the islands. When he saw Marettimo, which is concealed from Trapani at sea level by Levanzo, 'lying all highest up in the sea to the west', he realized that this was the island described in the *Odyssey* as Ithaca, as seen from the outside. Pantellaria, which is farther off towards Africa, he decided must be the island of Calypso. He went to the Grotta del Toro, where Ulysses hid his treasure, and had himself photographed standing in the cave of Polyphemus, and he identified the Asinelli and the Formiche near Trapani as the rocks hurled by the giant after Ulysses' retreating ship. 'I have satisfied myself of the exact position of Eumæus's hut and of the Hill of Mercury and of the fountain', he wrote from Rome on 30 August. 'All is perfectly clear and easily identifiable. . . . Scylla and Charybdis, though grossly exaggerated, are more genuine than I suspected. Scylla really did wreck a large steamer last year. . . . Charybdis really does prevent sailing vessels from going out, sometimes for three or four days together, and the two are very close to one another.' Wherever he went in Sicily, Butler found confirmation of his theories —everywhere local tradition connected the island with the *Odyssey*.

Meanwhile, in London, Lucie Dumas died at the French Hospital. During the last years of her life she had lived in Handel Street, near the Foundling Hospital in Bloomsbury, a circumstance, says Jones, that gave yet another significance to the epithet 'Handelian'. Butler arranged for her funeral, and accompanied her brother and Jones to Kensal Green. 'A very heavy blow to Jones also', he notes, 'as well as to myself.'

In July next year, 1893, Butler went down to Shrewsbury School for the Speech Day. Benjamin Jowett, the Master of Balliol, was also there and made a speech: 'It was a sermon not a speech', Butler comments, 'on the duties of a master and on those of a schoolboy.' Seeing how old, feeble and dull he had become, Butler determined to keep out of his way, even though he was asked to meet him at dinner. But in the drawing-room after dinner, Jowett 'toddled across the room' to him and the following conversation took place.

'I think I have had the pleasure of meeting you here before, Mr Butler.'

'Yes, Sir, but I did not think you would remember me.'

'Oh, I remember you very well; you know how heartily

we all laughed over your *Erewhon*—and moreover, there was a great deal of truth in that book.'

'It was like everything else, Sir, true, and not true.'

'Well, yes, I suppose that is it.'

'And then, *Erewhon* was published more than twenty years ago, and I have never succeeded in making you all laugh again.'

'But have you ever tried?'

'Oh, yes. I have written a good many books since *Erewhon*.'

'How is it, then, that I have never heard of any of them?'

'I suppose, Sir', I said, laughing, 'because they failed to attract attention; but a year ago I did myself the honour of sending you a pamphlet on the *Humour of Homer*, and another this spring on the Sicilian provenance of the *Odyssey*.'

'Ah, to be sure, I remember there was something of the kind, but I have so many of those things sent me that —well—to speak frankly I never read either of them.'

'Why should you, Sir? It was proper of me to send them as a mark of respect which I should have been sorry to omit, but I had very little idea that you would read them.'

Jowett then assured him that everyone interested in the classics would read his *Life of Dr Butler*.

By the middle of July Butler was in Italy again and spent some time in the Etruscan cities on his way to Rome and Naples. In Sicily he was asked to write some articles on the *Odyssey* for the *Rassegna della Letteratura Siciliana* and was elected a Socio Corrispondente of both Academies of science, letters and arts, at Aci Reale. He also wrote an article for *Il Lambruschini*, a scholarly periodical published at Trapani. The material of these articles was afterwards incorporated in *The Authoress*. At Trapani he went over all the Odyssean ground again, and decided that the bay of S. Cusumano must be the harbour Reithron and that the old city on the mountain must have been the original of Hypereia. He spent several days in Pantellaria, Calypso's island, making notes about the Cyclopean walls and other prehistoric remains. The English were extremely popular in Sicily at this time, for the British warships, sent to protect the English wine-merchants at Marsala, in 1860, had incidentally assisted the landing of Garibaldi and his thousand men, who then marched on Calatafimi and won their first victory in the liberation of Italy. But it was as the liberator of Nausicaa that Butler was welcomed by the Sicilians. He was welcomed particularly by Biagio Ingroja, who, as a young priest, had been a passionate adherent of Garibaldi and now became an equally passionate adherent of Butler. Ingroja was indefatigable in helping him to map out the topography of the *Odyssey* and looked forward to his yearly visits, Jones tells us, as to those of a brother. It was to this charming and enthusiastic man, who had by this time left the Church and become a schoolmaster, that *The Authoress of the Odyssey* is dedicated.

Returning home through Italy, Butler would not go to Varallo, as was his custom, as a protest against the substitution of a new plaster Christ for the original old wooden figure in Gaudenzio Ferrari's Crucifixion chapel on the Sacro Monte, and as soon as he got back to London he wrote a letter about it to *The Times*. As a result, there were complaints to Rome, and finally the grave old wooden Christ was replaced safely back on his original position on the cross.

'The Governor arrived home safely last evening', Alfred Cathie wrote to Jones on 22 September 1893. 'I thought him looking very well, only a little thin, but now he is home again he will pick it all up before Xmas.

I was very glad to see him after such a long absence, and so was he to see me again. I will not bully him more than I can help, but only a little teasing at times for that is only Alfred's nature and he does not really mean it.'

If Butler had found a daughter in Nausicaa, he was now to find another son when Jones returned from his summer holiday with a charming and ingenuous young Swiss, Hans Rudolph Faesch, who was coming to England to learn the language. Jones took him along to Clifford's Inn and Butler was at once attracted to him, and from that time, until he went to Singapore in February 1895, Hans spent his evenings with Butler and Jones and joined them on their Sunday walks in the country.

For the last twenty-three years Butler had had his little 'outings' regularly every Thursday and Sunday. On Thursdays he went with Alfred, on Sundays he was accompanied by Jones and Reggie Worsley. He used to say that he found a charm in the villages of Surrey, Kent and Sussex which he did not know where to rival, and his ordnance maps of the home counties gradually became covered with a spider's web of little red lines, tracing the walks he had taken. Whenever he found a village on the map he did not know, he made a point of visiting it on his next 'outing'. It was probably due to these regular country walks that he remained as well as he did and managed to get through so much work. One of the favourite walks with Hans was from Gravesend to Gadshill, stopping at The Falstaff Inn for a glass of beer. Gadshill was a favourite place with Butler because of its association with Falstaff. They would lunch there on their sandwiches and then walk on to a neighbouring station. During these expeditions Butler usually managed to get new laid eggs ('warm from the nest') from a farm on the plea of having an invalid wife. This joke was a

perennial source of amusement to the bachelors, though
Butler was known to crack slightly more *risqué* jokes with
the landladies of certain pubs, remarking on one occasion, as he edged his way gingerly out of a narrow passage,
his satchel full of new laid eggs, 'I must be careful as I go
out, you know; I feel like a woman in the family way.'
This delighted the two old ladies who kept the pub at
Harrow Weald, and they exclaimed: 'Get along with you!
What do you know about such things?' But it was with
the landlady of 'The Shakespeare' that Butler excelled
himself. This woman was 'a great sufferer', and Butler
always made a point of enquiring about her symptoms
in an almost professional bedside manner. On Sundays
the following dialogue sometimes took place.

'I trust, ma'am, you are feeling better?'
'Oh, Sir, I'm a great sufferer.'
'Are you sleeping fairly well?'
'Yes, thank you, Sir.'
'Is your appetite pretty good?'
'Yes, thank you, Sir.'
'You do not have palpitations?'
'No, Sir, thank you.'
'Are your——?'

But here, says Festing Jones, the enquiries became so
intimate that Hans, 'who had already disgraced himself,
had to be bundled out into the road as quickly as possible.'

In October Butler was robbed of his watch-chain in
Fetter Lane. The thief put his arms round him, snatched
at the chain, which broke at the swivel, left the watch in his
pocket and made off. 'It gave the Governor a dreadful
scare', Alfred told Jones. 'But I am by his side to comfort
him and cheer him and pull him through.' Butler wrote
a letter to *The Times* about it. Later, Alfred told him, he
saw the police and the members of the gang who robbed

people in the district, laughing and talking together in Fetter Lane. Alfred's letter is typical of his affectionate care for 'the poor old Governor', as he always called Butler. This care included leaving notes about in conspicuous places in Butler's rooms to remind him of what he had to do.

This is the last notice from Alfred to the effect that Samuel Butler Esqr is to buy himself a new Hat on Wednesday morning the 8th of November, 1893. Failing to do so there will be an awful scene on his return to Clifford's Inn.

Or he would slip a note into the 'Governor's' pocket, with 'Here, Sir, is a reminder for you; you must keep it in your waistcoat pocket and keep repeating it to yourself.' The note read: 'Dec. 1894. Please you are to change your flannels and socks tomorrow. Alfred.' Butler said that Alfred always made him feel like a basket that had been entrusted to a dog. When Alfred got married in 1894 he wrote to the 'Governor' who was in Sicily: 'The wedding went off very nicely and everybody said how nice we looked. I was under a top hat and felt very strange I can assure you. It was a lovely morning. We all met at church at 9.15, and when we came out got into a hansom cab to escape as much as possible the storm of rice. Mr King gave the lady away. It was a perfect success, and not the slightest thing occurred to mar the day's enjoyment.'

In return for this care, and also because he was very fond of him, Butler sometimes took Alfred abroad, where he never failed to act in character. He gave this up, however, after a trip to Switzerland, where Alfred showed a positively eighteenth-century horror of mountains, fearing that they might overbalance and bury him. On one occasion, after Butler had pointed out the different lakes and mountain ranges from the top of the Rigi, Alfred said: 'Yes, Sir, and thank you for telling me about it. And now, if you please, Sir, I should like to lie down on the grass here and have a read of *Tit-Bits*.' But on the whole, Butler found that after his marriage Alfred preferred to be given the money to take his wife ('the young woman whose property he now is') to the seaside in England. Three times a year Butler took him to the pantomime at Drury Lane, or the Lyceum, or to the Old Surrey Music Hall, and once Alfred took Butler to the Exhibition and made him go on the switchback, which he found 'damnable'. When Alfred was ill, he used to go and sit with him and showed the most tender concern for his baby and all its doings. 'Alfred's little baby is a very dear little person,' he wrote to Hans on one occasion. 'They say it has a very sweet temper, and it isn't a bit afraid. We have been having it vaccinated, which we did not like, for neither Alfred nor I believe for one moment in vaccination.' Such sympathy as is implied by this 'we' belies the idea that Butler retailed Alfred's sayings and doings merely as those of a comic servant. All his affection for Alfred comes out in the charming painting he did of him in 1888.

This affection was fully reciprocated. 'On the first day of every month', Alfred told A. G. Macdonell, who interviewed him as an old man in 1935, 'I had to draw two cheques—each for £16 13s 4d—one to Pauli and one to Jones. £200 a year, each, the Governor gave them. And Pauli launched with the Governor three days a week and never gave a Christmas box to any of the laundresses for years and years until at last one Christmas he gave Mrs Doncaster—after all those lunches, mind you—half-a-crown. The Governor was terribly upset over that half-crown. He was so generous himself. He used to give

Christmas boxes to all the laundresses in the building and
he never forgot any of the children's birthdays. There
was always five shillings for them. Yes, Charles Paine
Pauli. He was a queer one.'

On his third visit to Sicily in the summer of 1894,
Butler went to Marettimo, having heard that there were
remains of ancient walls there. He started at 10 p.m. on
14 August in the bi-weekly sailing post. 'I looked into
the hold where, among the hundred odd things that such
a boat was sure to contain, was a mattress spread for me,'
he wrote in an account of the trip. 'I smelt the hold and
shuddered. Many previous passengers to and from
Marettimo must have suffered from the effects of the
bumpy seas which the *vento maestro* raises. Cheese and
onions and rum, dirty clothes and barrels of pickled
sardines, cockroaches and blackbeetles, the ghosts of all
these things and the living presence of many more gave
me pause. I preferred the lovely moonlight and the fresh
breeze of the deck.' The voyage ought to have taken no
more than three or four hours, but soon after they left
Trapani harbour the breeze fell and they lay becalmed
while the moon set in the sea. 'I was dewy and salty but
not uncomfortable—only bored.' At last, at 3.30 a.m.,
Butler made up his mind to face the hold; he descended
and lay there till 6.30. It took eleven hours to reach
Favognana, the next island, where they spent the evening
and part of the night, during which Butler worked at his
translation of the *Odyssey*. At 4.30 a.m. they started again
and crept along in the heavy swell. The boys on board
caught some red mullet and the captain cooked them, and
Butler told the boys that they were like kittens and that
he was like an old cow. 'Then the sun set, and nothing
can be conceived more lovely; but the heat and monotony
were distressing and brought on a headache behind my
right eye which has been with me ever since.' At last,

about nine o'clock the breeze sprang up and they ran into Marettimo. It had taken them eighteen hours to do a distance of little more than twenty miles.

At Marettimo Ulysses was not a greater object of curiosity to the Phæacians, says Butler, than he found himself to the inhabitants. He had a letter of introduction to the brigadier in command of the island, where he found that his Odyssean theories had preceded him. A young man called Vincenzo took him everywhere and showed him the remains of a very ancient civilization. The defensive wall running round the island, Butler thought, possibly gave Nausicaa the idea for the wall running round the island of Aeolus. He went to dinner at the barracks with the brigadier who, with his two men, cooked the meal and did their best to honour the elderly English writer with that hospitality and charm Butler encountered everywhere in the Mediterranean world. They all ate together in the kitchen. 'First we had chicken broth, very fair and not untasty. Then came the chicken which had made the broth—such a poor little drunken drab of a thing as it must have been. Then four large plates of macaroni covered with tomatoes, mine being four times as much as I could by any conceivable means manage to eat. Then came another chicken, own brother to the one that had made the soup. Lastly, came what I took was the insides and entrails of the two chickens together. . . . And the wine was black and strong and had a taste of treacle and rum.' The brigadier told Butler that they had found some specimens of a kind of land-fish— 'it is really fish, but still they find it on land'—which filled the whole stomach with a divine and exquisite aroma that remained for days—'indeed, for a fortnight afterwards, when any little wind rises from the stomach, you can still taste it'. The description reminded Butler of the soothing herb which Helen puts into the mixing bowl

in the fourth book of the *Odyssey*. The land-fish turned
out to be snails, but Butler resolutely refused to try them,
and the meal ended with figs and pears. 'I was then taken
to the brigadier's room and the poor little man gave me
details as to the miseries of his life on Marettimo which
I can well believe.' After another uncomfortable, dawdling
return journey of thirteen hours he got back to Trapani.
He stayed a week with Count Agostino Pepoli at Le
Torri on Mount Eryx, charmed by the ravens with silver
bells round their necks, who flew in and out of the castle
windows and perched on the crazy wooden balconies over
precipices hundreds of feet deep. The count, he tells
Jones, 'has an imperfect lady here this year, lent him by
the Marchese, but it is understood she is more for show
than use. She is a very nice person and I should like her
very much if she did not exhibit so decided a desire that
I should take her back with me to London: an idea which
makes my backbone curdle. Still, she is exactly the person
we want. Shall I bring her after all?'

But the great event for which Butler had been waiting
was the midnight procession of the Personaggi—a con-
tinuation of some old rites of the Temple of Venus. First
came Night, a man dressed as a woman, with a black veil
and reclining before a background of clouds; next
Ashtaroth (that is, Venus) standing inside a huge open
bivalve with a cupid and two little girls going before her;
then Baal, then L'Apoteosi, personified by Julius Cæsar
('one of the finest looking, best-built young fellows
imaginable'); Aaron; The Sun; Faith; Christian Civilization; Eryx; Charity; Youth; and finally a triumphal car
in the form of a boat, in which were a band of little girl-
singers, surmounted by a canopy of the Madonna di
Custonaci. The procession began at 11 p.m. and slowly
wound its way through the streets all night until 5.30 the
next morning, many of the personages having by that

time fainted from exhaustion. 'The crowds, the perfect spontaneity, indigenousness, and heartiness (not a priest in the whole procession) made it a thing which I should be very sorry to have missed', Butler wrote to Jones. 'The whole thing was pagan with the slightest varnish of Christianity.'

At the end of September 1894 he paid a visit to his sisters at Shrewsbury. The strain of these visits was not felt by Butler alone. On his departure, his sisters retired to bed in a state of collapse, though, according to Butler, they irritated and persecuted him all the time he was there in all manner of petty ways. They gave him coffee for breakfast when they knew he liked tea, and although at the end of his visits he would say politely how much he had enjoyed himself, they never asked him to come again or said that he was always welcome. Perhaps, in this instance, his sisters were more honest than he was, graceless and sour as they must have been. He could not, however, help teasing them about their religion. He often wrote to them telling them of his travels or of people he met, and from time to time, he sent them small presents; but he never ceased to be hurt by their attitude to him.

The translation of the *Odyssey* was 'still on its rounds' from publisher to publisher, and *Dr Butler* had, 'in like manner, started on his way'. Nearly thirty publishers refused the *Odyssey* and the Cambridge University Press curtly declined even to consider *The Life and Letters of Dr Samuel Butler*. 'I shall go to Boulogne at Xmas with Gogin and I believe Jones will come too', he writes to his friend Mrs Bovill. 'There is something about Boulogne at Xmas which attracts me and I have been there regularly for a good many years. We are also finishing the Oratorio *Ulysses* which Jones and I began some few years ago and from which the *Odyssey* for a time deflected me. I therefore go to Rockstro once a fortnight [to study counterpoint]. Jones has some lovely things in it and, though it will probably fall as flat at *Narcissus*, than which nothing could well fall flatter, I shall be glad to have done it.'

If a certain weariness of tone crept into Butler's letters from time to time, it is hardly surprising. He had worked all his life, with unwearied application, at books which had been either ignored or viciously attacked, and whose sale had come nowhere near paying for the cost of production. After another year spent on cutting *Dr Butler* down to more manageable proportions—the original manuscript was reputed to be half a million words—and after he had published it at his own expense, it proved to be the only one of his books, apart from *Erewhon*, which brought him any kind of public recognition. *Ernest Pontifex* (renamed *The Way of All Flesh* by Streatfeild) he would not publish out of consideration for his sisters. *Alps and Sanctuaries* had had good reviews in the Roman Catholic papers and had won him the friendship of Mandell Creighton, Bishop of Peterborough and later Bishop of London, and after 1895 Butler became a frequent visitor to Fulham Palace. Dr Creighton's son, the Rev. Cuthbert Creighton, remembers his 'modest courtliness and gentleness' and 'the quaint old-fashioned way' he had of walking backwards when he left the room, 'bowing and smiling to the company'. Nothing, says the Rev. Cuthbert Creighton, who used to accompany Butler through the garden of the Episcopal Palace to Putney Bridge Station, could be less like the idea he had formed of a cranky, aggressive writer.

In February 1895 Hans Faesch left London for Singapore via Basel and Butler and Jones went to Holborn Viaduct station to see him off. They had both grown extremely fond of Hans, and this parting with their 'dear little fellow' was a great grief to both of them. What Butler felt about it may be gauged from the poem he brought for Jones to read next day at Staple Inn—the 'Calamus poem', Jones calls it:

IN MEMORIAM H.R.F.

14 February 1895

Out, out, out into the night,
With the wind bitter North East and the sea rough:
You have a racking cough and your lungs are weak,
But out, out into the night you go,
   So guide you and guard you, Heaven, and fare you well!

We have been three lights to one another, and now we are two
For you go far and alone into the darkness;
But the light in you was stronger and clearer than ours,
For you came straighter from God and, whereas we had
   learned,
You had never forgotten. Three minutes more and then
Out, out into the night you go;
   So guide you and guard you, Heaven, and fare you well!

Never a cross look, never a thought,
Never a word that had better been left unspoken;
We gave you the best we had, such as it was,
It pleased you well, for you smiled and nodded your head;
And now, out, out into the night you go.
   So guide you and guard you, Heaven, and fare you well!

Butler and Jones wept, standing on the platform, hand in hand, watching the train glide out, out into the night.

Therefore let tears flow on, for so long as we live
No such second sorrow shall ever draw nigh us,
Till one of us two leaves the other alone
And goes out, out, out into the night,
   So guard the one that is left, O God, and fare him well!

On the same day that Butler wrote 'In Memoriam', he also wrote to Hans: 'I never called you by your Christian name before, but I know I may do so now. We keep thinking of you all the time, and hoping that you got through your awful journey without the serious harm which such a terribly bleak night might easily do you. I woke often in the night, and after one o'clock I said to myself, "Thank heaven he is off the sea now." . . . What a beast I was for not taking you as far as Calais myself and helping you if you were ill. . . . Before I had done dressing I got out Bradshaw and noted your whereabouts, and glad indeed was I when it was half-past five and I could think of you as warm, and, I hope, being packed off straight to bed. In the evening I went up to Jones's, and we tried to talk of other things, but it was no use; we kept turning back to you again and again. . . . The sooner we all of us, as men of sense and sober reason, get through the very acute, poignant sorrow which we now feel, the better for us all. . . . I should be ashamed of myself for having felt as keenly and spoken with as little reserve as I have if it were anyone but you; but I feel no shame at any length to which grief can take me when it is about you. . . . I feel as if I had lost an only son with no hope of another. However—the sooner we can all take refuge in active employment the better for us all. Do not trouble to answer this. You will have much to do, and I have nothing.'

Then it occurred to him that perhaps the climate of Singapore would not suit Hans, who was tubercular, and a week later he is writing again with anxious care: 'Suppose you would come back, only do not quite see your way and do not wish to apply to your mother for fear of bothering her; then, my dear Hans, let me beseech you in the name of all the affection a dear father can bear to a very dear son, by the absurd, idiotic tears that you have wrung from me, by those we wrung from yourself, by the love which Jones bears you and which you bear towards him—if these things will not prevail with you nothing will —apply to me, and do so without delay in whatever way will ensure your getting the answer quickest which you will immediately receive—I mean *draw on me at once for your passage money and necessary expenses* and come home.' He concludes in a more jocular tone. 'As for me, I have a lusting after Gravesend and Gadshill. It will comfort me to know that the bowels of the landlady of the Shakespeare Inn are acting quite regularly. We think of you and love you always.'

Three weeks later, on 8 March, he wrote again. This letter, of which Jones gives an extract, shows still more clearly the abject state to which their love for Hans had reduced the two incarnate bachelors. 'I thought it *very* kind of you to send me a postcard as well as to Jones. "Why, if the dear fellow had not sent a postcard to either of us, we should never have wondered, for we should have known he could not manage it: but to send two was very good of him." Jones said, "It is exactly like him, he always does better than we could reasonably expect," and so you do, and I thank you. . . . Last night Jones and I dined at the house of some people of whom you have not heard us speak—they are very nice, but in the drawing-room after dinner the lady of the house said she did not begin to like people very much until they were about thirty years old. Did not Jones and I flare up just as much as we dared! and when we came away Jones said to me, "She would never have said that if she had known Hans." Of course she could not. . . . Jones and I never talk of anything else but you. It seems to me, the more I think of it, that the true life of anyone is not the one they live in themselves, and of which they are themselves conscious, but the life they live in the hearts of others; our bodies and brains are but the tools with which we work to make our true life which is not in the tool-box and tools we ignorantly mistake for ourselves, but in the work we do with them; and this work, if it be truly done, lives more in others than in ourselves.'

Hans wrote to Butler from the Mediterranean on the same day, his not very good English no doubt adding to the charm of his letter for Butler and Jones. 'I know that in every position of life I shall have you and Jones, which will help me with councels. . . . I feel I found a second father and I enjoi this idea. . . . Now we did not see any land for two days and in short time I shall be in Africa, there we shall have as hot as in hell and I hope the dozen priests who are on board will get it as hot as possible. Besides I made friendship with the most beastly looking of them. I told him some blooming lies and give him my brocken rosary to arrange. In the evening we plaid at cards and other young Swiss and I we cheated the pious man as good as we could.' Hans was puzzled at the devout, Tennysonian tone of Butler's 'In Memoriam'. 'I am not comfortable about publishing it', Butler wrote to him, 'but I wanted to set you and Jones and myself together as it were in a ring where we might stay and live together in the hearts of the kind of people we should have loved had we known them. Mrs Bovill, Jones, Gogin and myself are the only ones that know about it. . . . I think the lines are so obviously true and simple that the best people would like them and, finding Jones and Mrs Bovill agree with me, I decided to let the thing go.'[1] He

---

[1] As a matter of fact, 'In Memoriam' was never published in Butler's lifetime. 'About the poem, which I consider to be the best thing I ever wrote', he wrote to Hans on 6 June 1895, 'things have happened in England which make Jones and me decide not to publish it, even anonymously . . . At any other time it would probably have been all right. But people are such fools.' A note on the pressed copy of this letter states that the event referred to is the trial of Oscar Wilde.

reassured Hans that he has not become a believer in prayer 'and all that nonsense . . . but I know no words that express a very deeply felt hope so well as those I have used. . . . Jones and I both find that the moment we wake you are with us and so all day long till we go to sleep again.'

Every evening Butler thrashed out his Odyssean theories with Jones, convinced that he had within his grasp a vital clue that had eluded Homeric scholars for two thousand five hundred years, and that, given this, everything else in the *Odyssey* fell into place and just proportion. He anticipated and rehearsed every possible objection to his theories that the professional Greek scholars could raise and, in conversation with Jones, answered all of them. And Jones, knowing that he had been at work on the *Odyssey* all day, tried to distract him, but as soon as he talked of other things Butler grew silent and abstracted—'he was miles away, helping Nausicaa to wash her clothes at the salt-works of S. Cusumano; or sitting with Eumæus in his hut on the slopes of Monte Erice; or he would be going in and out of the house of Ulysses and seeing how like it was to the *stabilimento* at Selinunte'.

But this incessant application was beginning to affect his health more seriously than before. Going home sometimes at night from Staple Inn, he was overcome with giddiness and had to catch hold of the railings to keep himself from falling. 'It was all Homer and Dr Butler', he said. But when the doctor, who diagnosed 'rather serious brain fag', advised him to give up work for a few months, it occurred to him that he might break his routine and go abroad in the spring instead of the late summer and autumn. His work on the *Iliad* had made him want to see for himself how far the descriptions of landscape in the poem agreed with the reality, and he had rather dreaded going to Greece and Asia Minor in the autumn, fearing that it might be even more hot there than in Sicily. So, ill as he was, and fifty-nine years of age, he started for Greece, alone, in March. On the way he called upon the Faesch family as Basel. 'They have a lovely photo of Hans at about 19', he wrote to Jones, 'and some of him as a baby. I must borrow the 19 one and copy it with my camera.' Every postcard and letter exchanged with Jones is full of anxiety for 'our dear little man'. In April a card from Ceylon reached him, sent on by Alfred: 'Dear Mr Butler, I wished to-day all the time to have you on my side. I visited about ½ dozen churches of Budch in the beautiful country of Ceylon. Excuse this little card and have my best love. Also kind regards to Alfred and his baby'—to which Alfred added, a little maliciously, 'He does not say much, does he?'

Butler went on through Italy, calling at Casale to see the Avvocato Negri, who had been doing some independent research on Tabachetti; then on to Florence, where he stayed at the hotel kept by Isabella, now fat and aging, as she appears in the photograph of her at St John's. At Florence, also, he saw Helen Zimmern, who was editing the *Italian Gazette*, and she asked him for some articles on the *Odyssey*. At Corfu he found no recognizable Odyssean features at all, although, according to the majority of classical scholars, it was the original of Scheria. At Athens he met Jane Harrison, who had been so excruciated by his lecture on the *Humour of Homer*. Now she was sitting at the next table in the hotel, so Butler went up and apologized for the pain he had caused her by his lecture, reminding her that he 'had had to keep a roomful of working men in a good humour'. ' "Was I rude?" she answered. "Yes", said I laughingly, "very rude," so we made it up and smoked a couple of cigarettes.' They dined together during the rest of Butler's stay at

Athens, and he did his best to ingratiate himself, but 'it was uphill work'.

Next day he left his Homer pamphlets with Ernest Gardner at the British School of Archæology. Gardner asked him to lunch, but Butler could not get a definite opinion out of him on any subject. 'He had a horror of committing himself and was very correct, proper and prim.' Butler climbed the Acropolis and 'examined the bits of wall that are said to be Cyclopean—some of them may be, especially the bit near the Temple of Nike'. He was inclined to think that the bit of wall under the Pnyx was much more ancient than anything now remaining. 'But the antiques are soon seen', he told Jones on a card, 'and I have pretty well done them.' At Corinth some German professors got into the train with him and they discussed the *Odyssey*; when Butler said that in his view it was written by a woman they would have nothing to say to him. He drove out to Mycenæ with E. H. Burt and a Homeric scholar named Joyce ('academic from head to foot'), a pupil of Joyce's and five women. He saw the Treasury of Clytemnestra, the Gate of the Lions, and the Tomb of Atreus, of which he 'thought exactly as everyone else must do'. But he observed the ancient walls closely, noting whether they were worked with iron or not and calculated the date of the different buildings. Near one temple he found 'a mamma tortoise with a dear little baby tortoise, just like Alfred and his baby'. At Argos he talked to Joyce about the *Odyssey*, but 'could get nothing whatever out of him . . . it seemed that he had the fear-of-giving-himself-away disease badly'. At Smyrna he rode on a donkey up to the ruins on the heights above the town. Next day he went on with his translation of the *Iliad*. He was made to give up his books by the Turkish authorities at the Dardanelles and subjected to a rigorous examination, but the American and British consuls soon put things right and got him an interpreter, an escort and a horse, and he began his journey inland through the Homeric country.

The country seemed to him 'a good deal like that about Winchelsea and Rye' except for the 'strings of frowzy camels' and the birds, who seemed much tamer than in Europe. He noticed a great number of storks, some walking about in the growing corn, and many gull-like or hawk-like birds he had never seen before. But he suffered acute discomfort from his saddle, which was a Turkish one, for, his boots being so broad, he was only able to get the very tips of his toes into the stirrups and the back of the saddle was padded so that he had to ride almost standing on tip-toe with a bended knee. When he did succeed in wriggling his feet into the stirrups he could not get them out again and two knobs on the saddle bruised and chafed the inside of his thighs. Then, suddenly, the saddle slipped round so that Butler found himself hanging underneath the horse's belly. 'The good little horse saw in a moment what had happened', he says, 'and stood stock still till Yakoub Ahmed (the interpreter) and the zaptieh (the escort) came and extricated me. I had fallen on soft ground and was not even shaken. The men were all *very* good to me.' Butler called his horse Hans.

After a five hours' ride, during which they passed Renkoi, under the site of the ancient Orphrynium, looking down on Tenedos, Imbros and Samothrace, and the country getting more hilly and more beautiful, they reached the American consul's farm at Thymbra, where Butler spent the night. It was, he says, like a first-class New Zealand sheep station and about an hour from old Troy. In the morning, Mrs Calvert, the consul's wife, gave him an English saddle and he set off for Troy in comfort. When he reached Hissarlik, the site of the

193

ancient city, he was struck with the strong wind and was told that it was always blowing at Troy. Mr Calvert's nephew explained to him all the latest excavations of 1893-94, and Butler examined the walls and noticed that all of them were worked with an iron tool. 'Hissarlik is modern compared to Segni and Arpino', he notes. 'The walls cannot be earlier, one would say, than 1650 B.C. (the Mycenean age). They are not megalithic; they approach regular courses without reaching them; they appear at first sight poorly put together. On seeing the parts that have been sheltered from exposure, either by aspect or fallen earth, one perceives how beautifully built they really were; they are about 18 feet thick at top and thicker at bottom, and must have been very high.' He saw what he was told were traces of earlier cities—'great masses of earthen wall reddened and turned into brick earth in a way that nothing but fierce conflagration could effect. . . . I inclined to doubt there having been any considerable buildings at Hissarlik before the time of Priam's grandfather.' He was suspicious of some of Schliemann's conclusions. 'I was told that the Grecian fleet lay between Koumkaleh and the next point to the eastward. It may have been so—but if the Scamander in those days took the course marked for it in Schliemann's map the camp must have been half the year under water.'

As he was clambering about the dusty walls of Troy, he received a visit from the governor of the Dardanelles forts. Coffee and cigarettes were produced, and after satisfying himself that the elderly white-bearded gentleman in the dusty black baggy clothes and big boots was quite harmless—that is, that he was only interested in Homer and not at all interested in the position of the Turkish guns—the governor withdrew. Mounting Hans, Butler rode across the plains to the place where the Grecian fleet lay and decided that the *Iliad* was 'very substantially accurate . . . bar occasional gross poetical licences. Hector's running round the city is out of the question', but, on the other hand, 'Helen could perfectly well distinguish swells down below on the plain as in *Iliad* III.' When he visited the two great barrows known as the tomb of Achilles and Patroclus ('which they may or may not be'), he was told that a former British consul at great expense had bored down into one of them only to find a stone with a Latin inscription, which informed him that a Roman proconsul of the second or third century had opened the barrow and removed everything of value. After his tiring day, Butler went back to Mr Calvert's farm for the night.

Next day he explored the river-bed of the Scamander. 'Lots of lovely birds, almost as good as some of the bird-stuffers' windows in Oxford Street', he writes to Jones. 'Lovely English scenery, with cattle standing up to their middles in the Scamander and swishing their tails.' At Inea he saw the flight of some thousands of a large goose-like bird, flying about 150 feet above the ground. 'These, doubtless, are "the Strymonian cranes that wrangle in the air" of the *Iliad*', he notes. He spent the night at Byramich —'a filthy earthen floor, cobwebs in every angle of the small square box I had to sleep in; a sour-smelling sack or two of stale straw to lie on, covered, it is true, with a fair Turkish hearth-rug; nothing to wash in till I made them bring me an old tin petroleum box . . . need I go on? There was a place where they went to discharge their natural functions, but I would sooner marry Mrs X than go near it a second time.' But he had come to see the two springs, one hot and the other cold, at the source of the Scamander, mentioned by Homer, and he was determined to find out if Homer had told the truth.

Butler had already spent a week in the saddle, but he went on doggedly, paying the required courtesy visit to the local effendi, and receiving his visit in return at

8 o'clock in the morning. Ismail, the effendi, turned out to be a delightful man and accompanied him to the springs with an escort of thirteen soldiers. They rode through forests and defiles in the mountains and at last reached a level grassland full of flowers and abounding with brilliant birds, and here the carpets were spread beneath the trees, the trout cooked in egg, and they sat and ate 'cat's meat on skewers'. Ismail told Butler that he was fifty and a little troubled in his mind because he had never married, and he did not know whether he had done right or wrong. Butler replied that it was evidently the will of Allah that he should not marry, and Ismail lifted his hands to heaven and said it was a true word he had spoken. Butler then told him that a friend in England had asked the Archbishop of Canterbury the very same question and the Archbishop had replied (in the words of the old soldier in the train in Wales) that it was cheaper to buy milk than to keep a cow. 'Ah! Ah!' exclaimed the effendi, 'that is a most true word.' After that they exchanged presents: Ismail gave Butler his brass watch-chain and Butler gave him his silver match-box. Then he took Ismail's photograph and the photograph of all his men.

After his return to England, Butler received a letter addressed to: 'Mr Samuel Bueter, No. 15, Ciforzin Street [Ciforzin being not so far from Clifford's Inn in sound, particularly as Butler probably pronounced it Cliffords]: 'Ah my dear Brother', wrote Ismail, 'it is impossible for me to forget you. Under favourable circumstances I confess I must prefer you. Ah then, with the tears of gladness to be the result of the great love of our friendness. Ah my Sir, what pen can describe the meeting that shall be come with your second visit—if it please God. . . . Thank God to have your love and friendness with me and mine with your noble person.'

Butler returned from the Troad via Sicily and Varallo,

stopping at Basel to photograph the Faesch family. He had left England in a low state of health; he came back to London in June 1895 with his strength restored sufficiently to tackle the laborious task of shortening *The Life and Letters of Dr Samuel Butler*, to finish his translation of the *Iliad*, to prepare *The Authoress of the Odyssey* for the press, and to reconstruct the story behind Shakespeare's Sonnets with a bolder defiance of contemporary opinion than he had ever risked before. At one time, he had thought seriously of visiting Hans at Singapore, if only for a few days; but his 'dear little man' wrote begging him not to come, adding: 'There is nothing in that blasted hole [Singapore] who could interest me. No musik, no society, and nothing connected with any higher education.' In his reply, Butler asked Hans for a lock of his hair, on the pretence that it was wanted by a lady admirer. Next year, 1896, Hans moved to Saigon, which he describes as 'rather a beastly place'. He has, he says, made friends with a Frenchman, only he is a Catholic. Butler replied in July telling him not to worry about that, if his friend was a good fellow otherwise: 'I hate all that rubbish, whether Catholic or Protestant, more and more the older I grow—and so far from being more indifferent to it, the sense of the harm it does in a thousand ways and of its utter unworthiness impresses me more and more constantly. I loathe it—but at the same time I think we oppose it more effectually by treating it with silent contempt than by arguing about it.'

Hans returned to Switzerland for a holiday in 1898, and—as Jones puts it—'to make arrangements for a change in his life in the East'. As a matter of fact, he wanted to get married. Jones, who was staying in Basel, met his fiancée, Stephanie Rabe, and presented her with the locket he always wore on his watch-chain containing Hans's hair. 'You did very prettily about the locket',

Butler wrote to him. 'I had better share mine with you month by month, turn and turn about.' But Hans had to go back to Indo-China without his Stephanie and Jones, who had presented him with flowers on Butler's behalf, wrote on 3 August: 'When we returned last night there were the flowers on the table, and when poor Hans had read the labels his eyes filled with tears and he came and put his arms round me and kissed me in the presence of everybody. It was all I could do not to cry too.'

Longmans published *The Authoress*, at Butler's expense, towards the end of 1897. He supervised its production and sent Longmans a dummy and a sketch of the lettering on the spine, with the proviso 'you cannot keep it too simple'. The book was pretty generally attacked, though its main arguments were hardly so much as discussed. 'There was a very spiteful review in the *Academy*', Butler wrote to Jones on 4 December. 'I doubt not that it is by Andrew Lang, as also an equally spiteful review in the *Saturday Review* this morning. They are both by Lang I feel sure. Peel at Longmans thought the *Daily Chronicle* review was also by him, but about this I am not so sure. . . . You will have seen *The Times*, how spiteful it is. And *Literature* has given me a long article perhaps a shade less spiteful, but quite as silly as the others. . . . I am also glad to find that all this stupid and malicious stuff disturbs me so little. It is plain that all the more important reviewers have been much impressed with the book, and whether they like it or not it will stick by them.' Next year brought a bitter attack in *Longmans Magazine* by Andrew Lang—'the most unscrupulous I think that I have ever had of any book, unless perhaps Romanes' review of *Unconscious Memory*'. Curiously enough, the person to be most upset by the reviews was Pauli.

Butler had never cultivated the right people—indeed, he had made a point of *not* doing so. Certainly no publisher ever gave a nice little party to reviewers in order to 'launch' any of his books. Instead, he was content to wait in quiet confidence for the judgment of posterity. At any rate he persuaded himself that that was what he was doing.

CHAPTER VIII

THE MELLOWER SEASON

'IGET UP ABOUT 7, AND IMMEDIATELY, IN MY nightshirt, go into my sitting-room and light my fire', Butler wrote in November 1896 to Remi, the brother of Hans Faesch, who had asked him for an account of how he spent his day. 'I put the kettle on and set some dry sticks under it so that it soon heats enough to give me warm water for my bath. At 8 I make my tea and cook my breakfast—eggs and bacon, saúsages, a chop, a bit of fish or whatever it may be, and by 8.30 I have done my breakfast and cleared it all away.

'Then I read *The Times* newspaper, which takes me about 40-45 minutes. At 9.15 I do whatever little bit of work I can till Alfred comes at 9.30 and tells me all about the babies and whatever else interests him. We arrange what he is to do for the morning, and I get away to the British Museum as quickly as I can. I am there always about 10.15-10.30, according as I have any marketing to do or no.'

Having ordered his meat at a butcher named Darwin in Fetter Lane—he said that this was a proof of his forgiving disposition—Butler made his way through Lincoln's Inn to Bloomsbury. Ruddy and bearded like the pard in his baggy comfortable clothes and bulky boots, he climbed the wide Museum steps with his parcel of books and papers, advanced through the colonnade among the courting pigeons into the warm musty air of the Reading Room, where sound and light are subdued to the rustle of a turning page and the brownish gloom of an

English winter day. Meeting Dr Richard Garnett, his blue eyes twinkling mischievously behind the thick lenses of his pince-nez, Butler usually tried to think of something a little shocking to say. 'He asked me what we thought of doing when we had finished our present cantata. I said we should perhaps next try a sacred subject. He looked very proper and asked what one we had in view. I said demurely that we were thinking of The Woman Taken in Adultery. Mr Garnett did not quite like this.'

In those days there were still tables reserved for 'lady readers' in the Museum, but it was a standing joke that the ladies preferred to sit at the desks with the gentlemen. In fact, an acrimonious correspondence had developed on the subject in the columns of the *St James's Gazette*, the gentlemen complaining that the ladies were a nuisance, that they chattered, 'held little levées', read novels, painted pictures and rustled their silks. The ladies replied that the men were just as bad, and often went to sleep and snored.

Sitting at row B, Butler would begin revising his *Notebooks*—those observations and reflections originally jotted down, as they occurred to him, on little pads which fitted into his waistcoat pocket, which he then transcribed, revised and retranscribed into the famous bound volumes with their '225 pages of closely written sermon paper to each volume'. Butler wrote these in copying ink and deposited pressed copies of them with Jones, in case of fire.

After 1891 he made it a rule to spend an hour every morning re-editing his notes. He felt happier in the British Museum, he once said, than anywhere else. He is not alone in this feeling, for many another has sought refuge there from life behind a pile of books.

'I work at the Museum till 1, still at my Homer, which is done now, all but about eight days' work. Then I go out and dine, either at home or at a restaurant; but I never have more than one plate of meat and vegetables and no soup or sweets. I find the less I eat the better for me. Alfred and I generally waste half an hour or so till about 2.30 or 3, settling this, that, or the other.

'From 3 till 5 or 5.30 I write letters or work at home while Alfred typewrites for me, either my Homer, or notes for my commonplace book or whatever it may be, and at 4 we always have a cup of tea together. At 5.30 I have my real tea, which consists generally of a bit of fish and bread and butter, and after that I may smoke. I may smoke after 4, if anyone comes, or if I have to go calling anywhere, but never otherwise.

'From 6-8 I am alone and quiet, and at present I still go on with my Homer; but in a little while I hope to be able to get to my music again and finish my very difficult chorus which I have long put on one side. . . .

'At 8 I almost always go to Jones's, unless he comes to me; or we go out to a concert or theatre together, unless either of us has to go out to dinner. At 9.30 I leave him, come home, have some bread and milk, play two games of patience, smoke a cigarette and go to bed about 11. In bed I always read a scene or two of one of Shakespeare's plays till I find myself dropping off to sleep, and then goodnight.

'There! that is my normal day; but on Sundays and Thursdays I go out for the day, and before I go I fill the coal-scuttle and fetch up water and trim and fill the lamp etc., because my laundress, the good old woman who makes my bed and cooks for me when I am dining at home, will not have Alfred to help her. Jones goes out with me on Sundays and Alfred comes with me on Thursdays; on Sundays Alfred does not come at all to Clifford's Inn.

'There are also exceptions, when I have to go and

waste my afternoon paying calls; but my normal day is pretty much the same always, and I assure you it is a very happy one.'

Alfred, when A. G. Macdonell interviewed him in 1935, still had a vivid memory of Butler's habits. 'The Governor wasn't a Bohemian', he told Macdonell, 'he liked to arrange things in a routine. And the three things he didn't like were Drink, Late Hours, and Strange Company. . . . Often and often he would come to me and say, "Alfred, how do we stand at the bank? Have we any money, or are we pretty low?" And I would say, "We've got about a hundred pounds, sir", and he would say, "Good, then we can go to the pantomime tonight".'

Until he became too deaf, Butler enjoyed music halls and farces, but he avoided serious plays, detesting the northern gloom and social problems of Ibsen and not caring for the current flamboyant productions of Shakespeare. 'And by way of refinement', he concluded one of his letters to Robert Bridges in 1900, 'I am going to the Grand Pantomime at Islington this evening and heartily hope that it may be amusing as well as vulgar.' Mrs Boss, Worsley's laundress, was, of course, a music hall all to herself. Her sayings, said Butler, showed 'how Elizabethan a certain class of London old woman still is. As for her portrait, Rubens had painted her likeness very faithfully in the old woman near the lower left hand corner of his "Rape of the Sabines".' Mrs Boss represented for him, 'bravery, wit and poetry'—the kind of poetry endemic to London in which Walter Sickert so delighted. Butler also made bank holiday excursions to Clacton, and on one of these he met the Wife of Bath in person, as he has recorded in the *Notebooks*. For all his love of Italy, he was a confirmed Londoner. 'I have seen many foreign cities, but I know of none so commodious, or let me add, so beautiful', he writes in *Alps and Sanc-*

tuaries. 'I know of nothing in any foreign city to equal
the view down Fleet Street, walking along the north side
from the corner of Fetter Lane. It is often said that this
has been spoiled by the London, Chatham and Dover
Railway bridge over Ludgate Hill; I think, however, the
effect is more imposing now than it was before the bridge
was built. Time has already softened it; it does not
obtrude itself; it adds greatly to the sense of size, and
makes us doubly aware of the movement of life, the
colossal circulation, to which London owes so much of
its impressiveness.'

He had by now passed the spring of life, with its bitter
winds and its painful growth, and had come to the quiet
autumn—'the mellower season, and what we lose in
flowers, we more than gain in fruits'. It was in the last
decade of his life that he embarked upon the tremendous
task of his Odyssean researches, translated the *Odyssey*
and the *Iliad*, and did his edition of Shakespeare's
Sonnets, anticipating some of the most recent findings of
modern criticism. As if this was not enough, he undertook the labour and research necessary for the life of his
grandfather, Dr Butler of Shrewsbury; worked unre-
mittingly at the six volumes of the *Notebooks* and edited
the sixteen volumes of his general correspondence; prepared a new edition of *Erewhon* and brought his life to a
close in the serenity and tenderness of *Erewhon Revisited*.
Fruits of autumn, indeed! 'I am happier in the days of
my white beard', he wrote to an old schoolfellow, 'than
ever I was when I had a black one.'

He also still did much of his own housework, because
he disliked bothering other people—and also because it
was a relief to do something with his hands after so much
mental concentration. Mrs Doncaster, his laundress, was
an elderly woman and he would not allow her to come to
his rooms early enough to cook his breakfast; in the end,

when she became too drunken and verminous, he had to pension her off, and Mrs Cathie, Alfred's aunt, used to come and 'do' for him.

At Lewisham, Butler had houses in Queen's Villas, Mercy Terrace, Lily Villas, and Oglander Row. They did not bring him in much, as they were all mortgaged, and the bills for repairs were very heavy, as may be judged from his letter to the Lewisham Board of Works of 28 March 1895: 'I have laid out within the last 12 months as near as possible £600 on the above named property in the hope of getting a better class of tenants, and thus improving the neighbourhood, but though the houses have been more than six months ready for occupation I have not let a single one out of all the eleven.' Butler also owned considerable property at Shrewsbury, the Whitehall fields, which he had lately divided up into building land. The streets he named Bishop Street after his grandfather, Canon Street after his father, Clifford Street because he lived in Clifford's Inn, and Alfred Street. He also had to devote a good deal of time to the woods on the estate. But the situation was complicated by the fact that the Whitehall Manor had been sold by his father and his aunt Lloyd to his cousin Archdeacon Lloyd, while he was an undergraduate at Cambridge. Apart from the fact that the archdeacon was liable to interfere with the management of the woods, which were not his property, the whole subject of the Whitehall estate was a sore point, and was connected in Butler's mind with the whole complex of emotions centred on his father. 'It is valuable land', he had written to Miss Savage in 1881, 'and my father cannot take this from me.'

Like many bachelors, he was a confirmed cat-lover. But even here he was careful to see that his cats did not make too great an emotional demand upon him. 'No, I will have no Persian cat', he wrote to his sister, 'it is undertaking too much responsibility. I must have a cat whom I find homeless, wandering about the court, and to whom, therefore, I am under no obligation. . . . I have already selected a dirty little drunken wretch of a kitten to be successor to my poor old cat. I don't suppose it drinks anything stronger than milk and water but then, you know, so much milk and water must be bad for a kitten that age—at any rate it looks as if it drank; but it gives the impression of being affectionate, intelligent, and fond of mice, and I believe, if it had a home, it would become more respectable.' There was a plentiful supply of strays in Clifford's Inn, as people who wanted to get rid of their cats simply dropped them inside the railings of the garden and went away. There are many references to the habits of their respective cats in the correspondence with Miss Savage, and he told her on one occasion that Jones had 'a little love of a cat'.

Returning to his chambers one evening, Butler met William Morris and Emery Walker coming out of the Hall of Clifford's Inn where the Society of Arts and Crafts used to meet. Walker, whose office was next door to Butler's chambers, introduced the two writers. They shook hands and Morris said: 'Good evening, Mr Butler. I am much pleased to make your acquaintance. I have read your books with interest.' Butler replied: 'Good evening, Mr Morris. I am much pleased to make your acquaintance. I have read your books with interest.' After that each of them went on his way. But it is doubtful whether Butler had, in fact, read much of Morris, or whether he would have liked what he read. Curiously enough, both men had written Utopias about 'Nowhere', had translated the *Odyssey*, and the name of their best friend was Jones. But while Morris's translation of Homer is Victorian mediæval, Butler's is quite modern, and the difference between the two men comes out amusingly in their rendering of the same passage.

> O Circe, how wilt thou bid me to be kind and courteous
> When thou hast turned my fellow into swine within thine house?
> And for me, thou hast holden me here, and in thy craftihead
> Thou biddest me to thy chamber and to go up into thy bed,
> That thou may'st strip me of manhood and make me vile and base.
> Nay, never with my goodwill shall I go to thy bed and thy place.

Whereas Butler, translating the *Odyssey* frankly as a novel, had written:

> Circe, how can you expect me to be friendly with you when you have just been turning all my men into pigs? And now that you have got me here myself, you mean me mischief when you ask me to go to bed with you, and will unman me and make me fit for nothing.

Butler saw that to translate archaic Greek into pseudo-archaic English was not to come any nearer to the original. He used to say that 'The Ancient Mariner' would lose a good deal of its romantic appeal if it had been called 'The Old Sailor', but perhaps there is a little too much of the 'old sailor' about his rendering of the *Odyssey* into Tottenham Court Road English. Personally, Butler was timid and hesitant in manner, Morris explosive and dynamic, getting rid of much of his aggressiveness in his daily contacts, whereas Butler distilled his into satire. But there is no nostalgic Earthly Paradise sentiment in his books: they are as fresh and alive and down to earth as when they were first written. Since May Morris tells us that *Erewhon* was a household word at Kelmscott, one cannot help feeling that Morris might have been a little more cordial. But then this was the sort of thing that invariably happened whenever Butler met a fellow writer or artist. 'I heard Mr Morris lecture last week', Miss Savage had written in January 1884. 'Great nonsense he talked, but I enjoyed his pitching into the Radicals and middle-classes.'

As we have seen, Butler's Odyssean theories grew out of the writing and composing of the oratorio *Ulysses*. Re-reading the *Odyssey* suggested to him re-reading the *Iliad*, and, says Jones, these two great poems of antiquity suggested to him re-reading the greatest poet of modern times. He bought Shakespeare's works in the Temple edition, keeping the little red leather volumes in a light bookcase over his bed, and each night used to lull himself to sleep by reading them. In this way he read through all the plays, and then, some time in 1895, he began to puzzle over the Sonnets. As a prose man, Butler did not care for poetry, but he found Shakespeare 'as good as prose', and reading the Temple edition sent him to Stratford, just as the *Odyssey* sent him each year to Sicily, and the *Iliad* sent him to Troy. 'I met Jones at Stratford as arranged', he wrote to Hans on 9 August 1895, 'and we called on Shakespeare, but he was not at home'—an experience shared by most visitors to New Place.

'Fired by the success which, I believe, the simple method of studying text much and commentators little had obtained for me as regards the *Odyssey*', he writes in the preface to *Shakespeare's Sonnets Reconsidered*, 'it occurred to me that the Sonnets offered a problem on which the same method might be hopefully tried. . . . I resolved therefore that I would treat the Sonnets much as I had done the *Odyssey*, and as a preliminary measure began to commit them all to memory. By September 1898 I had them at my fingers' ends, and have daily from that time repeated twenty-five of them,

to complete the process of saturation.' Butler was nothing
if not thorough; one wonders how many other Shakespearean commentators have similarly soaked themselves
in their material. But, it should be noticed, it was not the
poetry of the Sonnets he was concerned with, but their
problem—that is to say, how much they reveal to us of
Shakespeare himself. Next, he got two copies of the
Sonnets and cancelled the odd numbers of the one and
the even numbers of the other, and laid them face up-
ward on a large table—as many, that is, as raised any
suspicion of displacement. Having laid them out, like a
game of patience, he shifted them again and again, until
he had them in the order in which he finally printed them.
This turned out to be the same as the original quarto,
except in the cases of Sonnets 35, 121, and 126-154.
The crux of the whole matter, in his view, lay in Sonnet
121.

Butler was not going to be swept out of his prosaic,
commonsensical attitude even by Shakespeare. He wanted
to arrive at the facts of Shakespeare's relations with W. H.
—a dangerous proceeding in his day, but that did not
daunt him. And although he came to love Shakespeare
as much as he loved Nausicaa, and almost as much as he
loved Handel, he was still going to tell the truth about
him. The whole force of Butler's interpretation derives
from his reading of the Sonnets as a series of love-letters;
he saw at once that here we come nearer to Shakespeare
than anywhere else.

The Sonnets cannot be precisely dated, though they
contain many parallel passages with the early plays, and
it is now generally supposed that they were written
between 1592 and 1598. Butler, however, dates them
1585-1588, and thinks they were Shakespeare's earliest
productions—a dating that is crucial to his whole interpretation. Butler's view has lately found support in

Professor Leslie Hotson's *Shakespeare's Sonnets Dated*.
Butler, like Hotson after him, argues that the great
'mortal moon' sonnet (107) must refer to the defeat of
the Armada, though he thinks that the 'moon' is Queen
Elizabeth; Hotson identifies the 'moon' with the battle
array of the Spanish ships, which sailed to attack in a
crescent formation. The most important similarity
between these two interpretations lies in their view that
the Sonnets are, as Hotson says, 'concrete and topical'
and 'an eloquent portrait of the artist as a young man'.
Butler also wrote that the Sonnets were 'dictated by the
feelings of the moment, and the circumstances of the
moment . . . and the more his [Shakespeare's] words are
taken *au pied de la lettre* the better they will be understood'.

It seems clear that Butler was drawn to the Sonnets in
the first instance by the parallel he must have seen
between them and his own relations with Pauli. Of Mr
W. H. he tells us: 'He was vain, heartless, and I cannot
think ever cared two straws for Shakespeare, who no
doubt bored him'—just as Butler knew he bored Pauli.
'Indeed, I have known cases', he says, 'in which a friend
has for years held himself the vassal of another whom he
believed to be absolutely dependent upon him.' But there
is nothing in the Sonnets to suggest that Shakespeare
ever thought Mr W. H. dependent upon him, and
Butler is certainly wrong in supposing that Shakespeare
was not attracted to the young man principally by his
good looks. 'From first to last it is plain that Shakespeare
assumed these were but the outward and visible signs of
an inward and spiritual grace. He could not believe that
any evil spirit should have so fair a house.' Sonnet 95
contradicts this Erewhonian morality. 'O what a mansion
have those vices got', exclaims the poet, 'which for their
habitation chose out thee.' When Butler cites Shakespeare's ironical praise of W. H.'s politic coldness in

Sonnet 94, he is again thinking of Pauli. Such, says Shakespeare:

> That do not do the thing they most do show,
> Who moving others, are themselves as stone,
> Unmoved, cold, and to temptation slow:
> They rightly do inherit heaven's graces,
> And husband nature's riches from expense,
> They are the Lords and owners of their faces,
> Others but stewards of their excellence:

The Sonnet ends with the warning:

> For sweetest things turn sourest by their deeds,
> Lilies that fester smell far worse than weeds.

By this time Shakespeare was beginning to turn somewhat sour himself.

'No doubt', says Butler, 'Shakespeare had his wild oats to sow' and the Sonnets are only 'excusable' if it can be shown that they were written by a very young man. The very fact, he thinks, that Shakespeare continually refers to himself as elderly and past his prime shows that he was in reality very young—for if he had been really old, or even middle-aged, he would not have mentioned it so often. It seems more likely, however, that when Shakespeare tells his mistress in Sonnet 138 that his days of love-making 'are past their best' and that 'age in love, loves not t'have years told', he may have been between thirty and forty. The Elizabethans matured far more quickly than we do today and men of forty were really considered old. Bacon even lamented that he was getting old at thirty, though the 'Beated and chopp'd with tann'd antiquity' of Sonnet 62 is perhaps carrying it a little too far. Butler argues that if Shakespeare thought of a man of forty as a dotard with one foot in the grave, he could not have been forty himself at the time of writing, or anywhere near it. His 'offence', he says, was therefore 'a sin of very early youth . . . towards which not a trace of further tendency can be discerned in any subsequent sonnet or work during five and twenty years of later prolific activity'. This 'offence', he tells us in the tone of a Victorian headmaster, writing of a somewhat wild but very promising boy, 'never went beyond intention and was never repeated'. As Mr Muggeridge remarks, Butler credited Shakespeare with sexual impulses as timid as his own. But Renaissance England was not Victorian England, which had sentenced Wilde to two years' hard labour in the year that Butler began to occupy himself with the Sonnets.

Wilde's *The Portrait of Mr W. H.* had appeared in *Blackwood's* in June 1889. Butler does not mention it, though it would be strange if he had not read it. This story Wilde expanded into a book of which he said 'our English homes will totter to their bases when my book appears'. But the manuscript was stolen at the sale of his effects at Tite Street while he was still on trial. Like Butler, he had argued that the Sonnets were addressed to William Hughes, but he identified him with a boy-actor for whom Shakespeare had written many of his feminine roles—particularly those parts in which a girl disguises herself as a man in order to follow her lover. He admitted, however, that he was 'almost afraid to turn the key that unlocks the mystery of the poet's heart'. Wilde shared Butler's morality of good looks, also his conception of immortality as the life we live after death on the lips of the living. This was apparently Shakespeare's idea of immortality too—'Where breath most breathes, even in the mouths of men'. This line Butler adapted in his own sonnet, 'Not on sad Stygian shore'. Wilde conjectures that Willie Hughes was 'lured away' from

Shakespeare's company by Marlowe to play Gaveston in *Edward II*, and that this explains the absence of his name in the list of players in the First Folio.

By taking the Sonnets *au pied de la lettre*, Butler arrived at a startling conclusion. It was some time, he says, before he saw how Sonnet 121 came to be placed after 120, instead of anywhere else, and until he had got hold of this he was aware that the riddle was as yet unread. But on placing it after Sonnet 32, he found everything explained itself. But if Sonnet 121 is to go after Sonnet 32, why not 120 and 119, which both deal with the same crisis? Characteristically, Butler ascribes many of the sonnets written to the black woman[1] to W. H.—and it may be that he is right, for we cannot place too much reliance upon the order in which they were printed.

In Sonnet 121, however, he discovered the central catastrophe of the whole series and the reason both for the poet's subsequent disgrace and his lameness. In this Sonnet he finds evidence of 'a cruel and most disgusting practical joke, devised by Mr W. H. in concert with others, but certainly never intended, much less permitted, to go beyond the raising coarse laughter against Shakespeare'. The joke was to ask Shakespeare to a rendezvous with W. H. and then to surprise him in a compromising situation. The jokers, he says, evidently manhandled Shakespeare, who managed to escape 'without his cloak' (*vide* Sonnet 34), but the beating he got at their hands made him temporarily lame—'Speak of my lameness and I straight will halt.' Unacceptable as this interpretation may appear at first, it is difficult to see what else Sonnet 121 means if it does not mean this, or something very like it:

[1] Usually referred to as the Dark Lady. Shakespeare is more precise and calls her 'black as hell'. She may have been a negress who acted in the Gray's Inn Revels.

213

'Tis better to be vile than vile esteemed,
When not to be receives reproach of being,
And the just pleasure lost, which is so deemed,
Not by our feeling, but by others' seeing.
For why should others' false adulterate eyes
Give salutation to my sportive blood?
Or on my frailties why are frailer spies,
Which in their wills count bad what I think good?
No, I am that I am, and they that level
At my abuses reckon up their own,
I may be straight though they themselves be bevel;
By their rank thoughts my deeds must not be shown;
    Unless this general evil they maintain,
    All men are bad and in their badness reign.

The writer is evidently defiant. He has lost his 'just pleasure' by being surprised *in flagrante delicto*, in what others regard as a disgraceful act, and he replies 'I am that I am'. Those who say he is bad should look to their own abuses. Mr Robert Graves, in his brilliant essay on 'The Sources of *The Tempest*',[1] accepts this interpretation, though he thinks that the plot was most likely hatched by the black woman in concert with W. H., probably with the assistance of Jonson and Chapman.

The whole affair is, after all, just what one might expect from the more roistering blades of Elizabethan London, and there is no reason why such a *dénouement* should not have been staged by Shakespeare's rivals to discredit him; though Butler's absurdly literal reading of the second line of Sonnet 34 ('And make me travel forth without my cloak') shows such crass insensitivity that it casts doubt upon his ability to understand poetry at all. Nevertheless, there is much to be said for a more common-sensical approach to poetry and it may be, as both he and Robert Graves assume, that the central tragedy of

[1] Reprinted in *The Common Asphodel*, 1949.

Shakespeare's life is to be read in the triangular relationship of the Sonnets.

It must be admitted that with Butler's interpretation
in mind everything does, as he claims, fall into place. So
Robert Bridges also discovered to his horror, when he
wrote to Butler on 25 January 1900: 'The more I read
the stronger your position seemed to be—but yet I was
not convinced. It only seemed to me that the refutation
was more difficult. . . . The hypothetical reconstruction of
facts which you have undertaken is impossible. . . . I am
very sorry indeed that you have been so clever as to make
up so good (so bad) a story—but I willingly recognize
that no one has brought the matter into so clear a light as
you have done.' Bridges thought that Shakespeare was
expressing ideal love and that it was 'the very absence of
sexual feeling which enabled him to use the sexual
imagery'. But how anybody can discover 'absence of
sexual feeling' in the Sonnets passes one's comprehen-
sion, though it was precisely the Victorian conception of
the impersonal Shakespeare, presented by Sidney Lee
and others, that Butler was out to destroy.[1] He replied to
Bridges: 'After a full two years, during which I have had
the Sonnets in my mind almost day and night, I formed
my conclusions concerning them, and I verily believe
that I have, to quote the Bishop of London's words to me
in writing about my book, "done all that can be done in
the name of commonsense". I am sorry that you dislike
my theory: I have made it clear that I do not like it
myself, but I believe it to be sound.' It was also customary
to say in Butler's time that the Sonnets had been written
to show that friendship is superior to love. 'My dear sir',
he exclaims impatiently in a letter to M. Fernand Henry,
who was translating them into French, 'take Sonnet 23;

[1] Butler rejects the identification of Mr. W. H. with Southampton
and accuses Sidney Lee of representing Shakespeare as a careerist.

215

how can it conceivably be taken as an attempt to show that friendship is superior to love? It says that Shakespeare wanted something which he is pleased to call "the perfect ceremony of love's rite", but which he cannot bring his tongue to utter in words, being afraid to trust his friend. This is what it says and what it means.[1] I disapprove as we all must do, but I am not going to hold up my hands in horror. . . . Take again Sonnets 57, 58. How can they be tortured into an attempt to proclaim the superiority of friendship over love? . . . They express bitter chagrin at his friend's not coming to see him, while Shakespeare was watching the clock hour after hour for his coming'—just as Butler had himself waited hour after hour for Pauli. Much that is hidden from us in Butler's life is revealed by his interpretation of the Sonnets.

Shakespeare's Sonnets Reconsidered was certainly a brave book to have written in the closing years of the Victorian era, with the hue and cry after Wilde still in the air. It appeared at Butler's expense under Longmans' imprint, though Charles Longman objected that it dealt with 'an unpleasant subject'. It was received for the most part in silence; in this case the silence was more embarrassed than usual. There was, however, 'an atrocious review' in the *Athenæum*, which, Butler suspected, came from the pen of Watts-Dunton. 'He tried to cotton on to me years ago in the old *Erewhon* days', he writes to Lilian Jones, 'but I detested him and would have none of him.' But Dr Furnivall, the Shakespearean scholar, who borrowed a copy of the book from Mr Bickley of the Manuscripts Department of the British Museum, was 'much interested' and asked Bickley to introduce him to Butler. The two

[1] As a matter of fact, as Mr Furbank points out to me, Shakespeare in Sonnet 23 does not say he *wants* 'The perfect ceremony of love's rite'. He says that he has forgotten to *say* it—that is, excess of emotion has made him unable to utter his love in sufficiently ceremonious words. A significant misinterpretation on Butler's part.

men met one afternoon in the Reading Room and adjourned for tea to an A.B.C. in Rathbone Place. To his surprise, Butler found Furnivall 'a most amiable, kindly old gentleman, absolutely free from "side" or affectation, and very sensible on some matters in respect of which most men are idiots'. Furnivall began by saying that he was under the impression that Butler had made Sonnet 107 refer to the Armada and had twisted everything else so as to make it fit in with this preconception. Not a very good beginning, perhaps; but he went on to say that in his opinion the Sonnets belonged to the *Hamlet* period, 'in view of their introspective and deeply philosophical character'. Butler did not reply directly to this, but inwardly commented that there was nothing in the Sonnets that might not have occurred long before he was twenty-one to any man who had been married against his will at eighteen and who had been greatly distressed for money. As they talked it transpired that Furnivall had not actually *read* Butler's book: he had only 'skimmed it'. But 'he was quite sure that there was nothing in the Sonnets to indicate that Shakespeare had been fonder of Mr W. H. than he should have been'. Then he admitted that he had never studied the Sonnets very closely. Butler parted from Furnivall after tea greatly depressed—'for I saw more plainly even than before that no one in my lifetime is likely to read, learn, and inwardly digest either my book or the immortal poems of which it treats'.

His translation of the *Odyssey* appeared in October 1900 and in November Hans was in London again, making his preparations for returning finally to Indo-China. Soon after his departure, Butler met Augustine Birrell at his friend Miss Sichel's. As usual in such cases, the meeting was not a success. Butler felt that he was to be 'exhibited' and arrived to tea tired and out of sorts. This was not the first time that Miss Sichel had tried to bring the two writers together, though about the only thing they had in common was their use of the English tongue. 'Now Birrell was a man whom I regarded as a self-advertising *poseur*, and whom I did not want to meet, feeling sure that, as in the case of several other lights of literature who at various times have made advances to me, he only wanted me to become one of his admirers and to tell him how clever he was', Butler comments in the *Notebooks*. 'Moreover he is a dissenter and a radical, and is review-puffed and in favour with *The Times*, and has married the late Lord Tennyson's daughter-in-law.' What could be worse? At Miss Sichel's Birrell entertained them with an account of how he went to lecture at Sheffield on literature and how the young men of the house where he was a guest, instead of going to his lecture, preferred to go to the circus to see some performing sea-lions—'And quite right too!' he added. To Butler it seemed that Birrell was all the time congratulating himself and rattling on like Pandarus in *Troilus and Cressida*. He laughed politely in the right places, but otherwise said nothing. Just as he was preparing to leave, however, something was said about Shakespeare and then, Miss Sichel told Jones afterwards, Birrell and Butler carried on a conversation which, though short, was as brilliant as any she had ever heard. But for his part, says Jones, when he saw Butler so nervous and uncomfortable, he was too anxious to get him away to pay much attention to anything else. How well one can share Butler's irritation with literary hostesses who insist on bringing antipathetic people together for the sake of witty conversation!

Butler was now engaged on his last work, *Erewhon Revisited*, and in it he was able to have his revenge, in the persons of Professors Hanky and Panky, on all the Birrells and Furnivalls and Andrew Langs and Huxleys

—on, in fact, the whole academic, ecclesiastical and scientific world which had either ignored or misrepresented him for the last thirty years. At the end of *Erewhon*, it will be recalled, Higgs escapes from the country in a balloon, which he had had made for him on the pretext that he is going to visit the air god and persuade him to end the drought. When he revisits the country in disguise twenty years later, he discovers that his ascent into heaven had been interpreted as a miraculous event and that he himself has been deified under the name of the Sunchild. Sunchildism is now the official religion of the country, complete with priesthood and mythology. But Higgs the Sunchild has now returned to Erewhon in person and threatens to reveal himself at the dedication of the magnificent new temple erected in his honour at Sunchildston. He is therefore in imminent danger of either being drowned at sight as a foreign devil or put to death as a heretic. His horror grows as he discovers bit by bit the whole fantastic structure of supernaturalism that has been built up round the perfectly natural events of his life. His most casual sayings have been published as sacred texts, his balloon has become a chariot drawn by the horses of the sun, and even their mythological manure is exhibited in a little heap of golden balls in the temple. Already there are schisms within the church, and different schools and sects who variously interpret his sayings. The villains of the piece are Hanky and Panky, Professors of Worldly and Unworldly Wisdom at the City of the People Who Are Above Suspicion; while talking to them, Higgs realizes that they do not really believe in the Sunchild, though they support the cult piously in public.

The most moving passage in the book is the meeting between Higgs in disguise and his son George by Yram, the daughter of the gaoler at Coldharbour, where he had been imprisoned on his first visit to Erewhon twenty years before. Since then, Coldharbour has become Sunchildston, the centre of the Sunchild cult, and Yram its mayoress. George confides to him at their first meeting that he regards Higgs as an impostor, but that if he were to return to Erewhon and to declare himself, he would not only accept him as his father but honour him to his dying day. So Higgs, longing to win his son's love and respect, even at the cost of death, determines to reveal himself at the dedication of the temple. It is a situation into which Butler put all his frustrated paternal emotion, and George is clearly modelled to a large extent on Hans. 'He dazzled me', confesses Higgs, 'with his comely debonair face, so full of youth, and health, and frankness.'

Meanwhile Hanky has discovered Higgs's identity and prepares his destruction. At the dedication ceremony Higgs reveals himself and is hurried away, on the instigation of George and Yram, as a harmless lunatic, but not before a stake has been erected for him in the temple square. Butler took Hanky's dedication sermon almost word for word from a letter to *The Times* by Sir George Gabriel Stokes and Lord Halsbury, asking for money for the Christian Evidence Society, and though in his preface he disclaimed any intention of satirizing Christianity, the parallel is so close that the disclaimer can have been no more than an elementary measure of precaution.

The central part of the book is devoted to Higgs's wanderings in Erewhon incognito, during which he meets the representatives of Erewhonian culture. There is Dr Downie, for example, Professor of Logomachy, 'who could say nothing in more words than any man of his generation'. His textbook on *The Art of Obscuring Issues* had passed through ten or twelve editions, and he had earned a high reputation for sobriety of judgment by resolutely refusing to have definite views on any subject.

Nevertheless, Downie appears as a far more pleasant character than Hanky and Panky, who represent all that is most sterile and hypocritical in the religious and academic life of the country. The scenes at the house of Yram and her husband, the Mayoress and Mayor of Sunchildston, are among the most charming pages Butler ever wrote and show how much he had mellowed since *Erewhon*. In *Erewhon Revisited* Butler did something he had never succeeded in doing before: he created a charming woman and family relations founded upon tolerance, affection and intelligence. The book is in every sense a final summing up of his life. If it lacks, to some extent, the spaciousness of *Erewhon*, with its magnificent descriptions of natural scenery and its genuine sense of the discovery of a new world, it exhibits a greater narrative power and power of characterization and an altogether firmer construction, and there is about it all the autumnal radiance and serenity of Butler's rich final period.

Longmans refused to publish *Erewhon Revisited*, even at Butler's expense, for fear of giving offence to the High Anglican party. So, 'on strong entreaty from Walker and Cockerell', he sent the book to Bernard Shaw and asked his advice. Shaw advised approaching one of the younger publishers. 'My own publisher', he wrote, 'is a young villain named Grant Richards who has no scruples of any kind. You had better let me show him to you on approval. If you will come to lunch with us at 1.30, say, on Wednesday or Thursday, I will invite Grant Richards, too. If you can persuade Walker or Cockerell or both to come along with you, do. . . . My wife is a good Erewhonian, and likes Handel; you won't find her in any way disagreeable. And 10 Adelphi Terrace is within easy reach.' Meanwhile Shaw warned Grant Richards that he would find Butler 'a shy old bird'. Richards agreed to publish *Erewhon Revisited* and to do a new edition of *Erewhon* itself. He was the first publisher to take a financial risk with any of Butler's books.

Butler now began 'editing his remains', and reliving all the most painful experiences of his life. While in Rome in the spring of 1898 he had written the long account of his relations with Pauli; in Switzerland in 1901 he also wrote much about his father and at least two of his sonnets on Miss Savage. During this year, too, he began transcribing all her letters, and some of his replies in order to give the letters coherence, with the idea of making them into a book which should be, as he wrote to his sister, 'a memorial of her, traced chiefly by her own hand'. He also carefully edited Festing Jones's letters. Jones's *Memoir*, with its air of frankness and informality, gives an enormous amount of detail about Butler, but on the all-important subject of his principal friendships it remains practically silent. The sonnet which Butler ironically called 'An Academic Exercise',[1] written when he was working on Shakespeare's Sonnets, tells us more about his feelings for Pauli—to whom, it has been assumed, it is addressed—than either he or Jones cared to do:

> We were two lovers standing sadly by
> While our two loves lay dead upon the ground;
> Each love had striven not to be first to die,
> But each was gashed with many a cruel wound.
> Said I: 'Your love was false while mine was true.'
> Aflood with tears, he cried: 'It was not so,
> 'Twas your false love my true love falsely slew—
> For 'twas your false love that was the first to go.'
> Thus did we stand and said no more for shame—
> Till I, seeing his cheek so wan and wet,

[1] First published in *Notebooks*, edited by Festing Jones (1912).

Sobbed thus: 'So be it; my love shall bear the blame;
Let us inter them honourably'. And yet
  I swear by all truth human and divine
  'Twas his that in its death throes murdered mine.

Mr Malcolm Muggeridge argues that this Sonnet was
in reality addressed to Jones and was an indication that
he and Butler had become estranged in the closing years
of Butler's life. Muggeridge quotes Alfred as saying that
Jones clung to Butler as long as he needed his money,
but that 'when he could stand on his own feet'—that is,
when he became well-to-do on his mother's death in 1900
—'he didn't want him any more'. Altogether, Alfred
seems to have had a poor opinion of Jones. 'He was
always crying', he told Muggeridge. 'The Governor
would excuse him by saying: "Alfred, he's Welsh!".'[1]
Muggeridge suggests that 'An Academic Exercise' was
written too long after Pauli's death to refer to him. But
Pauli did not die till 1897, and it was about this time that
the sonnet was written. In any case, the sonnets to Miss
Savage were written long after her death.

But that there was some estrangement between Butler
and Jones in the last year of Butler's life is shown by the
fact that when Jones went to Italy in the summer of 1901
he did not bother to let Butler know of all his various
changes of address. 'I am not uneasy about you', Butler
wrote to him from Clifford's Inn, 'for I think your not
sending an address is only due to forgetfulness—but it is
so unlike you to forget to send one, that I hardly quite
know what to make of it.' However, the rest of their
surviving correspondence is perfectly friendly in tone,
though it is clear that something had occurred to interrupt the flow of the old warmth and affection. It is only
too likely that Jones, after so many years, had begun to

[1] *The Earnest Atheist*, p. 166.

feel the need to stand on his own feet—a reaction that was, after all, perfectly natural.

At any rate, whether it was addressed to Pauli or to Jones, the 'Academic Exercise' arose out of the deepest emotional experience of Butler's life, after the love-hate relationship with his father, and contrasts sharply with the cruel humour of the third sonnet to Miss Savage, written at this time:

Had I been some young sailor, continent
Perforce three weeks and then well plied with wine,
I might in time have tried to yield consent
And almost (though I doubt it) made her mine.
Or had it been but once and never again,
Come what come might, she should have had her way;
But yielding once were yielding twice, and then
I had been hers for ever and a day.
Or had she only been content to crave
A marriage of true minds, her wish was granted;
My mind was hers, I was her willing slave
In all things else except the one she wanted:
    And here, alas! at any rate to me
    She was an all too, too impossible she. [1]

Witty and accomplished, no doubt; but inexcusable when applied to a woman whose influence, unlike the miserable Pauli's, had been entirely for good. For without Miss Savage's constant encouragement and criticism, it is doubtful whether we should have had *The Way of All Flesh* at all. As we have seen, the first half of the book, which was rewritten in the light of her criticism, is by far the best, and greatly superior to the second half, which was left unrevised after her death. But this was partly because in the earlier chapters Butler was recording, more or less accurately, things that had happened to him,

[1] First published in *Butleriana* (1932).

while the latter half called for more creative imagination than he possessed. There is, of course, no falling off in the quality of the actual writing, which remains admirably astringent.[1] But his act of putting the manuscript away and not touching it again after the death of 'the little lame lady' was a tacit recognition of the part she had played in the book. 'If I have been as selfish and egoistic to you as I was to her', he wrote to Jones, while editing her letters, 'it will explain a good deal.' After quoting this in the *Memoir*, Jones hastens to add: 'To me he was the dearest, kindest, most considerate friend that a man ever had. He was never selfish or egoistic, nor was there ever anything that required explanation.'

After passing the proofs of *Erewhon Revisited*, which were also read by Alfred and R. A. Streatfeild—an official in the British Museum whom he often consulted on literary matters and points of detail—Butler joined Jones at Pisa in the middle of May 1901. They went down through Rome to Naples and thence by sea to Palermo, then to Trapani and saw their friends, and it was all a triumphal progress. Next year the Communal Council of Calatafimi resolved by acclamation that the street leading from the Nuovo Mercato towards Segesta should be called Via Samuel Butler. The name of the hotel at Calatafimi was also changed from Albergo Centrale to Albergo Samuel Butler.

On the return journey Butler became very unwell, and could hardly do more than get into the train to travel by day and crawl into the hotel to sleep by night. But he would not alter his plans and, ill as he was, he went to all the places he had intended to visit. At Bologna he collapsed on to a seat in the picture gallery, but insisted on

---

[1] Butler's style is usually thought of as dry and witty. But he was sometimes capable of a lyrical impressionism, as in the long and beautiful note 'Sunday Morning at Soglio', which points forward to D. H. Lawrence.

Jones going round alone to see the pictures. They struggled on through Parma and Piacenza to Casale-Monferrato, where Butler at last consented to see a doctor. The doctor could not make out what was wrong with him, and as they journeyed north Butler's health improved. By the time they reached London in June he was almost himself again.

In the autumn he went to Switzerland, to Wassen, alone, where he stayed quietly sketching and 'editing his remains'. Here he fell ill again, and the doctor diagnosed malaria, though it is more likely that he was already suffering from the pernicious anæmia of which, next year, he died. By the end of September he was back at Clifford's Inn, and Jones returned to England with Remi Faesch, who had come to London to learn English like his brother. When in October *Erewhon Revisited* and the new edition of *Erewhon*, to which he had added about fifty pages, appeared and were favourably reviewed in *The Times* and *The Daily News*, Butler was staying with his sisters at Shrewsbury. He could not resist showing them the reviews. Harrie made 'some short slight remark indicating disapproval. May said not a word. . . . Next morning at breakfast there was no tea. May said: "Oh, Sam, I think you like tea for breakfast, do you not? We can have some made in a moment." I assured her that I liked coffee very much, which I do; it is not coffee, but Wilderhope coffee that I do not like. . . . But I could see I was in disgrace.' During the evening Butler was much amused by the *Life of Archbishop Benson*, which he had found in the house. When he came to the passage describing Benson's meeting with Gladstone, where the writer observes, 'His eyes alone afford sufficient reason for his being Prime Minister,' he 'tittered,' read the sentence aloud and remarked: 'It must have been his nose. The bishop must have written "nose" and young Dr

Benson changed it to "eyes". Harrie fired up and desired me not to read anything more to her.' At breakfast next morning, Harrie asked: 'You still continue to like coffee? We can have tea made for you if you like.' I still continued to like coffee. But when it proved that there was not enough to give me a second cup, I was firm, and she had to send for more. May was breakfasting in bed, so it rested with Harrie, who ate up all the four little pieces of toast without offering me a single one. The next day I was leaving, and I think it was felt that I had been sufficiently punished, for she insisted on my having two of the usual four pieces of toast.' (November, 1901.)

Christmas was spent as usual at Boulogne; afterwards Jones went to stay with his sister, Lilian, in her flat in Downshire Hill, Hampstead—it was in the ugly red brick block on the left hand side going up to Rosslyn Hill—where he developed pneumonia. Butler frequently made the journey up to Hampstead to visit his sick friend; but he was a sick man himself, and the weather was unusually severe, the journey long. When he could not go, he sent Jones or his sister long letters with accounts of his visits to music halls and the pantomime, and full of the semi-malicious gossip they both enjoyed. On 31 January he writes to Jones about the Surrey Pantomime. 'Victor Stevens was as good as ever and when he came on in full fig I was quite surprised to see how young he still was. His "No no no no no no no no no NO!" was as quick as ever, but the vulgarity was a good deal toned down from what it was in the old days. True, there was still *some* vulgarity—the dear old familiar allusions to delirium tremens, of which there had been no trace at the Grand or at Drury Lane, were at the Surrey once more in evidence: indeed one man made quite a long speech whilst he "had got them". There was a bath and wash-house scene in which Victor Stevens in stays, bathing drawers and long dishevelled black hair, as also all the other protagonists in extreme *deshabillé*, came almost up to the old Grecian level. Talking of plays, Meo[1] came to tea last Wednesday, and told me that he had been to see a play by Mr Bernard Shaw—a private performance of a piece that would not be permitted to be done in public. If the play was anything like what Meo said it was, I cannot understand how a man who considered himself a gentleman should have chosen to be bothered with writing it.'

This was *Mrs Warren's Profession*, which was performed privately in January 1901. It is curious to see that Butler, in common with other men of his prudish age, delighted in bawdy jokes and frequented prostitutes, but would not tolerate any serious discussion of prostitution on the stage. Shaw's first play was *Widowers' Houses*, dealing with slum property; as a slum landlord himself, this could hardly have made any greater appeal to Butler. 'I am to lunch at Shaw's tomorrow', he writes to Lilian Jones on 4 February, 'and have said I will eat vegetarian. I shall then hear what courses he recommends re my projected work on Tabachetti. When I last lunched there I met a man named Salt who has sent a prospectus of "The Humanitarian League" of which he is honorary secretary, and a card for a lecture by Mrs Leighton Cleather on "Wagner as a pioneer of Humanitarianism". . . . He has also sent me a pamphlet on Animals' Rights —"The immediate question that claims our attention is this: if men have rights, have animals their rights also?" This sentence, on which I lighted at random, is so

[1] Gaetano Meo, the painter, whom Butler had known since they were fellow students at Heatherley's. He used to have supper with Butler every alternate Saturday and Butler called at 47 Downshire Hill every alternate Sunday on his way up to Jack Straw's Castle, where he had his lunch. Gaetano's little girls used to play Handel to him when he visited Downshire Hill.

obviously suggestive of the Rights of Animals chapter which I have intercalated into my enlarged *Erewhon* that Mr Salt (who published his pamphlet in 1900) may be excused for thinking that I had him in view when writing my own chapter—but I am innocent of all knowledge of his pamphlet. By the way, Shaw said that he regarded my chapter on the Rights of Vegetables as a direct attack upon himself—but he was not serious.' The Salt referred to here is Henry Salt, who, with his colleague J. L. Joynes, had been a master at Eton and was later associated with Morris in the Social Democratic Federation. Butler had never liked Shaw, in spite of his friendliness, and when Emery Walker first brought him to Clifford's Inn, on the score that he was a great lover of Handel, 'he did nothing but cry down Handel and cry up Wagner. I did not like him and am sure that neither did he like me.' Butler could never forgive Shaw for attacking Shakespeare in favour of Bunyan in his *Saturday Review* articles. 'If he means it, there is no trusting his judgment,' he writes in the *Note-books*. 'If he does not mean it I have no time to waste on such trifling. . . . There is something uncomfortable about the man which makes him uncongenial to me.'

As he was leaving the Museum one afternoon he met McColl, formerly editor of the *Athenæum*, 'looking very dull and cross and heavy', he wrote to Lilian Jones. 'They handed him his coat and I helped him put it on, but as I had my umbrella and packet of papers in my hands, I did not do it well, and several stitches cracked as he struggled to get his arm in. Of course I ought to have put my umbrella down before I helped him on, but I was too lazy; and I was not altogether sorry that the stitches cracked. He walked with me to the gate, or rather shambled, for he does not walk, and on the way said he had seen my sonnet in the *Athenæum* ("Not on sad Stygian shore") and had thought it very fine. He asked Rendall who wrote it, and when I heard this I was quite sorry about the stitches.'[1] This sonnet, though somewhat conventional, is for that reason, perhaps, usually considered to be Butler's best poem. It is as follows:

> Not on sad Stygian shore, nor in clear sheen
> Of far Elysian plain, shall we meet those
> Among the dead whose pupils we have been,
> Nor those great shades whom we have held as foes;
> No meadow of asphodel our feet shall tread,
> Nor shall we look each other in the face
> To love or hate each other being dead,
> Hoping some praise, or fearing some disgrace.
> We shall not argue saying ' 'Twas thus' or 'Thus',
> Our argument's whole drift we shall forget;
> Who's right, who's wrong, 'twill be all one to us;
> We shall not even know that we have met.
> > Yet meet we shall, and part, and meet again,
> > Where dead men meet, on lips of living men.

The continued spell of cold weather had stopped Butler's Sunday and Thursday outings, 'So I am not quite at my best', he tells Jones in February, 'and have stuck too closely to editing correspondence and copying and scoring music. . . . My knees continuing very stiff and rheumatic, I went to Jaeger's and bought myself a pair of woollen knee-warmers which I hope will mend matters, price 2s. 9d. . . . I have settled my correspondence now as far as the death of my father, 29 December, 1886, and am thankful to have done so, for the period is not a pleasant one to resuscitate, and I think I shall find all subsequent years easier and quicker editing.' Grant Richards not caring to undertake a new edition of *Ex Voto*, Butler was preparing to write a short work on

---

[1] 'I do not think McColl disliked or dislikes me; but he was not a pleasant person to deal with, and often gave my books to reviewers who he perfectly well knew would slate them of set purpose.' (Note of February, 1902).

Tabachetti to be called *Jean de Wespin* and to incorporate in it a good deal of the old material.

In March he started for Sicily, where it was arranged
that he should meet the Fuller Maitlands and show them
the country of the *Odyssey*. Jones was not yet well enough
to go, but was to meet Butler on his return journey in
North Italy. On the boat, crossing to Calais, Butler met
a man who told him that Eustatius, the earliest mediæval
commentator on Homer, wrote that Homer took much
of his poems from a poem written by a woman, which
was preserved in the temple of Memphis in Egypt. At
Casale-Monferrato Butler found himself 'so unaccount-
ably weak' that he sent for a doctor and remained there
a few days. His Italian friends tried to persuade him to
stay longer, but he replied that he had promised to go to
Sicily and intended to keep his promise, even if it cost
him his life. He reached Rome tired out, but met the
Fuller Maitlands and discussed plans for going to Sicily.
In Rome he saw a homœopathic doctor who diagnosed
malarial fever and dosed him with quinine 'to an extent
which I thought heroic'. He went to the Collegio Romano
and there he found confirmation of the story he had been
told crossing to Calais. 'Tis said that one Naucrates has
recorded how a woman of Memphis, named Phantasia,
a teacher of philosophy, daughter of Nicharchus, composed the stories of the war before Ilium and the wandering of Ulysses, and placed the books in the temple of
Hephæstus at Memphis. Whereon Homer came there
and having obtained copies of the originals wrote the
Iliad and the *Odyssey*. Some say that he was an Egyptian
born, or travelled to Egypt and taught the people there.'
This Butler regarded as no more than an interesting
corruption of the truth.

Staying at the same hotel in Rome was an English
doctor, a Dr Rowland Thurnam, who had just returned

from Sicily. Butler told him that he was on his way there himself and the conversation turned to Trapani and the *Odyssey*. 'Oh! in that case', said Dr Thurnam, 'you ought to talk to old Butler.' 'I am old Butler', said Butler, and after that they sat and talked until three in the morning. This meeting with an enthusiastic admirer did him so much good that Butler thought himself well enough to go on to Naples and thence by boat to Palermo, where he arrived on 12 April and met the Fuller Maitlands. 'No, I am not better', he wrote to Jones, 'and must stay here a day or two, I think: but will see how I am tomorrow and let you know.' He remained at Palermo a month, telling Jones that he was better; but after he had been there a fortnight, the doctor insisted on his having a nurse, and he wrote saying that he had 'turned the corner'. Early in May the nurse took him to Naples, and he sent for Alfred to take him home. As it happened a yacht belonging to one of Harrie's nephews was lying off the coast at the time. But, as Mrs Garnett puts it, Harrie 'dared not expose a young man to the contaminating influence of the infidel'.

From Naples, Butler wrote to the Fuller Maitlands that there was no doubt that he was far more gravely ill than had been suspected, and was 'only being hurried home as a prelude to consultations, operations, and artificial prolongations of what Christian charity should curtail. . . . The doctor fully believes that I may reach London much as now, and there may be weeks or even months before the end comes, but I can see that he has not the faintest doubt what the end is to be. Therefore with infinite thanks for infinite kindness received from both of you and every cordial wish for many years of happiness and health to you both, I bid you both heartily farewell. No answer, please.'

To Jones at Ancona he wrote on 15 May: 'I don't see

why you should come home sooner than you naturally would. Alfred and the nurse will get me home. I am feeling more hopeful today about getting home alive, about which yesterday I was almost despairing.'

Alfred arrived and they travelled straight back to England, dropping the nurse at Calais and reaching London on 19 May. Two days later Butler wrote to Jones at Basel: 'I feel sure that I shall not ask you to do anything that does not commend itself to your sense of our ultimate happy relations. However, I shall be very glad to see you on your return.' Next day he wrote to the editor of the Sicilian paper *Quo Vadis*: 'I salute my Trapanese friends, I embrace them, I raise my hat and I bid them a cordial farewell.' It was really the end. He was moved from Clifford's Inn to a nursing home in Cavendish Square, 'shrunk, feeble and shockingly pale'. His complexion had always been florid, now he was as white as the sheets on his bed.

Jones had still not returned to England by 24 May and Alfred wrote to him: 'Mr Butler will be very grateful if you could come home as soon as you can.' This card was contradicted next day by a telegram from Butler telling Jones not to hurry back. Then, hearing that he was already on the way, Butler wrote to him at Staple Inn on 28 May advising him to see his [Butler's] solicitor, Russell Cooke, before coming to the nursing home. 'I think it will be better all round', he wrote. There is no hint in the *Memoir* that relations between Butler and Jones had become strained. However, when Jones did finally reach the bedside of his dying friend all difficulties were apparently smoothed away and on 4 June Butler wrote to Harrie about his new will of 31 May: 'I have left Jones, with whom I have made up all estrangement, £500. We are now as good friends as ever.' Nevertheless, he made Streatfeild, not Jones, his literary executor; and, according to Muggeridge, made Jones promise to pay back to his estate all the money he had given him, saying: 'I do not intend to have a second Pauli.' To Alfred he bequeathed £2,000 and most of his furniture, and to Mrs Cathie, his laundress, £1 a week for life; to Streatfeild he left all his manuscripts, and to Gogin an annuity of £100. In all this it must be remembered that Butler regarded Jones's health as now too seriously impaired for him to be entrusted with the management of his books, and that during the last year of his life he had come to rely more and more upon Streatfeild's judgment and advice. As his other executor he appointed Reginald Worsley. To Jones, however, he left the copyrights of the works in which they had collaborated. The bulk of his estate, which was ultimately valued at over £33,000, went to his nephew, Henry Thomas Butler, who had settled in Florida, though he left legacies of £200 each to his sisters, and the income of his estate at Watford Gap, Northampton, to his sister-in-law. He specified, however, that the legacy to Alfred and Gogin's and Mrs Cathie's annuities should have priority over all other bequests.

Butler was not comfortable in the nursing home in Cavendish Square and was moved to another in St John's Wood. 'I am much better today', he said to Jones soon after this. 'I don't feel at all as though I were going to die; of course, it will be all wrong if I do get well, for there is my literary reputation to be considered. First, I write *Erewhon*—that is my opening subject; then, after modulating freely through all my other books and the music and so on, I return gracefully to my original key and publish *Erewhon Revisited*. Obviously now is the proper moment to come to a full close, make my bow and retire; but I believe I am getting well, after all. It's very inartistic, but I cannot help it. However, we shall see.'

Jones told him that his recovery would give him an
opportunity for a coda of considerable length on a tonic
pedal.

But there was to be no coda. In spite of his brave high
spirits, he was far worse than he had ever been. One day
he asked Jones to bring him the piano score of *Solomon*
that he might refresh his memory of the harmonies of
'With thee th'unsheltered moor I'd tread'; but Jones
knew that he was unequal to reading a score, and next
day he had forgotten all about it. The doctor told him
that when he got better he should give up his rooms in
Clifford's Inn and move to a more airy situation for his
convalescence, and he discussed with Jones whether he
should take a flat or a house. A house was finally decided
upon and Jones and Alfred set about looking for houses
in Hampstead, for of course if Butler moved Jones would
have to move too. They found one for sale freehold at
£1,500 and Reginald Worsley was sent to inspect it. 'I
am not behaving like a man who is going to die', said
Butler, 'I make a will, and tell my sisters all about it, and
then here I am buying a freehold house at Hampstead!'
A second doctor was called in, who diagnosed pernicious
anæmia and acute intestinal catarrh. Butler lay in bed
quite cheerful and in no pain, but growing weaker each
day. One day he said that he did not suppose he would
ever drink another glass of wine or smoke another
cigarette, but Jones assured him that when he recovered
he would soon be returning to all his old vices. He smiled,
but he was not convinced.

On 18 June he had difficulty in breathing and Jones
and Alfred lifted him out of bed and sat him in an arm-
chair. He dozed, and when he woke he said: 'I'm going
away soon. I'm to be left alone.' Jones said: 'I've brought
Reggie to tell you about your house. He has been to
Hampstead and seen it.' Butler asked if the drains were

all right and told Worsley to get in touch with his solicitor. They discussed the house for a little while and then he said he knew he was dying. As Jones left the room, he said he would come to see him in the morning and Butler replied that he did not suppose he would be there in the morning. Jones remained below, and presently Alfred came to fetch him. When Butler saw them he said that it was a dark morning. In reality, it was a fine summer evening about 8 o'clock. 'Have you brought the cheque book, Alfred?' he said. Then he took off his spectacles and put them down on the table. 'I don't want them any more,' he said, and his head fell back and he died.

Sixteen mourners—Butler's sisters were not among them, though they included Gaetano Meo, R. A. Streatfeild, Gogin, Richard and Reginald Worsley, Jason Smith, Russell Cooke, Edward Tanner (who used to collect his rents) and of course Alfred and Jones—met at Waterloo Station on 21 June. At Woking they drove to the Crematorium. Festing Jones describes the scene: 'The coffin was put on trestles, there was no pall, there were no flowers, and there was no service. We waited. Presently the doors were opened and the coffin was taken through and put into the furnace.'

The problem now arose of what to do with the ashes. At one time Butler had wished them to be scattered over the grass plot at Clifford's Inn. But, when they had discussed it, Jones pointed out that there would be calcined bones among the ashes, and they could not scatter these over the lawn: they would have to borrow a spade and dig them in and this might lead to trouble. Besides, adds Jones, he did not like the idea of putting Butler's ashes where the laundresses dumped their unwanted cats. Alfred had said, too, that he would like to keep the Governor's ashes on his mantelpiece. Butler had agreed to this and nothing more was said. Later Alfred changed his mind and told Butler that he did not think he would care to have his ashes after all. Butler thereupon directed that his body should be burnt and the ashes not preserved. Accordingly, Jones and Alfred returned to the Crematorium on the Saturday after the funeral and were given the remains of their friend in a little jar. This they took into the garden, a hole was dug among the bushes, and the ashes were thrown into it with nothing to mark the spot.

Butler had always looked upon his body as little more than a tool-box. What mattered to him was the work done; in that work, and in the thoughts of future generations, lay his hope of immortality. His epitaph, if he is to have one, should be the sonnet, 'Not on sad Stygian shore'. But, half-humorously, he expected another kind of immortality in the classical sense. 'If on my descent to the nether world', he had written in the *Notebooks*, 'I were to be met and welcomed by the shades of those to whom I have done a good turn while I was here, I should be received by a fairly illustrious crowd. There would be Giovanni and Gentile Bellini, Leonardo da Vinci, Gaudenzio Ferrari, Holbein, Tabachetti, Paracca, and D'Enrico: the authoress of the *Odyssey* would come and Homer with her; Dr Butler would bring with him the many forgotten men and women to whom in my memoir I have given fresh life; there would be Buffon, Erasmus Darwin, and Lamarck; Shakespeare also would be there and Handel. I could not wish to find myself in more congenial company and I shall not take it too much to heart if the shade of Charles Darwin glides gloomily away when it sees me coming.'

CHRONOLOGY

1835	Born 4 December.
1843	First visit to Italy.
1846–48	School at Allesley, near Coventry.
1848–54	School at Shrewsbury.
1851	H. F. Jones born.
1853	Second visit to Italy.
1854	Goes to St John's College, Cambridge.
1858	Bracketed twelfth in Classical Tripos.
1858–59	Contributes to *The Eagle*.
	Working in parish of St James's, Piccadilly, as preparation for ordination.
	Returns to Cambridge and takes drawing lessons.
1859	Refuses to be ordained.
	Emigrates to Canterbury Settlement, New Zealand.
1860–64	Studies Darwin and the Gospels in New Zealand.
	Contributes to New Zealand *Press* (1862-64).
	A First Year in Canterbury Settlement (1863) published by his father from material from his letters home.
	Meets Charles Paine Pauli.
1864	Returns to England and settles in Clifford's Inn.
	Paints 'Family Prayers'.
1865	*Evidence for the Resurrection of Jesus Christ, As Given By The Four Evangelists, Critically Examined*, published anonymously as a pamphlet.
	Lucubratio Ebria, published in New Zealand *Press* (July).

1866	Sits for his portrait (in profile) to G. W. Sharp
1867	Studying painting at Heatherley's School of Art, Newman Street. Meets Miss Savage.
1869–76	Exhibiting at Royal Academy.
1870	Begins *Erewhon*.
1871	Extant correspondence with Miss Savage begins.
	Meets Isabella Zanetti at Arona, Maggiore.
1872	Meets Lucie Dumas ('Madame') in Islington.
	Begins *The Way of All Flesh*.
	Erewhon published (May) anonymously. Second edition in same year under his own name.
	Sunday 'outings' begin with visit to Haslemere.
	First visit to Darwin at Down (May). Second visit in November.
1873	*The Fair Haven* by 'the late John Pickard Owen' published. Second edition in same year under Butler's name.
	His mother dies at Menton.
	Invests in Hoare's companies.
1874	Collapse of Hoare's companies. Goes to Canada (1874–75).
	'Mr Heatherley's Holiday' exhibited at Royal Academy.
1876	Begins *Life and Habit: An Essay After a Completer View of Evolution*.
	Meets Henry Festing Jones.
1877	'Here my career as an art-student, for I was never more, may be said to end. It fizzled out. . . .'
	Begins using the British Museum Reading Room regularly.
1878	*Life and Habit* published.

1878   *A Psalm of Montreal* published in *The Spectator* (May).

1879   *Evolution, Old and New: Or, the Theories of Buffon, Dr Erasmus Darwin and Lamarck, as compared with that of Mr Charles Darwin* published.

1880   Quarrels with Darwin. Letter to *Athenæum* 31 January.
Unconscious Memory.

1880–83   Rewriting *The Way of All Flesh.*

1882   *Alps and Sanctuaries* published, with illustrations by Butler, Jones and Gogin.

1883   Begins writing music.

1884   The cantata *Narcissus* begun.
Selections from Previous Works published.

1885   Death of Miss Savage.
Gavottes, Minuets, Fugues, and Other Short Pieces for the Piano, in collaboration with Festing Jones.

1886   His father dies.
Holbein's *La Danse.*
Applies for Slade Professorship of Fine Arts at Cambridge.

1887   Engages Alfred Emery Cathie as clerk and valet.
Luck or Cunning, As the Main Means of Organic Modification?
Takes up photography.

1888   *Ex Voto: An Account of the Sacro Monte or New Jerusalem at Varallo-Sesia.* Illustrated with Butler's photographs of work by Gaudenzio Ferrari, Tabachetti and Paracca.
Narcissus: A Cantata in the Handelian form, in collaboration with Festing Jones.

1891   Begins translating the *Odyssey.*

1892	Delivers lecture *The Humour of Homer* at the Working Men's College, Great Ormond Street.
	First visit to Sicily.
	Death of Lucie Dumas.
1893	Meets Hans Faesch.
1894	Italian edition of *Ex Voto*.
1895	Visits Greece and the Troad.
	Begins work on Shakespeare's Sonnets.
1896	*The Life and Letters of Dr Samuel Butler.*
	Gogin paints his portrait.
1897	*The Authoress of the Odyssey.*
	Death of Pauli.
1898	*The Iliad Rendered into English Prose.*
1899	*Shakespeare's Sonnets Reconsidered and in part Rearranged,* with a reprint of the original edition of 1609.
1900	*The Odyssey Rendered into English Prose.*
1901	*Erewhon Revisited Twenty Years Later.* New and enlarged edition of *Erewhon*.
	Writes Sonnets on Miss Savage.
1902	Last illness and death, 18 June.
1903	*The Way of All Flesh,* edited by R. A. Streatfeild.
	Death of Hans Faesch.
1904	*Essays on Life, Art and Science.*
	Ulysses, An Oratorio, in collaboration with Festing Jones.
1909	*God the Known and God the Unknown,* articles from *The Examiner*.
1912	*Note-Books.* A selection arranged and edited by H. Festing Jones.
1913	*The Humour of Homer, and Other Essays.*
1917	Butler Collection at St John's College, Cambridge, inaugurated.

1919   *Samuel Butler: Author of Erewhon: A Memoir.* By Henry Festing Jones.

1923–26   *The Shrewsbury Edition of the Complete Works of Samuel Butler,* edited by H. F. Jones and A. T. Bartholomew, 20 vols. (Jonathan Cape).

1928   Death of Henry Festing Jones.

1932   *Butleriana,* edited by A. T. Bartholomew.

1934   *Further Extracts from the Note-Books of Samuel Butler,* edited by A. T. Bartholomew.

1935   *Letters Between Samuel Butler and Miss E. M. A. Savage,* 1871–1885, edited by Geoffrey Keynes and Brian Hill.

1951   *Samuel Butler's Notebooks,* further extracts edited by Geoffrey Keynes and Brian Hill.

1960   *Darwin and Butler: Two Versions of Evolution,* by Basil Willey (Chatto & Windus).

1962   *The Family Letters of Samuel Butler,* edited by Arnold Silver (Jonathan Cape).

1964   *Ernest Pontifex or The Way of All Flesh,* edited from the original manuscript by Daniel F. Howard (Methuen).

INDEX